# 4 ★ All-Star

## Linda Lee

### Kristin Sherman ★ Grace Tanaka ★ Shirley Velasco

## Second Edition

Mc
Graw
Hill

*Connect
Learn
Succeed*™

The McGraw·Hill Companies

Connect
Learn
Succeed™

ALL-STAR 4 STUDENT BOOK

Published by McGraw-Hill, a business unit of The McGraw-Hill Companies, Inc., 1221 Avenue of the Americas, New York, NY, 10020. Copyright © 2011, 2006 by The McGraw-Hill Companies, Inc. All rights reserved. No part of this publication may be reproduced or distributed in any form or by any means, or stored in a database or retrieval system, without the prior written consent of The McGraw-Hill Companies, Inc., including, but not limited to, in any network or other electronic storage or transmission, or broadcast for distance learning.

Some ancillaries, including electronic and print components, may not be available to customers outside the United States.

This book is printed on acid-free paper.

1 2 3 4 5 6 7 8 9 0 WDQ/WDQ 1 0 9 8 7 6 5 4 3 2 1 0

ISBN 978-0-07-719713-1

MHID 0-07-719713-5

ISE ISBN 978-0-07-131385-8

ISE MHID 0-07-131385-0

Vice president/Editor in chief: *Elizabeth Haefele*
Vice president/Director of marketing: *John E. Biernat*
Director of Sales and Marketing, ESL: *Pierre Montagano*
Director of development: *Valerie Kelemen*
Developmental editor: *Kathleen Ossip, Nancy Jordan, Laura LeDrean*
Marketing manager: *Kelly Curran*
Lead digital product manager: *Damian Moshak*
Digital developmental editor: *Kevin White*
Director, Editing/Design/Production: *Jess Ann Kosic*
Lead project manager: *Susan Trentacosti*
Senior production supervisor: *Debra R. Sylvester*
Designer: *Srdjan Savanovic*
Senior photo research coordinator: *Lori Kramer*
Photo researcher: *Allison Grimes*
Digital production coordinator: *Cathy Tepper*
Illustrators: *Alyta Adams, Andrew Lange, Jerry Zimmerman, Jerry Gonzalez, Michael Hortens, Bot Roda, Maureen Cavallo, Daniel Rubenstein*
Typeface: *11.5/12.5 Frutiger LT Std 45 Light*
Compositor: *Laserwords Private Limited*
Printer: *Worldcolor*
Cover credit: *Andrew Lange*
Credits: *The credits section for this book begins on page 229 and is considered an extension of the copyright page.*

The Internet addresses listed in the text were accurate at the time of publication. The inclusion of a Web site does not indicate an endorsement by the authors or McGraw-Hill, and McGraw-Hill does not guarantee the accuracy of the information presented at these sites.

www.mhhe.com

# ACKNOWLEDGMENTS

The authors and publisher would like to thank the following individuals who reviewed *All-Star Second Edition* at various stages of development and whose comments, reviews, and field-testing were instrumental in helping us shape the second edition of the series:

Carlos Alcazar, Newport-Mesa USD Adult School, Costa Mesa, CA ★ Isabel V. Anderson, The English Center, Miami, FL ★ Carol Antunano, The English Center, Miami, FL ★ Ted Anderson ★ Josefina Aucar, Miami Beach Adult and Community Education Center, Miami, FL ★ Veronica Pavon-Baker, Miami Dade County Public Schools, Miami, FL ★ Barry Bakin, Pacoima Skills Center, Pacoima, CA ★ Michael Blackman, Reseda Community Adult School, Reseda, CA ★ Taylor H. Blakely, Newport-Mesa USD Adult School, Costa Mesa, CA ★ Marge Bock, Sweetwater USD Adult Education, Chula Vista, CA ★ Lusine Bokhikyan ★ Rothwell H Bouillon, Pacoima Skills Center, Pacoima, CA ★ Ian Brailsford, South Piedmont Community College, Monroe, NC ★ Roy Carl Brungardt, Riverside Adult School, Riverside, CA ★ Paul Buczko, Pacoima Skills Center, Pacoima, CA ★ Gemma S Burns, Riverside Adult School, Riverside, CA ★ Kathleen Bywater, Riverside Adult School, Riverside, CA ★ Helen Canellos, Milwaukee Area Technical College, Milwaukee, WI ★ Richard H Capet, Pimmit Hills Adult Education Center, Falls Church, VA ★ Waldo Cardenas, Miami Dade County Public Schools, Miami, FL ★ Gemma Santos Catire, Miami Beach Adult and Community Education Center, Miami, FL ★ Julio Chow, Pacoima Skills Center, Pacoima, CA ★ Claire Cirolia, Fairfax County Adult ESL Program, Fairfax, VA ★ Sabine Cooke, Riverside Adult School, Riverside, CA ★ Jeffrey R Corrigan, Newport-Mesa USD Adult School, Costa Mesa, CA ★ Don Curtis, Oakland USD Adult Education, Neighborhood Centers, Oakland, CA ★ Angela DeRocco, Sweetwater USD Adult Education, Chula Vista, CA ★ Jorge de la Paz, Miami Sunset Adult Center, Miami, FL ★ Deborah Ebersold, Pacoima Skills Center, Pacoima, CA ★ Fernando Egea, Miami Sunset Adult Center, Miami, FL ★ Marilyn Farrell, Riverside Adult School, Riverside, CA ★ Lora Finch, Newport-Mesa USD Adult School, Costa Mesa, CA ★ Pat Fox, Montgomery College, Rockville, MD ★ Antoinette Galaviz, Reseda Community Adult School, Reseda, CA ★ Elizabeth Gellatly, Newport-Mesa USD Adult School, Costa Mesa, CA ★ Dennys Gonzalez, Miami Dade College, Miami, FL ★ Amber G Goodall, South Piedmont Community College, Monroe, NC ★ Amy Grodzienski, Reseda Community Adult School, Reseda, CA ★ Ana Guadayol, Miami-Dade College VESOL, Miami, FL ★ Diane Helvig, Sweetwater USD Adult Education, Chula Vista, CA ★ Kristine Hoffman, Newport-Mesa USD Adult School, Costa Mesa, CA ★ Dr. Coral Horton, Miami-Dade College, Miami, FL ★ Valerie Johnson, Reseda Community Adult School, Reseda, CA ★ Ali Kiani, Reseda Community Adult School, Reseda, CA ★ Donna Kihara, Reseda Community Adult School, Reseda, CA ★ Angela Kosmas, Wilbur Wright College, Chicago, IL ★ Alida Labiosa, Newport-Mesa USD Adult School, Costa Mesa, CA ★ Lourdes A. Laguilles, Reseda Community Adult School, Reseda, CA ★ Holly Lawyer, Elgin Community College, Elgin, Illinois ★ Lia Lerner, Burbank Adult School, Burbank, CA ★ Mae F Liu, Chinese American Planning Council, New York, NY ★ Levia Loftus, College of Lake County, Grayslake, IL ★ Nancy Magathan, Reseda Community Adult School, Reseda, CA ★ Monica Manero-Cohen, Miami Beach Adult and Community Education Center, Miami, FL ★ Matilda Martinez, Miami Beach Adult and Community Education Center, Miami, FL ★ Suzette Mascarenas, Newport-Mesa USD Adult School Costa Mesa, CA ★ Sara McKinnon, College of Marin, Kentfield, CA ★ Ibis Medina, Miami Sunset Adult Center, Miami, FL ★ Alice-Ann Menjivar, Carlos Rosario International Public Charter School, Washington, DC ★ Kathleen Miller, Reseda Community Adult School, Reseda, CA ★ Kent Minault, Pacoima Skills Center, Pacoima, CA ★ Pedro Monteagudo, Miami Beach Adult and Community Education Center, Miami, FL ★ Jose Montes, The English Center, Miami, FL ★ Ilene Mountain, Newport-Mesa USD Adult School Costa Mesa, CA ★ Mary Murphy-Clagett, Sweetwater USD Adult Education, Chula Vista, CA ★ Fransisco Narciso, Reseda Community Adult School, Reseda, CA ★ Anita Nodarse, Miami Dade College, Miami, FL ★ Zoila Ortiz, Miami Sunset Adult Center, Miami, FL ★ Phil Oslin, Sweetwater USD, Adult Education, Chula Vista, CA ★ Nancy Pakdel, Newport-Mesa USD Adult School, Costa Mesa, CA ★ Eduardo Paredes-Ferro, Miami Sunset Adult Center, Miami, FL ★ Virginia Parra, Miami Dade College, Interamerican Campus, Miami, FL ★ Elaine S Paris, Chinese American Planning Council, New York, NY ★ Ellen R. Purcell, Public Schools/Pimmit Hills, Falls Church, VA ★ Michelle R Quiter, Austin Community College, Austin, TX ★ Sandra Ramirez, Pacoima Skills Center, Pacoima, CA ★ Corinne Rennie, Newport-Mesa USD Adult School, Costa Mesa, CA ★ Barbara Rinsler ★ Ray Rivera, South Dade Adult Education Center, Homestead, FL ★ Abdali Safaei, Reseda Community Adult School, Reseda, CA ★ Bernard Sapir, Reseda Community Adult School, Reseda, CA ★ Amy Schneider, Pacoima Skills Center, Pacoima, CA ★ Delisa Sexton, Pacoima Skills Center, Pacoima, CA ★ Norma S Smith, Pacoima Skills Center, Pacoima, CA ★ Mandi M Spottsville, Newport-Mesa USD Adult School ★ Helen G Stein, Miami Dade College, Miami, FL ★ Jennifer C Storm, College of Lake County, Grayslake, IL ★ Terri L Stralow, South Piedmont Community College, Monroe, NC ★ Dina P Tarrab, Reseda Community Adult School, Reseda, CA ★ Maliheh Vafai, East Side Adult Education, San Jose, CA ★ Rosanne Verani, Riverside Adult School, Riverside, CA ★ Kermey Wang, Riverside Adult School, Riverside, CA ★ Cynthia Whisner, Riverside Adult School, Riverside, CA ★ Duane Wong, Newport-Mesa USD Adult School, Costa Mesa, CA

# SCOPE AND SEQUENCE

## LIFE SKILLS

| UNIT | Listening and Speaking | Reading and Writing | Critical Thinking | Vocabulary | Grammar |
|------|------------------------|---------------------|-------------------|------------|---------|
| **Pre-Unit**<br>**Getting Started**<br>*page 2* | • Express opinions<br>• Introduce yourself<br>• Interview your classmates<br>• **WB:** Talk about your family<br>• **WB:** Show interest<br>• **WB:** Talk about job history | • Preview the book<br>• **WB:** Complete a resume | • Evaluate<br>• Choose the best alternative<br>• Preview | • Introductions<br>• Information questions | |
| **Unit 1**<br>**Skills and Abilities**<br>*page 4* | • Talk about continuing education<br>• Talk about personal and professional goals<br>• Listen to telephone conversations and messages<br>• Talk about telephone behavior<br>• Talk about job interviews | • Complete a class registration form<br>• Read about types of skills<br>• Write about types of skills<br>• Write telephone messages<br>• Read an article on non-verbal communication<br>• Read about career plans<br>• Preview a reading<br>• Read and interpret a course schedule<br>• Write about goals<br>• Read a college website<br>• Make inferences<br>• Write business letters<br>• **WB:** Write a cover letter and a thank you note for a job interview<br>• **WB:** Read about the role of parents in their child's education<br>• **WB:** Write a note to your child's teacher | • Evaluate<br>• Apply knowledge<br>• Analyze | • Types of courses<br>• Educational and professional goals<br>• **WB:** Adjectives to describe skills<br>• **WB:** Professions<br>• **WB:** Skills | • Present Perfect vs. Simple Past<br>• Compound Sentences with *so, too, not either, neither* and *but*<br>• *Either...or, Both... and*, and *Neither... nor* |
| **Unit 2**<br>**Getting Around**<br>*page 18* | • Talk about types of transportation<br>• Talk about solving transportation problems<br>• Talk about automobile insurance<br>• Listen to conversations regarding a traffic accident and car repair<br>• **Pron:** Blending words in questions with *you*<br>• **WB:** Give directions | • Read an insurance policy<br>• Read automobile insurance terms<br>• Read a bus schedule<br>• Read about travel options<br>• Identify the topic and main idea<br>• Compound subjects, verbs, and objects<br>• Compound sentences<br>• **WB:** Read entertainment listings<br>• **WB:** Interpret maps and directions<br>• **WB:** Write directions | • Make inferences<br>• Compare information<br>• Analyze<br>• Interpret | • Automobile insurance terms<br>• Car accident checklist<br>• Pausing expressions<br>• **WB:** Adjectives and adverbs<br>• **WB:** Car-related words<br>• **WB:** Recreational events | • Articles<br>• Indirect Questions<br>• Modals of Possibility, Probability, and Logical Conclusion<br>• Requests and Offers |

# CORRELATIONS TO STANDARDS

| Civics Concepts | Math Skills | CASAS Life Skills Competencies | SCANS Competencies (Workplace) | EFF Content Standards | Florida | LAUSD |
|---|---|---|---|---|---|---|
| • **WB:** Understand the elements of a resume | | • 0.1.2, 0.2.1, 2.7.2, 4.1.2 | • Decision making<br>• Sociability<br>• Knowing how to learn | • Communicate so that others understand<br>• Reflect on and reevaluate your opinions and ideas | | • 1a, 2 |
| • Identify educational opportunities<br>• Recognize personal and professional goals<br>• Recognize personal job skills and abilities<br>• Recognize appropriate interviewing behavior<br>• Ability to take and interpret telephone messages<br>• Recognize do's and don'ts of phone use<br>• Understand public school enrollment procedures | • Understand how to pay on an installment plan | • **1:** 2.5.5, 2.8.2, 2.8.3, 4.1.4<br>• **2:** 4.4.1, 4.4.2, 7.3.1<br>• **3:** 2.1.7, 2.1.8,<br>• **4:** 2.5.5, 4.1.4, 4.1.8, 4.4.5, 7.1.1<br>• **5:** 4.6.2<br>• **6:** 0.1.1, 4.1.7, 7.2.4<br>• **WB:** 0.1.2, 0.2.3, 2.5.5, 4.4.1, 4.5.4 | • Understand systems<br>• Reasoning<br>• Organize and maintain information<br>• Problem solving<br>• Self-management<br>• Decision making<br>• Work well with others | • Create vision of future<br>• Plan and renew career goals<br>• Pursue personal self-improvement<br>• Reflect on and reevaluate your opinions and ideas<br>• Develop a sense of self that reflects your values | • **1:** 5.03.05, 5.03.12,<br>• **2:** 5.03.07,<br>• **3:** 5.01.07,<br>• **4:** 5.03.02, 5.03.05, 5.03.13,<br>• **5:** 5.01.01<br>• **WB:** 5.03.03 | • **1:** 38(b), 11 (a),<br>• **3:** 15 (a, b),<br>• **4:** 11 (b, c) 42,<br>• **5:** 35 (a, b), 45<br>• **WB:** 4 (b), 8(c), 10 (a, b), 14<br>• **RC:** 1a |
| • Interpret information about automobile insurance<br>• Understand what to do in case of an accident | | • **1:** 1.9.7, 2.2.3, 5.3.7, 5.5.6, 7.3.1, 7.3.2<br>• **2:** 1.9.8<br>• **3:** 1.9.7, 2.2.3, 2.2.4, 2.2.5, 2.6.3, 5.3.1<br>• **4:** 1.9.7, 2.1.2, 2.5.1, 5.5.6, 7.3.1, 7.3.2, 7.3.3<br>• **5:** 7.2.1, 7.2.3<br>• **WB:** 2.2.1, 2.6.1, 2.6.2, 3.4.2, 4.3.3 | • Participate as a member of a team<br>• Acquire and evaluate information<br>• Understand systems<br>• Know how to learn<br>• Organize and maintain information<br>• Creative thinking<br>• Interpret and communicate information | • Reflect on and reevaluate opinions and ideas<br>• Find and use community resources and services<br>• Communicate so that others understand<br>• Participate in group processes and decision making | • **1:** 5.06.02,<br>• **2:** 5.07.02,<br>• **3:** 5.06.01, 5.06.03<br>• **5:** 5.06.01<br>• **RC:** 5.06.05 | • **3:** 13, 25 (b), G20<br>• **4:** G7, 25a<br>• **WB:** 4a, 16, 18 |

CASAS, Florida, and LAUSD standards: Numbers in bold indicate lesson numbers. • **G:** Grammar • **WB:** Workbook • **RC:** Online Teacher's Resource Center

# SCOPE AND SEQUENCE

## LIFE SKILLS

| UNIT | Listening and Speaking | Reading and Writing | Critical Thinking | Vocabulary | Grammar |
|---|---|---|---|---|---|
| **Unit 3**<br>**Your Health**<br>*page 32* | • Talk about a health emergency<br>• Talk about types of health care professionals<br>• Listen to phone conversations between patients and doctors' offices<br>• Talk about food labels and nutrition<br>• Talk about healthy and unhealthy diets<br>• Role-play phone call to 911<br>• Interrupt politely<br>• **WB:** Schedule a doctor's appointment<br>• **WB:** Read entertainment listings: Describe medical symptoms to a doctor | • Read about health care professionals and specialties<br>• Read nutrition labels<br>• Read an appointment card<br>• Read a medical bill<br>• Use context clues<br>• Use punctuation marks<br>• **WB:** Read about emergency room procedures<br>• **WB:** Read an appointments calendar<br>• **WB:** Read about health insurance<br>• **WB:** Read a workers' health and safety quiz<br>• **WB:** Read and write a personal note<br>• **WB:** Complete a medical history form<br>• **WB:** Read a drug label<br>• **WB:** Complete an insurance claim form | • Classify<br>• Analyze<br>• Make inferences<br>• Use context clues<br>• Prioritize | • Types of health care professionals and specialties<br>• Nutritional labels<br>• Ways to interrupt politely<br>• **WB:** Body parts, internal organs<br>• **WB:** Medical symptoms | • Present Perfect Continuous<br>• Gerunds vs. Infinitives as Objects of Verbs<br>• *Used to*<br>• *Because, since,* and *so* |
| **Unit 4**<br>**Rights and Responsibilities**<br>*page 46* | • Talk about Washington, DC<br>• Talk about marches and protests<br>• Talk about rights and responsibilities<br>• Discuss social issues<br>• Listen to conversations about the U.S. educational system<br>• Express agreement and disagreement<br>• Talk about unions | • Read about marches and protests<br>• Read and take notes on rights and responsibilities<br>• Read charts about education in the U.S.<br>• Read and write about work unions<br>• Scan a reading<br>• Adjust your reading speed<br>• Identify purpose for writing business letters<br>• **WB:** Interpret a map<br>• **WB:** Read about the Bill of Rights<br>• **WB:** Read a portion of the OSHA website<br>• **WB:** Read about the U.S. Congress<br>• **WB:** Read about tenants' rights<br>• **WB:** Read about voting rights<br>• **WB:** Complete a voter registration application | • Analyze<br>• Rank information<br>• Summarize<br>• Predict<br>• Apply knowledge to new situations | • U.S. Constitutional rights and responsibilities<br>• Educational system<br>• Workers' rights<br>• Unions<br>• **WB:** Noun/verb/adjective forms | • Present Passive<br>• Past Passive<br>• Passive with Present Perfect<br>• Passive with Modals |
| **Unit 5**<br>**Consumer News and Views**<br>*page 60* | • Discuss advertising<br>• Talk about shopping and comparison shopping<br>• Listen to conversations between customers and salespeople<br>• Role-play conversations between customers and salespeople<br>• Talk about finding housing<br>• Express doubt<br>• Listen to phone messages about housing<br>• **Pron:** Intonation in tag questions<br>• **WB:** Return an item to a store<br>• **WB:** Ask about total price | • Read advertisements<br>• Read housing ads<br>• Write a classified ad<br>• Use a dictionary<br>• Write a letter of complaint<br>• **WB:** Read about misleading advertising techniques<br>• **WB:** Complete a merchandise return form<br>• **WB:** Read about postal services<br>• **WB:** Read about consumer resources | • Analyze advertisements<br>• Use context clues<br>• Compare<br>• Evaluate | • Advertisements<br>• Shopping terms<br>• Housing ads<br>• **WB:** Adjectives to describe defective merchandise | • Adjectives with –*ed* and –*ing*<br>• Tag Questions<br>• Reported Speech |

| Civics Concepts | Math Skills | CASAS Life Skills Competencies | SCANS Competencies (Workplace) | EFF Content Standards | Florida | LAUSD |
|---|---|---|---|---|---|---|
| • Understand when to call 911<br>• Understand types of health care professionals<br>• Determine who to see for different health issues<br>• Understand and analyze food labels<br>• Analyze personal health habits<br>• **WB:** Interpret warnings on drug labels<br>• **WB:** Complete an insurance claim form | • Convert numbers to percentages | • **1:** 2.1.2, 2.5.1, 3.6.2, 3.6.3,<br>• **2:** 3.1.4, 3.1.5, 3.5.6, 3.6.2, 3.6.3<br>• **3:** 3.1.2, 3.4.2<br>• **4:** 1.6.1, 3.5.1, 3.5.2, 3.5.9 0.2.3<br>• **WB:** 3.1.1, 3.2.1, 3.2.3, 3.3.2 | • Decision making<br>• See things in the mind's eye<br>• Self-management<br>• Acquire and evaluate information<br>• Organize and maintain information<br>• Know how to learn<br>• Reasoning<br>• Creative thinking<br>• Problem solving | • Provide for physical needs<br>• Participate in group processes and decision making<br>• Organize and maintain information<br>• Communicate so that others understand<br>• Reflect on and reevaluate opinions and ideas<br>• Find, interpret, and analyze diverse sources of information<br>• Give and receive support outside the immediate family<br>• Help self and others | • **3:** 5.01.06<br>• **6:** 5.01.08<br>• **WB:** 5.05.01, 5.05.04<br>• **RC:** 5.05.05, 5.05.06 | • **1:** 12,<br>• **2:** 29 (a, b),<br>• **4:** 28, G5<br>• **3:** 7d, G12 (b), G13 (b)<br>• **5:** G3<br>• **WB:** 4a, 8 (b), 31 |
| • Identify U.S. Constitutional rights and responsibilities<br>• Understand the U.S. educational system<br>• Understand educational rights and options<br>• Understand protests and marches<br>• **WB:** Understand tenants' rights<br>• **WB:** Understand voting rights<br>• **WB:** Understand electoral politics | • Understand bar and line graphs | • **1:** 5.2.1, 5.2.6, 5.6.1, 7.2.4<br>• **2:** 5.1.1, 5.6.3<br>• **3:** 0.1.2, 2.8.1,<br>• **4:** 4.2.2, 4.2.6, 6.7.2, 7.2.4,<br>• **5:** 6.8.1,<br>• **6:** 5.1.6, 5.1.7, 5.6.1, 7.3.1, 7.3.2,<br>• **WB:** 0.1.3, 0.2.3, 0.1.4, 1.4.5, 1.4.7, 1.4.8, 2.5.1, 2.5.2, 3.4.2, 4.3.3, 5.1.2, 5.1.4, 5.3.2 | • Participate as a member of a team<br>• See things in the mind's eye<br>• Know how to learn<br>• Reasoning<br>• Acquire and evaluate information<br>• Organize and maintain information<br>• Problem solving<br>• Understand how systems work<br>• Work within the system<br>• Interpret and communicate information | • Reflect on and reevaluate opinions and ideas<br>• Find and use community resources and services<br>• Recognize and understand your human and legal rights and civic responsibilities<br>• Communicate so that others understand<br>• Participate in group processes and decision making<br>• Figure out how systems work | • **1:** 5.01.03<br>• **2:** 5.02.04<br>• **3:** 5.02.08<br>• **4:** 5.03.09<br>• **WB:** 5.02.01<br>• **RC:** 5.02.07 | • **1:** 5 (a),<br>• **3:** 7 (c), 5 (b),<br>• **2:** G11 (a)<br>• **3:** 7a, G11 (b)<br>• **5:** 43, G5 (c)<br>• **WB:** 23, 26 (a), 26 (b)<br>• **RC:** 26 (c) |
| • Engage in comparison shopping<br>• Understand impulse buying<br>• Analyze advertisements<br>• Analyze personal shopping behavior<br>• **WB:** Understand postal services<br>• **WB:** Identify consumer resources | | • **1:** 1.2.1, 7.2.2<br>• **2:** 0.1.8, 1.2.6, 1.3.1, 1.5.2, 1.6.3<br>• **3:** 0.1.2<br>• **4:** 1.4.1, 1.4.2,<br>• **5:** 7.4.4, 7.4.5<br>• **6:** 1.6.2, 1.6.3<br>• **7: WB:** 2.4.2, 2.4.3, 5.2.1, 5.3.2 | • See things in the mind's eye<br>• Understand how systems work<br>• Analyze and communicate information<br>• Creative thinking<br>• Decision making<br>• Acquire and evaluate information<br>• Organize and maintain information<br>• Problem solving<br>• Participate as a member of a team<br>• Reasoning<br>• Use resources wisely | • Participate in group processes and decision making<br>• Provide for physical needs<br>• Identify and monitor problems<br>• Listen to and learn from others' experiences and ideas<br>• Communicate with others inside and outside the organization<br>• Find and use community resources and services<br>• Put ideas and directions into action<br>• Teach children | • **1:** 5.01.03, 5.04.03<br>• **2:** 5.04.09<br>• **Review:** 5.04.06<br>• **WB:** 5.04.02<br>• **TRC:** 5.01.09 | • **1:** 9,<br>• **2:** G16<br>• **3:** G24<br>• **6:** 21 (a,b), G19<br>• **WB:** 8a, 17 (a, b), 26 (b) |

CASAS, Florida, and LAUSD standards: Numbers in bold indicate lesson numbers. • **G:** Grammar • **WB:** Workbook • **RC:** Online Teacher's Resource Center

# SCOPE AND SEQUENCE

## LIFE SKILLS

| UNIT | Listening and Speaking | Reading and Writing | Critical Thinking | Vocabulary | Grammar |
|---|---|---|---|---|---|
| **Unit 6**<br>**Rules and Laws**<br>*page 74* | • Talk about courtrooms and people in them<br>• Summarize<br>• Talk about types of crime and common laws<br>• Listen to recorded messages<br>• Listen to information about getting a marriage and driver's license<br>• Talk about getting a marriage and driver's license<br>• Paraphrase<br>• Talk about traffic tickets<br>• Talk about neighborhood problems<br>• **Pron:** Reduction of past modals<br>• **WB:** Agreeing to terms | • Read roles of people in a courtroom<br>• Read journal entries<br>• Read checklists about getting a marriage and driver's license<br>• Take notes on prerecorded instructions<br>• Read about traffic citations<br>• Write details about traffic citations<br>• Read about community involvement<br>• Read about Neighborhood Watch<br>• Write about community problems<br>• Recognize cause and effect<br>• Use graphic organizers for writing<br>• **WB:** Read a newspaper article about a trial<br>• **WB:** Read a biographical article<br>• **WB:** Read and complete a rental agreement | • Sequence<br>• Summarize<br>• Compare<br>• Paraphrase<br>• Interpret | • Courtroom language<br>• Types of crimes<br>• Instructions to obtain a marriage license<br>• Instructions to obtain a driver's license<br>• Citations<br>• **WB:** Words related to a rental agreement | • *Could, Should*, and *Ought to* for Advice<br>• *Should Have, Could Have*, and *Must Have*<br>• *Be Supposed to*<br>• *Had Better* and *Had Better not* |
| **Unit 7**<br>**Career Paths**<br>*page 88* | • Talk about workplace situations<br>• Talk about workplace responsibilities and behavior<br>• Talk about interviews<br>• Listen to job interviews<br>• Role-play job interviews<br>• Discuss ideal employees and employers<br>• Expand responses to questions | • Read work rules<br>• Read online job postings<br>• Write a job description<br>• Write job tasks<br>• Read an employment application<br>• Read an article about a successful businessman<br>• Read a resume<br>• Identify a sequence of events<br>• **WB:** Read a fable<br>• **WB:** Interpret a bar graph<br>• **WB:** Write career planning advice<br>• **WB:** Complete a work progress report<br>• **WB:** Read a workplace accident report | • Solve problems<br>• Analyze<br>• Evaluate<br>• Rank job benefits<br>• Solve problems based on new information<br>• Make inferences<br>• Sequence<br>• Brainstorm | • Workplace skills and behavior<br>• Classified job postings<br>• Sequence words | • Past Perfect<br>• Phrasal Verbs<br>• Past Perfect Continuous |

| Civics Concepts | Math Skills | CASAS Life Skills Competencies | SCANS Competencies (Workplace) | EFF Content Standards | Florida | LAUSD |
|---|---|---|---|---|---|---|
| • Interpret basic court procedures<br>• Understand requirements for obtaining licenses<br>• Understand different types of crimes<br>• Understand information about traffic tickets<br>• **WB:** Understand rental agreements<br>• **WB:** Interpret worker protection laws | | • **1:** 5.3.3, 5.6.3<br>• **2:** 5.3.7<br>• **3:** 1.9.2, 5.4.5<br>• **4:** 2.5.8, 2.7.3, 5.6.1, 5.6.2<br>• **5:** 5.3.7, 7.2.2<br>• **6:** 6.6.5,<br>• **WB:** 1.4.3, 2.7.2, 5.2.1, 5.3.1, 5.3.5, 5.3.6 | • Know how to learn<br>• See things in the mind's eye<br>• Analyze and communicate information<br>• Decision making<br>• Responsibility<br>• Integrity and honesty<br>• Acquire and evaluate information<br>• Organize and maintain information<br>• Problem solving<br>• Work well with others | • Participate in group processes and decision making<br>• Identify and monitor problems, community needs, strengths, and resources<br>• Develop a sense of self that reflects your history, values, beliefs, and roles in the larger community<br>• Reflect on and reevaluate your opinions and ideas<br>• Get involved in the community and get others involved<br>• Define common values and goals and resolve conflict<br>• Listen to and learn from others' experiences and ideas<br>• Use technology<br>• Recognize and understand your human and legal rights and civic responsibilities | • **2:** 5.07.02<br>• **3:** 4.02.06, 5.01.08<br>• **4:** 5.02.02<br>• **6:** 5.05.02<br>• **WB:** 5.04.04, 5.06.05 | • **1:** G8<br>• **4:** G10<br>• **WB:** 24, 26 (b) |
| • Understand and analyze appropriate workplace behavior<br>• Understand how to interview effectively<br>• Understand and rank job benefits<br>• **WB:** Understand accident reports | • Compute averages | • **1:** 4.4.1, 4.6.3<br>• **2:** 4.1.3, 4.4.4,<br>• **3:** 4.1.2, 4.1.5, 4.1.7,<br>• **4:** 4.2.5, 6.7.5, 7.2.4<br>• **5:** 7.2.4<br>• **6:** 4.1.2, 7.2.6<br>• **WB:** 0.1.1, 4.1.3, 4.1.5, 4.1.7, 4.1.8, 4.2.1, 4.2.4, 4.3.4, 4.4.1, 4.4.4, 4.6.1, 4.6.4, 4.6.5, 4.8.6, 7.1.3, 7.3.1, 7.3.2, 7.5.1 | • Interpret and communicate information<br>• See things in the mind's eye<br>• Reasoning<br>• Work well with others<br>• Know how to learn<br>• Acquire and evaluate information<br>• Organize and maintain information<br>• Self-management<br>• Creative thinking<br>• Use resources wisely<br>• Self esteem | • Participate in group processes and decision making<br>• Pursue personal self-improvement<br>• Create a vision of the future<br>• Plan and renew career goals<br>• Balance and support work, career, and personal goals<br>• Organize, plan, and prioritize work and use resources<br>• Reflect on and reevaluate your opinions and ideas<br>• Find and get a job<br>• Communicate with others inside and outside the organization | • **2:** 5.03.02<br>• **6:** 5.03.03<br>• **WB:** 5.01.02, 5.03.04, 5.03.06, 5.03.08<br>• **RC:** 5.03.03 | • **3:** 1 (b), 3, 35 (a, b, c), G6<br>• **4:** 40 (b), 43,<br>• **6:** 37<br>• **WB:** 7 (d), 8 (d), 34, 36, 38 (c), 39 (a, b), |

CASAS, Florida, and LAUSD standards: Numbers in bold indicate lesson numbers.   •   **G:** Grammar   •   **WB:** Workbook   •   **RC:** Online Teacher's Resource Center

# SCOPE AND SEQUENCE

## LIFE SKILLS

# CORRELATIONS TO STANDARDS

| Civics Concepts | Math Skills | CASAS Life Skills Competencies | SCANS Competencies (Workplace) | EFF Content Standards | Florida | LAUSD |
|---|---|---|---|---|---|---|
| • Understand the use of credit<br>• Understand a budget<br>• Understand interest rates<br>• Understand banking services<br>• **WB:** Recognize causes of government debt<br>• **WB:** Interpret a phone bill | • Understand rates | • **1:** 1.5.1, 6.0.4, 6.1.5<br>• **2:** 1.8.5, 1.8.6, 7.2.1, 7.2.7<br>• **3:** 0.1.6, 1.8.1, 1.8.3<br>• **4:** 1.2.4, 4.2.1<br>• **5:** 7.2.1<br>• **6:** 1.5.2<br>• **7: WB:** 1.4.4, 1.5.3, 1.8.3, 5.8.1, 5.8.2, 5.8.3 | • See things in the mind's eye<br>• Acquire and evaluate information<br>• Reasoning<br>• Problem solving<br>• Analyze and communicate information<br>• Use resources wisely<br>• Understand how systems work | • Manage resources<br>• Provide for physical needs<br>• Educate self and others | • **1:** 5.04.01, 5.04.08<br>• **3:** 5.04.07 | • **1:** 19,<br>• **2:** G18<br>• **3:** 20 (a, b), G18<br>• **4:** 40 (a)<br>• **WB:** 22 (a-c) |
| • Understand a work schedule<br>• Understand an employee performance evaluation<br>• **WB:** Understand the process for reporting hazards in the workplace | | • **1:** 4.3.4,<br>• **2:** 4.4.3<br>• **3:** 4.1.9, 4.4.1, 4.4.2, 7.1.1<br>• **4:** 4.4.4, 4.6.1<br>• **5:** 4.4.2<br>• **6:** 4.1.3<br>• **WB:** 3.4.2, 4.3.3, 6.7.4, 7.3.2 | • Problem solving<br>• Reasoning<br>• Integrity/Honesty<br>• Interpret and communicate information<br>• Sociability<br>• Responsibility<br>• Self-esteem<br>• Exercise leadership<br>• Acquire and evaluate information<br>• Use computers to process information | | • **1:** 5.03.15, 5.07.01,<br>• **3:** 5.03.14<br>• **4:** 5.03.11<br>• **6:** 5.03.01 | • **1:** 32, 33,<br>• **3:** 38 (a)<br>• **2:** G2<br>• **3:** 34b<br>• **4:** 34a, 39 (c), 41<br>• **WB:** 40(c)<br>• **RC:** 32, 33 |
| • Understand cultural differences<br>• Understand dinner party etiquette<br>• Recognize bias and stereotyping | | • **1:** 2.7.1, 2.7.2<br>• **2:** 2.7.2, 2.7.9, 4.2.6, 6.7.2, 7.5.5<br>• **3:** 2.7.2, 2.7.9<br>• **4:** 2.7.2, 4.8.7<br>• **5:** 2.8.1, 7.2.3<br>• **6:** 4.6.2<br>• **WB:** 4.8.7, 8.2.1, 8.2.3, 8.2.5, 8.2.6 | • See things in the mind's eye<br>• Reasoning<br>• Sociability<br>• Acquire and evaluate information<br>• Organize and maintain information<br>• Interpret and communicate information | | • **1:** 5.01.05, 5.02.03,<br>• **3:** 5.01.01,<br>• **4:** 5.01.04<br>• **WB:** 5.03.10 | • **1:** G22<br>• **4:** G15 |

CASAS, Florida, and LAUSD standards: Numbers in bold indicate lesson numbers.    •    **G:** Grammar    •    **WB:** Workbook    •    **RC:** Online Teacher's Resource Center

# TO THE TEACHER

*All-Star Second Edition* is a four-level, standards-based series for English learners featuring a picture-dictionary approach to vocabulary building. "Big picture" scenes in each unit provide springboards to a wealth of activities developing all of the language skills.

An accessible and predictable sequence of lessons in each unit systematically builds language and critical thinking skills around life-skill topics. *All-Star* presents family, work, and community topics in each unit and provides alternate application lessons in its workbooks, giving teachers the flexibility to customize the series for a variety of student needs and curricular objectives. *All-Star* is tightly correlated to all of the updated major national and state standards for adult instruction.

## New to the Second Edition

- **Updated content** provides full coverage of all major *revised* standards including CASAS, Florida, LAUSD, EFF, and Texas.
- **NEW comprehensive, carefully sequenced grammar program** connects target grammar to the content to enrich learning and provide full coverage of grammar standards.
- **NEW robust listening program** addresses the latest CASAS standards and prepares students for the types of listening items on CASAS tests.
- **NEW Work-Out CD-ROM with complete student audio** provides a fun, rich interactive environment with over 25 hours of learning and the entire *All-Star Second Edition* student audio program in downloadable MP3 files.
- **NEW Teacher Resource Center** offers downloadable and printable Study Guides and Learner Persistence Worksheets, EZ-Tests, Big Picture PowerPoint Slides, full Teacher Audio for Tests in downloadable MP3 files, and other materials to support teaching.
- **NEW Interactive Correlations Chart** allows teachers to easily cross-reference standards with Student Book, Workbook, and Study Guide pages.

## Hallmark *All-Star* Features

- Dynamic Big Picture scenes present life-skills vocabulary and provide lively contexts for activities and discussions that promote all-skills language development.
- Predictable sequence of seven two-page lessons in each unit reduces prep time for teachers and helps students get comfortable with the format of each lesson.
- Flexible structure, with application lessons addressing family, work, and community topics in both the Student Book and Workbook, allows teachers to customize each unit to meet a variety of student needs and curricular objectives.
- Comprehensive coverage of key standards, such as CASAS, Florida, LAUSD, EFF, and Texas, prepares students to master a broad range of critical competencies.

- Multiple assessment measures like CASAS-style tests and performance-based assessment offer a variety of options for monitoring and assessing learner progress.

## The Complete *All-Star* Program

- The **Student Book** features ten 14-page units that integrate listening, speaking, reading, writing, grammar, math, and pronunciation skills with life-skills topics, critical thinking activities, and civics concepts.
- The **Student Work-Out CD-ROM with full student audio** extends the learning goals of each Student Book unit with an interactive set of activities that build vocabulary, listening, reading, writing, and test-taking skills. The CD-ROM also includes the full Student Book audio program.
- The **Teacher's Edition with Tests** includes:
  - Step-by-step procedural notes for each Student Book activity
  - Notes on teaching the Target Grammar Pages
  - Expansion activities addressing multi-level classes, literacy, and students that need to be challenged
  - Culture, Grammar, and Pronunciation Notes
  - Two-page written test for each unit (Note: Listening passages for the tests are available on the Teacher Audio with Testing CD and on the Online Teacher Resource Center)
  - Audio scripts for all audio program materials
  - Answer keys for Student Book, Workbook, and Tests
- The **Workbook** includes supplementary practice activities correlated to the Student Book. As a bonus feature, the Workbook also includes two alternate application lessons per unit that address the learner's role as a worker, family member, and/or community member. These lessons may be used in addition to, or as substitutes for, the application lessons found in Lesson 4 of each Student Book unit.
- The **Teacher Audio with Testing CD** contains recordings for all listening activities in the Student Book as well as the listening passages for each unit test.
- The **Online Teacher Resource Center** provides teachers with the tools to set goals for students, customize classroom teaching, and better measure student success. It includes:
  - EZ-Tests that allow teachers to create customized online tests
  - An Interactive Correlations Chart that allows teachers to easily cross-reference standards with Student Book, Workbook, and Study Guide pages
  - Big Picture PowerPoint slides that present the Student Book Big Picture scenes
  - A Learner Persistence Kit that sets and tracks student achievement goals
  - A Post-Testing Study Guide that moves students toward mastery and tracks their progress using the reproducible Study Guide Worksheets
  - Downloadable MP3 files for the Testing audio programs

# Overview of the *All-Star Second Edition* Program

## UNIT STRUCTURE

The *Welcome to All-Star Second Edition* guide on pages xvi–xxi offers teachers and administrators a visual tour of one Student Book unit and highlights the exciting new features of the Second Edition.

*All-Star Second Edition* is designed to maximize flexibility. Each unit has the following sequence of seven two-page lessons:

- Lesson 1: Talk about It
- Lesson 2: Vocabulary in Context
- Lesson 3: Listening and Speaking
- Lesson 4: Application
- Lesson 5: Reading Strategy
- Lesson 6: Writing Skill
- Lesson 7: Review and Assessment

Each unit introduces several grammar points. A Target Grammar icon

**Target Grammar**
Expressing preferences  page xxx

in the lessons refers teachers and students to the Target Grammar Pages at the back of the book where they can find explanations of the grammar points and contextualized practice.

## SPECIAL FEATURES OF EACH UNIT

- **Target Grammar Pages:** Throughout each unit, students are directed to the Target Grammar Pages in the back of the book, where the grammar point they have been exposed to in the lesson is presented and practiced in manageable chunks. Students learn the target grammar structure with clear charts, meaningful examples, and abundant practice activities.

  This approach gives teachers the flexibility to introduce grammar in any of several ways:
  - At the beginning of a lesson
  - At the point in the lesson where the grammar appears in context
  - As a follow-up to the lesson

- **CASAS Listening:** Each unit has at least two activities that simulate the CASAS listening experience.

- **Window on Pronunciation.** This special feature, which appears in the Listening/Speaking lesson, addresses issues of stress, rhythm, and intonation so that the students' spoken English becomes more comprehensible.

- **Window on Math.** Learning basic math skills is critically important for success in school, on the job, and at home. As such, national and state standards for adult education mandate instruction in basic math skills. Across the book, an orange box called Window on Math is dedicated to helping students develop the functional numeracy skills they need for basic math work.

## TWO-PAGE LESSON FORMAT

The lessons in *All-Star* are designed as two-page spreads. Lessons 1–3 follow an innovative format with a list of activities on the left-hand page of the spread and picture dictionary visuals supporting these activities on the right hand page. The list of activities, entitled Things to Do, allows student and teachers to take full advantage of the visuals in each lesson, enabling students to achieve a variety of learning goals.

## "BIG PICTURE" SCENES

Each unit includes one "big picture". This scene is the visual centerpiece of each unit, and serves as a springboard to a variety of activities in the Student Book, Teacher's Edition, and Work-Out CD-ROM. In the Student Book, the "big picture" scene introduces the topic and serves as a prompt for classroom discussion. The scenes feature characters with distinct personalities for students to enjoy, respond to, and talk about. There are also surprising and fun elements for students to discover in each scene.

The Teacher's Edition includes a variety of all-skills "Big Picture Expansion" activities that are tied to the Student Book scenes. For each unit, these expansion activities address listening, speaking, reading, writing, and grammar skills development, and allow teachers to customize their instruction to meet the language learning needs of each group of students.

## CIVICS CONCEPTS

Many institutions focus direct attention on the importance of civics instruction for English language learners. Civics instruction encourages students to become active and informed community members. Throughout each *All-Star* unit, students and teachers will encounter activities that introduce civics concepts and encourage community involvement. In addition, Application lessons provide activities that help students develop in their roles as workers, parents, and citizens. Those lessons targeting the students' role as citizen encourage learners to become more active and informed members of their communities.

## CASAS, SCANS, EFF, FLORIDA, TEXAS, LAUSD, AND OTHER STANDARDS

Teachers and administrators benchmark student progress against national and/or state standards for adult instruction. With this in mind, *All-Star* carefully integrates instructional elements from a wide range of revised standards including CASAS, SCANS, EFF, LAUSD, Texas, and the Florida Adult ESOL Standards. Unit-by-unit correlations of these standards appear in the scope and sequence. Here is a brief overview of our approach to meeting the key national, state, and district standards.

- **CASAS.** Many U.S. states, including California, tie funding for adult education programs to student performance on the Comprehensive Adult Student Assessment System (CASAS). The CASAS (www.casas.org) competencies identify more than 300 essential skills that adults need in order to succeed in the classroom, workplace, and community. Examples of these skills include identifying or using appropriate nonverbal behavior in a variety of settings, responding appropriately to common personal information questions, and comparing price or quality to determine the best buys. *All-Star* comprehensively integrates all of the CASAS Life Skill Competencies throughout the four levels of the series.

- **SCANS.** Developed by the United States Department of Labor, SCANS is an acronym for the Secretary's Commission on Achieving Necessary Skills (wdr.doleta.gov/SCANS/). SCANS competencies are workplace skills that help people compete more effectively in today's global economy. The following are examples of SCANS competencies: works well with others, acquires and evaluates information, and teaches others new skills. A variety of SCANS competencies is threaded throughout the activities in each unit of *All-Star*. The incorporation of these competencies recognizes both the intrinsic importance of teaching workplace skills and the fact that many adult students are already working members of their communities.

- **EFF.** Equipped for the Future (EFF) is a set of standards for adult literacy and lifelong learning developed by The National Institute for Literacy (www.nifl.gov). The organizing principle of EFF is that adults assume responsibilities in three major areas of life—as workers, as parents, and as citizens. These three areas of focus are called "role maps" in the EFF documentation. In the parent role map, for example, EFF highlights these and other responsibilities: participating in children's formal education and forming and maintaining supportive family relationships. *All-Star* addresses all three of the EFF role maps in its *Application* lessons.

## NUMBER OF HOURS OF INSTRUCTION

The *All-Star* program has been designed to accommodate the needs of adult classes with 70–180 hours of classroom instruction. Here are three recommended ways in which various components in the *All-Star* program can be combined to meet student and teacher needs.

- **70–100 hours.** Teachers are encouraged to work through all of the Student Book materials. Teachers should also look to the Teacher's Edition for teaching suggestions and testing materials as necessary. Students are encouraged to "Plug in and practice" at home with the Work-Out CD-ROM for each unit.
*Time per unit: 7–10 hours*

- **100–140 hours.** In addition to working through all of the Student Book materials, teachers are encouraged to incorporate the Workbook and Work-Out CD-ROM activities for supplementary practice. Students are encouraged to "Plug in and practice" at home with the Work-Out CD-ROM for each unit.
*Time per unit: 10–14 hours*

- **140–180 hours.** Teachers and students working in an intensive instructional setting can take advantage of the wealth of expansion activities threaded through the Teacher's Edition to supplement the Student Book, Workbook, and Work-Out CD-ROM materials. Students are encouraged to "Plug in

and practice" at home with the Work-Out CD-ROM for each unit.
*Time per unit: 14–18 hours.*

## ASSESSMENT

The *All-Star* program offers teachers, students and administrators the following wealth of resources for monitoring and assessing student progress and achievement:

- **Standardized testing formats.** *All-Star* is correlated to the CASAS competencies and many other national and state standards for adult learning. Students have the opportunity to practice answering CASAS-style listening questions in Lesson 7 of each unit. Students practice with the same item types and bubble-in answer sheets they encounter on CASAS and other standardized tests. Student also practice CASAS-style listening items in the Work-Out CD-ROM Listening and Practice Test sections.

- **Achievement tests.** The *All-Star Teacher's Edition* includes end-of-unit tests. These paper-and-pencil tests help students demonstrate how well they have learned the instructional content of the unit. Adult learners often show incremental increases in learning that are not always measured on the standardized tests. The achievement tests may demonstrate learning even in a short amount of instructional time. Twenty percent of each test includes questions that encourage students to apply more academic skills such as determining meaning from context, making inferences, and understanding main ideas. Practice with these question types will help prepare students who may want to enroll in academic classes.

- **EZ Test Online.** *All-Star's* online test generator provides a databank of assessment items from which instructors can create customized tests within minutes. The EZ Test Online assessment materials are available at www.eztestonline.com. For EZ Test tutorials, go to http://mpss.mhhe.com/eztest/eztotutorials.php.

- **Performance-based assessment.** *All-Star* provides several ways to measure students' performance on productive tasks, including the Spotlight: Writing, located in the Workbook in the second edition. In addition, the Teacher's Edition suggests writing and speaking prompts that teachers can use for performance-based assessment. These prompts derive from the "big picture" scene in each unit and provide rich visual input as the basis for the speaking and writing tasks asked of the students.

- **Portfolio assessment.** A portfolio is a collection of student work that can be used to show progress. Examples of work that the instructor or the student may submit in the portfolio include writing samples, audio and video recordings, or projects. Every Student Book unit includes several activities that require critical thinking and small-group project work. These can be included in a student's portfolio. The Teacher's Edition identifies activities that may be used as documentation for the secondary standards defined by the National Reporting System.

- **Self-assessment.** Self-assessment is an important part of the overall assessment picture, as it promotes student involvement and commitment to the learning process. When encouraged to assess themselves, students take more control of their learning and are better able to connect the instructional content with their own goals. The Student Book includes *Learning Logs* at the end of each unit, which allow students to check off the vocabulary they have learned and the skills they feel they have acquired. In the Workbook, students complete the Practice Test Performance Record on the inside back cover.

- **Other linguistic and nonlinguistic outcomes.** Traditional testing often does not account for the progress made by adult learners with limited educational experience or low literacy levels. Such learners tend to take longer to make smaller language gains, so the gains they make in other areas are often more significant. These gains may be in areas such as self-esteem, goal clarification, learning skills, access to employment, community involvement and further academic studies. The SCANS and EFF standards identify areas of student growth that are not necessarily language based. *All-Star* is correlated with both SCANS and EFF standards. Like the Student Book, the Workbook includes activities that provide documentation that can be added to a student portfolio.

## About the author and series consultants

**Linda Lee** is lead author on the *All-Star* series. Linda has taught ESL/ELT in the United States, Iran, and China, and has authored or co-authored a variety of successful textbook series for English learners. As a classroom instructor, Linda's most satisfying teaching experiences have been with adult ESL students at Roxbury Community College in Boston, Massachusetts.

**Grace Tanaka** is professor and coordinator of ESL at the Santa Ana College School of Continuing Education in Santa Ana, California, which serves more than 20,000 students per year. She is also a textbook co-author and series consultant. Grace has 25 years of teaching experience in both credit and non-credit ESL programs.

**Shirley Velasco** is principal at Miami Beach Adult and Community Education Center in Miami Beach, Florida. She has been a classroom instructor and administrator for the past 28 years. Shirley has created a large adult ESL program based on a curriculum she helped develop to implement state/national ESL standards.

# Welcome to *All-Star*

## Second Edition

*All-Star* is a four-level series featuring a "big picture" approach to meeting adult standards that systematically builds language and math skills around life-skill topics.

## Complete Standards Coverage Using the "Big Picture" Approach

**ACCESSIBLE, TWO-PAGE LESSON FORMAT** follows an innovative layout with a list of activities labeled "Things to Do" on the left and picture-dictionary visuals on the right.

**COMPREHENSIVE COVERAGE OF REVISED KEY** standards, such as CASAS, Florida, Texas, LAUSD, and EFF prepares students to master critical competencies.

**PREDICTABLE UNIT STRUCTURE** includes the same logical sequence of seven two-page lessons in each unit.

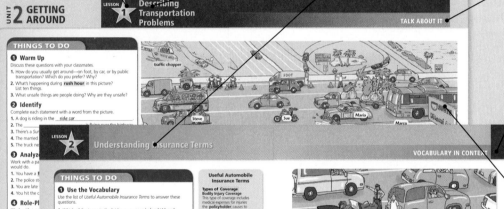

**"BIG PICTURE" SCENES** are springboards to the lesson and to a wealth of all-skills expansion activities in the Teacher's Edition and *NEW* Work-Out CD-ROM.

**HIGHLIGHTED LIFE-SKILLS VOCABULARY** is presented through compelling realia, illustrations, and in rich contextual environments.

**TARGET GRAMMAR** points students to the Target Grammar Pages where they find manageable chunks of grammar with clear examples and plentiful follow up activities.

# *NEW* Comprehensive Grammar Program

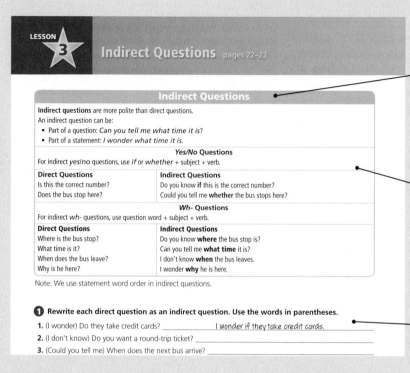

**CAREFULLY SEQUENCED GRAMMAR** covers grammar standards and introduces, builds on, and practices grammar throughout the book and series.

**GRAMMAR CHARTS** with clear presentations and examples make it easy to learn the target grammar.

**CONTEXTUALIZED GRAMMAR PRACTICE** helps students internalize the grammar.

# *NEW* Work-Out CD-ROM with Interactive Activities and Complete Student Audio

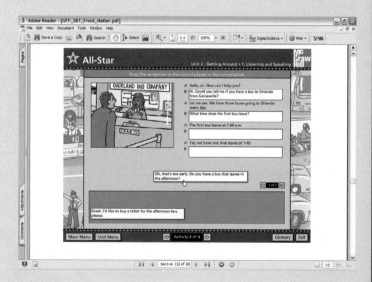

- Over 25 hours of listening, reading, writing, and grammar activities
- Voice record activities
- Entire student audio program MP3s for download

# Integrated Skills with Enhanced Listening

**READING STRATEGY** presents and practices a reading strategy, developing both reading and critical thinking skills.

**REALIA-BASED READINGS AND NARRATIVE SELECTIONS** such as maps, advertisements, descriptive paragraphs, and short stories provide the basis for developing reading skills.

**LISTENING ACTIVITIES** prepare students for a variety of situations including the types of listening items found on the CASAS test.

**COMMUNICATION STRATEGY** boxes present specific strategies that improve students' ability to communicate effectively, helping them become more fluid, natural speakers.

**WRITING SKILL** guides students through a writing task, leading them to practical writing outcomes.

**ABUNDANT OPPORTUNITIES FOR WRITING** prepare students for a variety of academic and real-world writing challenges, such as completing standard forms and writing complete sentences.

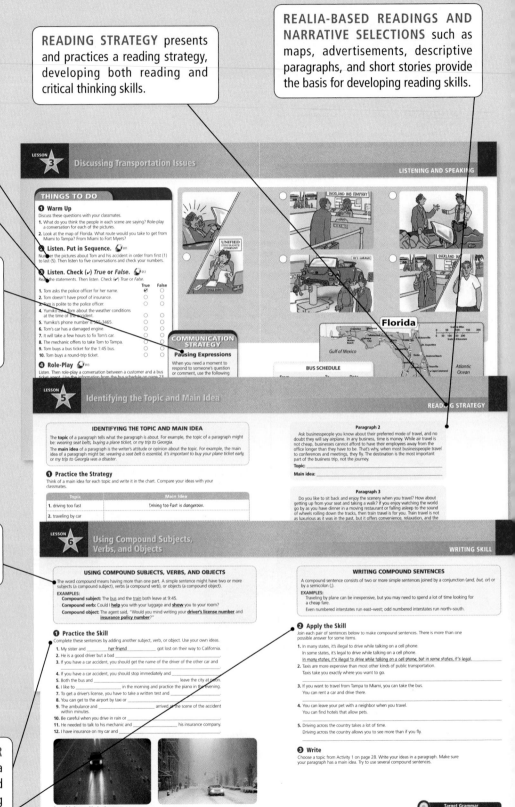

# Real World Applications

**APPLICATION LESSON IN EACH UNIT** focuses on developing the students' roles in life as workers, parents, and citizens.

**REAL-WORLD DOCUMENTS AND SITUATIONS** are highlighted in the Application lesson, exposing students to critical concepts they encounter at work, at home, and in the community.

**CRITICAL THINKING** activities such as evaluating and classifying, allow students to interact with the content in a meaningful way.

**WINDOWS ON PRONUNCIATION** help students produce sounds in English and address issues of stress, rhythm, and intonation.

**ALTERNATE APPLICATION LESSONS IN THE WORKBOOK** provide a flexible approach to addressing family, work, and community topics.

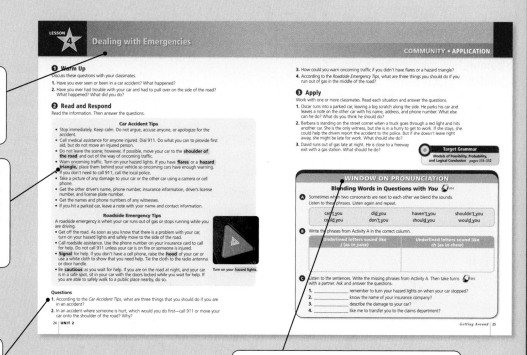

# Multiple Opportunities for Assessment

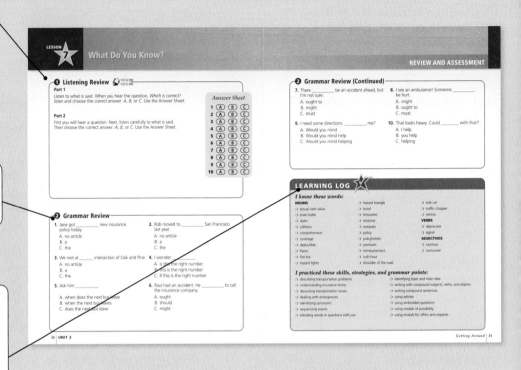

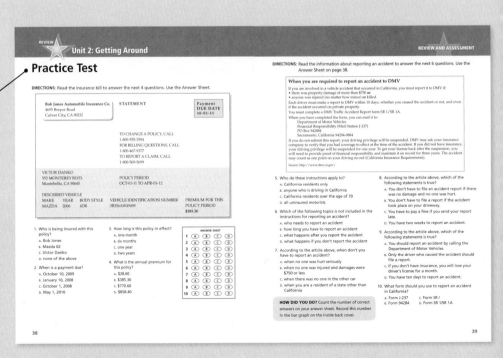

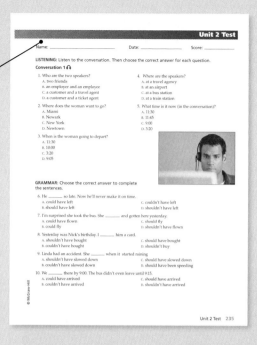

UNIT TEST in the Teacher's Edition rounds out the assessment program.

# *NEW* Teacher Resource Center

- EZ Test Online bank of 500+ test questions for teachers to create customized tests.

- Study Guide reproducible worksheets support a portfolio-based approach to assessment.

- Persistence Kit includes reproducible worksheets that promote student goal setting and achievement.

- Interactive Correlations Chart allows teachers easy and immediate access to standards coverage in the *All-Star Second Edition* program.

# GETTING STARTED

## ★ Have We Met Before?

## ➊ Evaluate

How can you start a conversation with someone you don't know? Read and evaluate the conversations below. Check (✔) *Good start* or *Not a good start*.

**1**

Nice weather today.

Sure is.

Do you live around here?

Yes, I do. I live on the East Side. What about you?

❑ Good start
❑ Not a good start

**2**

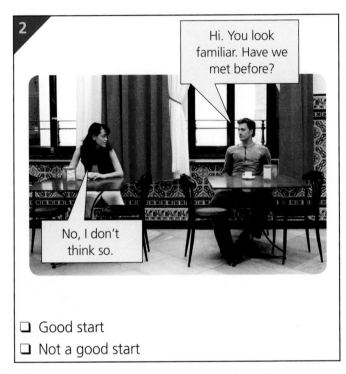

Hi. You look familiar. Have we met before?

No, I don't think so.

❑ Good start
❑ Not a good start

**3**

Hi, my name is Scott.

Hi, Scott. I'm Eva. Where are you from, Scott?

I'm from Mexico. And you?

❑ Good start
❑ Not a good start

**4**

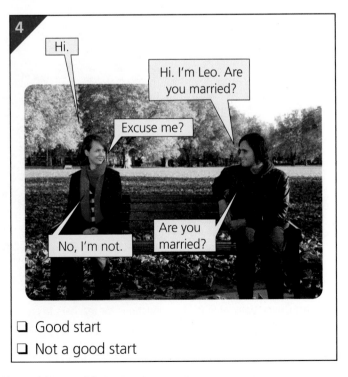

Hi.

Hi. I'm Leo. Are you married?

Excuse me?

Are you married?

No, I'm not.

❑ Good start
❑ Not a good start

What did you like and dislike about each conversation? Share ideas with your classmates.

## ❷ Talk about It

Talk to a classmate. Take turns asking and answering questions 1 to 4 in the chart below. Write your classmate's answers. Then repeat with two more classmates.

Example:  A: Hi. My name's Oscar.

B: Hi, Oscar. My name's Shirin. It's nice to meet you.

A: Nice to meet you, too. Where are you from, Shirin?

B: I'm from Iran. And you?

A: I'm from Mexico.

B: Oh, that's an interesting country. What languages do you speak?

A: I speak Spanish and English. What about you?

B: I speak French, Farsi, and English.

A: Wow! How long have you been here?

B: For about a year. And you?

A: I've been here for two years.

B: What classes are you taking?

A: I'm taking this class, a history class, and physics. What about you?

B: I'm just taking this class for now.

A: That's great. I think it will be a good class.

B: I think so, too. Well, nice talking with you.

A: Nice to talk to you, too.

| Name | 1. Where are you from? | 2. What languages do you speak? | 3. How long have you been here? | 4. What classes are you taking? |
|---|---|---|---|---|
| 1. | | | | |
| 2. | | | | |
| 3. | | | | |

## ❸ Look It Over

What's in this book? Look at the Scope and Sequence, or Table of Contents, on pages iv–xi and answer the questions below.

**1.** Most textbooks are divided into chapters or units. How many units are there in this book? _____

**2.** What is the topic of Unit 5? _____

**3.** What page does Unit 3 begin on? _____

**4.** If you want to find the words that appear on the audio recording, where can you look? _____

**5.** If you have a question about grammar, on what pages can you look for the answer? _____

## LESSON 1 — Exploring Continuing Education

### THINGS TO DO

### ❶ Warm Up

Discuss these questions with your classmates.

1. What are three things you would like to learn to do?

2. Which class in the picture would you like to take? Why?

3. What jobs could the classes prepare you for?

### ❷ Identify the Class

Look at the picture. Complete the sentences with the correct class name. Remember to use capital letters.

1. The teacher is fixing part of a machine in <u>Small Engine Repair</u>.

2. The students are exercising in _____.

3. The students are making vases and bowls in _____.

4. A student is reading a paper in _____.

5. The students are preparing food in _____.

6. The teacher is giving a presentation from his laptop in _____

_____.

### ❸ Discuss

Look at the class schedule with a classmate. Talk about classes you would like to take. Give your reasons.

**Example:**  *I would like to take Italian Cooking because I love to eat.*

### ❹ Write

Complete the registration form with information about yourself. Choose two courses from the schedule.

Name _____

Address _____

City/State/Zip _____

Course 1 _____

Course 2 _____

Tuition total: $ _____

Writing II

| Continuing Education Course Schedule *Wednesday Evening Classes* | | | | |
|---|---|---|---|---|
| COURSE | WKS | TIME | TUITION | ROOM |
| Auto Body Repair | 12 | 6:30–9:30 | $245 | Th12 |
| Basic Computer Skills | 10 | 7:00–9:00 | $224 | 307 |
| Careers in Banking | 8 | 6:30–9:00 | $209 | B223 |
| Computer Repair | 10 | 6:30–9:30 | $249 | B234 |
| Website Design | 12 | 7:45–10:00 | $250 | PE22 |
| Drawing Workshop | 8 | 6:30–9:00 | $224 | W453 |
| Interviewing Skills | 12 | 6:00–9:30 | $265 | Th43 |
| Italian Cooking | 10 | 7:00–8:30 | $189 | 304 |
| Keyboarding | 8 | 7:00–8:00 | $220 | B231 |
| Photography | 8 | 6:45–9:45 | $249 | 303 |
| Pottery I | 8 | 6:00–8:30 | $209 | 308 |
| Public Speaking | 8 | 7:00–9:00 | $209 | 302 |
| Small Engine Repair | 12 | 7:00–9:00 | $265 | 306 |
| Stress Management | 12 | 4:00–5:00 | $189 | W233 |
| Tai Chi | 10 | 7:00–8:30 | $175 | 305 |
| Writing II | 10 | 7:00–9:00 | $224 | 301 |

Pottery I

Basic Computer Skills

Small Engine Repair

Public Speaking

Tai Chi

OFFICE

Photography

Italian Cooking

303

Work-Out CD-ROM

Unit 1: Plug in and practice!

*Skills and Abilities* | 5

# Identifying Interpersonal Skills

## THINGS TO DO

### ❶ Warm Up

Discuss these questions with your classmates.

**1.** What skills do you need to be successful at work?

**2.** What skills do you need to be a good parent?

**3.** Read about the skills shown in the pictures. How have these skills helped you in your personal life? At work?

### ❷ Read and Respond

Read the information in boxes 1 to 4 on page 7. Circle your answer to each question. Then discuss your answers with a partner.

**Example:** *My listening skills are very good. I concentrate on what the speaker is saying. My writing skills are not very good. I'm not very concise.*

### ❸ Match

Match the words on the left to the correct definition on the right. Write the letter on the line.

**1.** _c_ share      **a.** very good at

**2.** ____ distracted      **b.** focus

**3.** ____ concentrate      **c.** part of something

**4.** ____ comprehend      **d.** understand

**5.** ____ leave out      **e.** not focused

**6.** ____ proficient      **f.** not include

### ❹ Read and Identify

Read each statement. Decide which interpersonal skill the person needs to work on. Write the skill.

**1.** No one understands Dan when he explains things. __oral communication skills__

**2.** Ann never did her share of the work when she worked with her group. _____

**3.** Kelly often thinks about other things when people are talking to her. _____

**4.** Kato has sent me many confusing emails lately. _____

### ❺ Listen and Identify 🎧 002

Listen to the conversations. For each conversation, check *Good* if the person is good at the skill or *Not very good* if the person is not good at it.

|  | Good | Not very good |
|---|---|---|
| **1.** Listening skills | ○ | ○ |
| **2.** Oral communication skills | ○ | ○ |
| **3.** Team skills | ○ | ○ |
| **4.** Writing skills | ○ | ○ |

**Target Grammar**

Present perfect vs. Simple past
*pages 144–145*

**1**

### Listening Skills

Good listeners **concentrate** on what the speaker is saying; they don't get **distracted** by their own thoughts or by other things. They don't interrupt the speaker either. Instead, they show the speaker that they are interested in what the speaker is saying.

How good are your listening skills?

| Very good | Good | OK | Not very good |
|---|---|---|---|
| 1 | 2 | 3 | 4 |

**2**

### Oral Communication Skills

People with good speaking skills are able to express their ideas **clearly.** They use specific vocabulary and **leave out** unnecessary details.

How good are your oral communication skills?

| Very good | Good | OK | Not very good |
|---|---|---|---|
| 1 | 2 | 3 | 4 |

**3**

### Writing Skills

**Proficient** writers are able to express their ideas clearly and **concisely.** They don't use unnecessary words. Because their writing is easy for others to **comprehend**, good writers don't leave their readers confused.

How good are your writing skills?

| Very good | Good | OK | Not very good |
|---|---|---|---|
| 1 | 2 | 3 | 4 |

**4**

### Team Skills

People with good team skills are **cooperative**. They work well together. They are also **flexible**. They will change their plans or ideas to help the team succeed. Finally, people with good team skills **take responsibility for** doing their **share** of the work. They don't **expect** other people to do their work for them.

How good are your team skills?

| Very good | Good | OK | Not very good |
|---|---|---|---|
| 1 | 2 | 3 | 4 |

# Taking Telephone Messages

## THINGS TO DO

### ❶ Warm Up

Discuss these questions with your classmates.

1. Do you use voicemail on your home phone or cell phone? What does your outgoing message say?

2. Read the list of Telephone Dos and Don'ts. Add two more ideas to each list.

### ❷ Listen for General Information  003

Listen to six telephone calls. Number them in order from first (1) to last (6).

_____ Someone calls to ask about a job.

_____ Someone calls to apologize for something.

\_\_1\_\_ Someone calls to ask a favor.

_____ The caller is going to be home late.

_____ Someone calls to invite someone to something.

_____ The caller is returning a call.

### ❸ Listen for Specific Information  004

Read the telephone messages on page 9. Listen to the six telephone calls again. Add the missing information to the messages.

### ❹ Role-Play  005

Listen. Then choose a reason for calling a classmate. Practice leaving a message on his or her answering machine. Then ask your classmates to evaluate your message. Use the Communication Strategy on this page.

Example:　A: **You have reached the Li family. Please leave a message.**

　　　　　B: **Hi. This is Rick Martinez calling for Jim. Jim, I'm calling to get the homework assignment for English class. Could you please call me at 555-8933? Thanks. Bye.**

## Telephone Dos and Don'ts

**Do**

- speak clearly.
- identify yourself when you leave a telephone message.
- be concise when you leave a message.
- avoid using filler words such as *you know, um,* and *like.*
- speak softly when you use a cell phone in a public place.
- _____
- _____

**Don't**

- use a cell phone in a restaurant.
- hang up without saying "Good-bye."
- keep anyone on hold for more than a few seconds.
- _____
- _____
- _____

## COMMUNICATION STRATEGY

### Stating Your Purpose

When you call someone on the phone, it helps to first state your name and purpose for calling.

I'm calling to…

My purpose for calling is to…

The reason I'm calling is to…

(1) Pat,

Leila called again. She has called three times. She wants to know if you can

Call her at 805-555-         .

Don

(2) Dad:

Mom isn't going to be

_____

_____ .

(3)

**WHILE YOU WERE OUT**

FOR: Mr. Takase

DATE: June 15    TIME: 12:30

FROM: _____

OF: _____

PHONE: _____

EMAIL: _____

☐ Telephoned         ☒ Will Call Again

☒ Returned Call      ☐ Please See Me

☐ Please Call        ☐ Important

MESSAGE: Mr. Lee said he will

_____

_____

_____ .

(4) Jan,
Maria called to _____
_____
_____

                    Mario
                    7:30

(5) FROM  Betty

DATE  June 12

TIME  2:30

TO _____

MESSAGE  Called to

_____ on

[day] _____ at

[time] _____ . Her number is

555- _____ .

(6)

**WHILE YOU WERE OUT**

FOR: Ms. Parker

DATE: June 14    TIME: 10:30

FROM: Sam

OF: _____

PHONE: _____

EMAIL: _____

☐ Telephoned         ☐ Will Call Again

☐ Returned Call      ☐ Please See Me

☐ Please Call        ☐ Important

MESSAGE: Called to _____

_____

_____

Would like you to call back
when convenient.

# Setting Goals for Learning New Skills

## ❶ Warm Up

Read. Then discuss the questions with your classmates.

Ellen has been a receptionist for ten years. She wants a change and is looking for a new career path. She has taken some courses at the community college to become more proficient in English and writing. She wants to be an accountant.

QUESTIONS   What can Ellen do to reach her goals? What steps should she take? Make a plan for her to reach her goals.

## ❷ Read and Respond

Read the information. What course or courses should Ellen take?

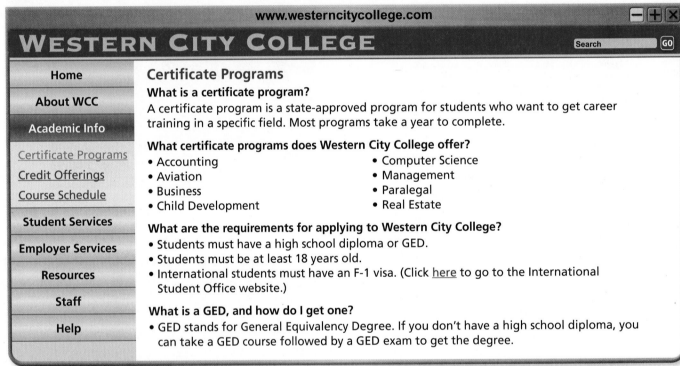

www.westerncitycollege.com

**WESTERN CITY COLLEGE**     Search  GO

| Home |
| About WCC |
| Academic Info |
| Certificate Programs |
| Credit Offerings |
| Course Schedule |
| Student Services |
| Employer Services |
| Resources |
| Staff |
| Help |

**Certificate Programs**

**What is a certificate program?**
A certificate program is a state-approved program for students who want to get career training in a specific field. Most programs take a year to complete.

**What certificate programs does Western City College offer?**
- Accounting
- Aviation
- Business
- Child Development
- Computer Science
- Management
- Paralegal
- Real Estate

**What are the requirements for applying to Western City College?**
- Students must have a high school diploma or GED.
- Students must be at least 18 years old.
- International students must have an F-1 visa. (Click here to go to the International Student Office website.)

**What is a GED, and how do I get one?**
- GED stands for General Equivalency Degree. If you don't have a high school diploma, you can take a GED course followed by a GED exam to get the degree.

## ❸ Write

Answer the questions in complete sentences.

**1.** What are the requirements for applying to Western City College?

_____

**2.** How long do most certificate programs last?

_____

**3.** Why do students apply to a certificate program?

_____

**4.** What do international students have to do to apply to Western City College?

_____

## ❹ Apply 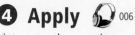 006

Listen to the students discuss their goals and their plans for learning new skills. Complete the chart.

| Student | Goal | Skills Needed | Courses and Certificate Programs |
|---|---|---|---|
| Jan | be a real estate agent | Internet<br>oral communication | basic computer skills<br>website design<br>public speaking |
| Maria | | | |
| Julio | | | |
| Frank | | | |

## ❺ Write

Think about a goal you have. Write it on the line. Then list the skills you need to achieve your goal. Finally, write some ideas about how you can learn these skills.

**Goal**

_____

**Skills needed**

_____

_____

_____

_____

**How I can learn these skills**

Example: *Take a course in _____. Enroll in a certificate program in _____.*

_____

_____

_____

_____

_____

_____

## MAKING INFERENCES

A fact is a piece of information that you can show is true. An inference is what you can guess is true based on the facts you have read.

**Examples:**

**Fact:**      Oscar found the problem with my computer and fixed it.
**Inference:**   Oscar is a good problem solver.

**Fact:**      Oscar always gets to work on time.
**Inference:**   Oscar is dependable.

When you read, it's important to be able to make logical inferences from the facts you read.

## ❶ Practice the Strategy

Read each fact. Then check (✔) the logical inference.

**1. Fact:** Everyone in the class failed the test.

   **Inference:**      ◯ The test was very difficult.

                ◯ Everyone in the class understood the material.

**2. Fact:** It's about 200 miles from Boston to New York.

   **Inference:**      ◯ You can't fly from Boston to New York.

                ◯ It takes about 4 hours to drive from Boston to New York.

**3. Fact:** Carlos spoke Spanish to his grandmother.

   **Inference:**      ◯ Carlos is bilingual.

                ◯ Carlos's grandmother understands Spanish.

**4. Fact:** Taka wants to take a computer course.

   **Inference:**      ◯ Taka has excellent computer skills.

                ◯ Taka wants to improve her computer skills.

## ❷ Preview

Read the title of the article on the next page. What do you think the article is about?
Write your answer on the line below.

I think this article is about

_____

**Target Grammar**

Compound sentences with *so, too, not either, neither,* and *but*   *page 146*

# ❸ Listen and Read  007

Listen to the article as you read along.

## *Talking Without Words*

Most employers say that they know whether they like a candidate for a job before he or she says a word. A good posture, firm handshake, and bright smile communicate confidence and a positive attitude, two qualities most employers look for in an employee.

Nonverbal communication, or body language, can say more about you than your résumé or the words you speak. Do you cross your arms in front of your body or look away when you are speaking to someone? These actions communicate that you are feeling closed off or defensive. If you tilt your head to one side or play with your hair, it shows you might be romantically interested in the person you're talking to.

Some experts say that nonverbal communication is more convincing than words. For instance, if a man nods his head yes while saying, "I'm not guilty," a jury is likely to believe he is guilty. Or if a woman holds her shoulders high up by her ears while saying, "I'm totally relaxed," we're likely to believe she is not relaxed at all. In these cases, it's true that actions speak louder than words.

# ❹ Understand the Reading

Match the nonverbal messages with the physical actions.

**1.** \_\_\_\_\_ I'm interested in dating you.      **a.** shoulders held up by ears

**2.** \_\_\_\_\_ I'm confident.      **b.** arms crossed over body

**3.** \_\_\_\_\_ I'm closed off and defensive.      **c.** good posture

**4.** \_\_\_\_\_ I'm not relaxed.      **d.** tilting head to one side

# ❺ Apply the Strategy

Based on the facts in each statement, write an inference.

**1.** During the interview, Kelly sat with good posture and smiled.

    *Kelly wants to show a positive attitude to the interviewer.*

**2.** Dan doesn't look at people when he talks to them, and he crosses his arms over his body, too.

**3.** Mary plays with her hair and tilts her head when she talks to Hector.

**4.** Jorge smiles all the time.

## WRITING BUSINESS LETTERS

A business letter has six main parts.

**Heading:**
The heading includes the writer's complete address and the full date.

**Inside Address:**
The inside address should include the name and complete address of the person and/or the company to whom you are writing.

**Salutation:**
The salutation goes below the inside address. Some common salutations are
**Dear Mr. or Ms. _____:** or **Dear Hiring Manager:**

**Body:**
The body of the letter gives your reason for writing. This information should be clear and concise.

**Closing:**
The closing is below the body of the letter. Common closings for a business letter are
**Very truly, Sincerely,** or **Warm regards.** Use a comma at the end of the closing.

**Signature:**
The writer's signature goes under the closing. The writer's name is typed under the signature.

## ❶ Practice the Skill

Label the parts of the letter.

4355 Bryson Avenue      _Heading_
Chicago, IL 60607
November 14, 2010

Ms. Anna Phillio      _____
Director, Student Records
Southside High School
4335 West Wilson Avenue
Chicago, IL 60625

Dear Ms. Phillio:      _____

I am applying to a certificate program and need to show proof of my successful completion of high school.
I'm writing to request a copy of my transcripts for the years I attended Southside, 2004-2008. Please send
one copy directly to me, and one copy to Northwestern Community College. I have included an envelope
addressed to Northwestern along with a check for $25.00 for my transcripts.      _____

If you need any more information, you can either call me at (708) 555-8142 or email me at *KarenM@dmail.com*.

Best regards,      _____

*Karen Miller*      _____

Karen Miller

**Email vs. Business Letter**

Most business correspondence is done through email. However, there are some types of business communications that must be handled through a signed letter. For example, requests for legal documents such as school transcripts or medical records and requests for a change of address at your bank and the post office must be made through a signed letter or by filling out a form.

## ❷ Write

Type and sign a letter requesting your medical records from your doctor. Imagine that you are moving to a new city, and you want to take your records with you because you haven't found a new doctor yet. Address your letter to:

Dr. Jane Goldsmith
3636 California Street
San Francisco, CA 94109

---

### WINDOW ON MATH

#### Paying Tuition on an Installment Plan

**A** Read the information.

Some colleges and universities will allow you to pay your tuition on an installment plan. In most cases, you'll make an **initial** payment. Then the rest of tuition will be split into monthly payments. You can calculate the monthly installments by subtracting the initial payment from the total, then dividing the remaining amount by the number of months in the semester.

Tuition = $1,200
Initial Payment = $400
Remaining Amount = $800 ÷ Months in a semester = 4
800/4 = 200, or $200 per month.

**B** Calculate the installment amounts.

1. Kelly wants to go to summer school. Tuition is $900. The initial payment is $300. The summer semester is three months long. If Kelly pays her tuition on an installment plan, how much will she pay each month? _____

2. Devon applied for a certificate program in business at the local community college. He needs to pay the first semester's tuition on an installment plan. The tuition is $1,600. The semester is four months long. The initial payment is $500. What will Devon's monthly tuition payment be? _____

**Target Grammar**

*Either…or, both…and,*
and *neither…nor* *page 147*

## ① Listening Review  008

### Part 1

First, you will hear a question. Next listen carefully to what is said. You will hear the question again. Then choose the correct answer: *A, B,* or *C.* Use the Answer Sheet.

### Part 2 🎧 009

You will hear the first part of a conversation. To finish the conversation, listen and choose the correct answer: *A, B,* or *C.* Use the Answer Sheet.

**Answer Sheet**

1  Ⓐ  Ⓑ  Ⓒ
2  Ⓐ  Ⓑ  Ⓒ
3  Ⓐ  Ⓑ  Ⓒ
4  Ⓐ  Ⓑ  Ⓒ
5  Ⓐ  Ⓑ  Ⓒ
6  Ⓐ  Ⓑ  Ⓒ
7  Ⓐ  Ⓑ  Ⓒ
8  Ⓐ  Ⓑ  Ⓒ
9  Ⓐ  Ⓑ  Ⓒ
10  Ⓐ  Ⓑ  Ⓒ

## ② Grammar Review

Circle the correct answer: A, B, or C.

**1.** They _____ in Dallas for three years. Now they live in Los Angeles.

A. have lived
B. lived
C. has lived

**2.** You can register for the course _____ at the school or online.

A. neither
B. both
C. either

**3.** Lin _____ three classes last year.

A. has taken
B. took
C. takes

**4.** She _____ here since January.

A. been
B. has been
C. was

**5.** Lara _____ to Canada five times.

A. was
B. have been
C. has been

**6.** I _____ Mexico when I was a child.

A. visited
B. have visited
C. have been

## ❷ Grammar Review (continued)

**7.** Dan smiles a lot, and so _____.

   A. does Jun

   B. Jun doesn't

   C. Jun, too

**8.** Sue likes to talk, but _____.

   A. Andy does, too

   B. Andy doesn't

   C. neither does Andy

**9.** Both phone messages _____ emails should be short.

   A. but

   B. nor

   C. and

**10.** _____ teachers nor students came to the picnic.

   A. Either

   B. Neither

   C. Both

## LEARNING LOG

### *I know these words:*

| NOUNS | VERBS | ADJECTIVES | ADVERBS | OTHER |
|---|---|---|---|---|
| ○ installment plan | ○ concentrate | ○ cooperative | ○ clearly | ○ take responsibility for (something) |
| ○ share | ○ comprehend | ○ concise | ○ concisely | |
| | ○ expect | ○ distracted | | |
| | ○ leave out | ○ flexible | | |
| | | ○ initial | | |
| | | ○ proficient | | |

### *I practiced these skills, strategies, and grammar points:*

○ exploring continuing education

○ identifying interpersonal skills

○ listening for general information

○ listening for specific information

○ taking phone messages

○ researching certificate programs

○ setting goals for learning new skills

○ making inferences

○ writing business letters

○ paying tuition on an installment plan

○ reviewing present perfect vs. simple past

○ using compound sentences with *so, too, not either, neither,* and *but*

○ using *either…or, both…and,* and *neither…nor*

**Work-Out CD-ROM**

**Unit 1: Plug in and practice!**

## THINGS TO DO

### ❶ Warm Up

Discuss these questions with your classmates.

**1.** How do you usually get around—on foot, by car, or by public transportation? Which do you prefer? Why?

**2.** What's happening during **rush hour** in this picture? List ten things.

**3.** What unsafe things are people doing? Why are they unsafe?

### ❷ Identify

Complete each statement with a word from the picture.

**1.** A dog is riding in the __side car__.

**2.** The _____ is flying over the highway.

**3.** There's a *Sun Pass* sign on the _____.

**4.** The married couple is riding in the _____.

**5.** The truck next to the police car is pulling a _____.

### ❸ Analyze

Work with a partner. For each situation, describe what you would do.

**1.** You have a **flat tire**.

**2.** The police stop you for speeding.

**3.** You are late for a meeting and stuck in traffic during rush hour.

**4.** You hit the car in front of you.

### ❹ Role-Play

Work with a partner. Role-play a short conversation between the people in the picture.

**Example:** *Maria: Can't you go any faster? I have to get to the airport.*
*Taxi Driver: Sorry, miss. There's nothing I can do. It's rush hour.*

**1.** Officer Goode and Tom

**2.** Andy and the person he's calling

**3.** Maria and the taxi driver

**4.** Takeshi and Mia

**5.** The married couple in the limousine

traffic chopper

Steve

boat trailer

Kyle

## THINGS TO DO

### ❶ Use the Vocabulary

Use the list of *Useful Automobile Insurance Terms* to answer these questions.

1. Which of the terms in the list have you seen before? Where?
2. What is the difference between collision and comprehensive coverage?

### ❷ Find the Synonym

Find a synonym on pages 20–21 for these words. There may be more than one correct synonym for some words.

yearly _____     belongings _____

car _____     driver _____

crash _____     payment _____

### ❸ Evaluate

Study the insurance **policy** on page 21. Complete the statements.

1. This policy lasts for _____ months.
2. The policyholder drives about _____ miles each year.
3. Tom pays a total premium of $_____ each year.
4. If Tom has an accident with someone who is not insured, $_____ of his own medical payments will be covered.
5. If Tom's car is destroyed in a fire, he will have to pay a deductible of $_____ before he is paid a reimbursement.
6. Tom's collision coverage is the _____ value of his car.

### ❹ Listen 🎧 010

Listen to the conversations. Check (✔) *True* or *False*.

|  | True | False |
|---|---|---|
| 1. The caller is asking about his premium. | ○ | ○ |
| 2. The recording describes how to submit an application for insurance. | ○ | ○ |
| 3. The insurance agent is describing bodily injury coverage. | ○ | ○ |
| 4. Mr. Rideout's car has depreciated $20,000. | ○ | ○ |

## Useful Automobile Insurance Terms

**Types of Coverage**

**Bodily Injury Coverage**
This type of coverage includes medical expenses for injuries the **policyholder** causes to someone else.

**Collision Coverage**
This type of coverage includes damage to the policyholder's car from any collision. The collision could be with another car, a building, a sign post, etc.

**Comprehensive Coverage**
This type of coverage includes damage to the policyholder's car from something other than a collision, such as theft or fire.

**Personal Injury Coverage**
This covers the treatment of injuries to the driver and passengers of the policyholder's **vehicle**.

**Property Damage Coverage**
This type of coverage includes the damage the policyholder causes to someone else's property.

**Uninsured Motorist Coverage**
This pays for treatment and property damages of the policyholder if he or she has a collision with an uninsured driver.

**Other Useful Terms**

**Actual Cash Value**
The cost to replace a vehicle minus the amount it has **depreciated**, or decreased in value, since you bought it.

**Claim**
The policyholder's request for **reimbursement**, or payment, by their insurance policy.

**Deductible**
The amount that you pay if you have an accident.

**Premium**
The amount of money you pay for your insurance coverage.

### Target Grammar

*A, an, some, and **the***
*pages 148–149*

## UNIFIED AUTOMOBILE INSURANCE COMPANY
3833 Bradbury Road   Fredericksburg, VA 22401

Policyholder and Address:
Thomas Rideout
564 Philips Street
Miami, FL 33136

Policy Number: 00044 44 244 443 5
POLICY PERIOD (12:01 A.M. Standard Time)
**EFFECTIVE** October 01, 2012 TO October 01, 2013

Description of Covered Vehicle

| YEAR | MAKE | MODEL | ANNUAL MILEAGE | VEHICLE IDENTIFICATION NUMBER |
|------|------|-------|----------------|-------------------------------|
| 2009 | VOLKSWAGEN | BEETLE | 10,000 | WP0CA29894U612345 |

| Description of Coverage | | | Deductible | Annual Premium |
|---|---|---|---|---|
| Bodily Injury (other driver and passengers) | | | | |
|    Each Person | $300,000 | | | |
|    Each Accident | $600,000 | | | $500 |
| Property Damage (other person's property) | | | | |
|    Each Accident | $50,000 | | | $200 |
| Personal Injury (policyholder and passengers) | | | | |
|    Each Person | $10,000 | | | $30 |
| Uninsured Motorist | | | | |
|    Bodily Injury | | | | |
|       Each Person | $300,000 | | | |
|       Each Accident | $600,000 | | | $250 |
|    Physical Damage | | | | |
|       Comprehensive Coverage | Actual Cash Value | | $500 | $250 |
|       Collision Coverage | Actual Cash Value | | $500 | $450 |
| | | | | |
| Total Annual Premium | | | | $1,680 |

## THINGS TO DO

### ❶ Warm Up

Discuss these questions with your classmates.

1. What do you think the people in each scene are saying? Role-play a conversation for each of the pictures.

2. Look at the map of Florida. What route would you take to get from Miami to Tampa? From Miami to Fort Myers?

### ❷ Listen. Put in Sequence.  011

Number the pictures about Tom and his accident in order from first (1) to last (5). Then listen to five conversations and check your numbers.

### ❸ Listen. Check (✔) *True* or *False*.  012

Read the statements. Then listen. Check (✔) *True* or *False*.

|  | True | False |
|---|---|---|
| 1. Tom asks the police officer for her name. | ✔ | ○ |
| 2. Tom doesn't have proof of insurance. | ○ | ○ |
| 3. Tom is polite to the police officer. | ○ | ○ |
| 4. Yumiko asks Tom about the weather conditions at the time of the accident. | ○ | ○ |
| 5. Yumiko's phone number is 555-3465. | ○ | ○ |
| 6. Tom's car has a damaged engine. | ○ | ○ |
| 7. It will take a few hours to fix Tom's car. | ○ | ○ |
| 8. The mechanic offers to take Tom to Tampa. | ○ | ○ |
| 9. Tom buys a bus ticket for the 1:45 bus. | ○ | ○ |
| 10. Tom buys a round-trip ticket. | ○ | ○ |

### ❹ Role-Play  013

Listen. Then role-play a conversation between a customer and a bus ticket agent. Use the information from the bus schedule on page 23 and the expressions from the Communication Strategy box.

A: Blueway Bus Service. Can I help you?

B: Yes. Could you tell me if you have a bus to Tampa from downtown Miami leaving around <u>9:00 in the morning</u> tomorrow?

A: <u>Around 9:00?</u> Let me see . We have a bus that departs <u>at 9:45</u>.

B: Can you tell me what time it arrives?

A: Just a minute . Uh, looks like it arrives at <u>4:00</u>.

## COMMUNICATION STRATEGY

### Pausing Expressions

When you need a moment to respond to someone's question or comment, use the following expressions:

Let me see.

Just a minute.

Hold on a minute.

⊙ **Target Grammar**

Indirect questions  *page 150*

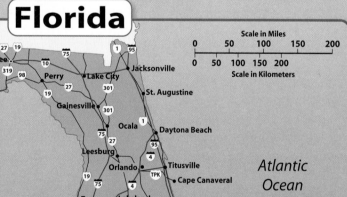

## Florida

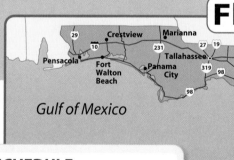

### BUS SCHEDULE

| From | To | Date |
| --- | --- | --- |
| Miami, Downtown, FL | Tampa, FL | 10/14 |

| Departs | Arrives | Duration | Transfers |
| --- | --- | --- | --- |
| 07:55a | 05:55p | 10h, 0m | 0 |
| 09:45a | 05:55p | 8h, 10m | 0 |
| 11:55a | 09:00p | 9h, 5m | 0 |
| 01:35p | 11:15p | 9h, 40m | 0 |
| 01:45p | 11:15p | 9h, 30m | 1 |
| 04:10p | 12:10a | 8h, 0m | 0 |
| 10:10p | 05:30a | 7h, 20m | 1 |

# Dealing with Emergencies

## ❶ Warm Up

Discuss these questions with your classmates.

**1.** Have you ever seen or been in a car accident? What happened?

**2.** Have you ever had trouble with your car and had to pull over on the side of the road? What happened? What did you do?

## ❷ Read and Respond

Read the information. Then answer the questions.

### Car Accident Tips

- Stop immediately. Keep calm. Do not argue, accuse anyone, or apologize for the accident.
- Call medical assistance for anyone injured. Dial 911. Do what you can to provide first aid, but do not move an injured person.
- Do not leave the scene; however, if possible, move your car to the **shoulder of the road** and out of the way of oncoming traffic.
- Warn oncoming traffic. Turn on your hazard lights. If you have **flares** or a **hazard triangle,** place them behind your vehicle so oncoming cars have enough warning.
- If you don't need to call 911, call the local police.
- Take a picture of any damage to your car or the other car using a camera or cell phone.
- Get the other driver's name, phone number, insurance information, driver's license number, and license plate number.
- Get the names and phone numbers of any witnesses.
- If you hit a parked car, leave a note with your name and contact information.

### Roadside Emergency Tips

A roadside emergency is when your car runs out of gas or stops running while you are driving.

- Get off the road. As soon as you know that there is a problem with your car, turn on your hazard lights and safely move to the side of the road.
- Call roadside assistance. Use the phone number on your insurance card to call for help. Do not call 911 unless your car is on fire or someone is injured.
- **Signal** for help. If you don't have a cell phone, raise the **hood** of your car or use a white cloth to show that you need help. Tie the cloth to the radio antenna or door handle.
- Be **cautious** as you wait for help. If you are on the road at night, and your car is in a safe spot, sit in your car with the doors locked while you wait for help. If you are able to safely walk to a public place nearby, do so.

Turn on your hazard lights.

## Questions

**1.** According to the *Car Accident Tips*, what are three things that you should do if you are in an accident?

**2.** In an accident where someone is hurt, which would you do first—call 911 or move your car onto the shoulder of the road? Why?

**3.** How could you warn oncoming traffic if you didn't have flares or a hazard triangle?

**4.** According to the *Roadside Emergency Tips*, what are three things you should do if you run out of gas in the middle of the road?

## ❸ Apply

Work with one or more classmates. Read each situation and answer the questions.

**1.** Oscar runs into a parked car, leaving a big scratch along the side. He parks his car and leaves a note on the other car with his name, address, and phone number. What else can he do? What do you think he should do?

**2.** Barbara is standing on the street corner when a truck goes through a red light and hits another car. She is the only witness, but she is in a hurry to get to work. If she stays, she could help the drivers report the accident to the police. But if she doesn't leave right away, she might be late for work. What should she do?

**3.** David runs out of gas late at night. He is close to a freeway exit with a gas station. What should he do?

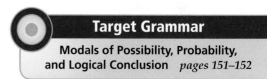

**Target Grammar**

Modals of Possibility, Probability, and Logical Conclusion   *pages 151–152*

---

## WINDOW ON PRONUNCIATION

### Blending Words in Questions with *You* 🎧 014

**A** Sometimes when two consonants are next to each other, we blend the sounds. Listen to these phrases. Listen again and repeat.

| | | | |
|---|---|---|---|
| can't you | did you | haven't you | shouldn't you |
| could you | don't you | should you | would you |

**B** Write the phrases from Activity A in the correct column.

| Underlined letters sound like *j* (as in *juice*) | Underlined letters sound like *ch* (as in *chew*) |
|---|---|
| | |
| | |
| | |

**C** Listen to the sentences. Write the missing phrases from Activity A. Then take turns with a partner. Ask and answer the questions. 🎧 015

**1.** _____ remember to turn your hazard lights on when your car stopped?

**2.** _____ know the name of your insurance company?

**3.** _____ describe the damage to your car?

**4.** _____ like me to transfer you to the claims department?

# Identifying the Topic and Main Idea

## IDENTIFYING THE TOPIC AND MAIN IDEA

The **topic** of a paragraph tells what the paragraph is about. For example, the topic of a paragraph might be: *wearing seat belts, buying a plane ticket,* or *my trip to Georgia.*

The **main idea** of a paragraph is the writer's attitude or opinion about the topic. For example, the main idea of a paragraph might be: *wearing a seat belt is essential, it's important to buy your plane ticket early,* or *my trip to Georgia was a disaster.*

## ❶ Practice the Strategy

Think of a main idea for each topic and write it in the chart. Compare your ideas with your classmates.

| Topic | Main Idea |
|---|---|
| **1.** driving too fast | Driving too fast is dangerous. |
| **2.** traveling by car | |
| **3.** buying auto insurance | |
| **4.** making travel plans | |
| **5.** driving while drunk | |
| **6.** traveling by plane | |
| **7.** hitchhiking | |

## ❷ Listen and Read 🎧 016

Listen as you read each paragraph. Write the topic and main idea of each paragraph.

### Paragraph 1

Traveling is something that most people enjoy, but the way people travel differs greatly. Some people like to (or have to) travel by plane. People who travel for business often have to travel by plane so that they can get to and from their destinations as quickly as possible. Some people enjoy traveling by train. In some places, this can be the most affordable way to get from city to city or from country to country. Still, many people prefer to travel by car. Usually people travel by car when they want independence and flexibility. Finally, many people choose to travel by bus. Depending on where you live, traveling by bus can be affordable and convenient. What mode of transportation do you prefer?

Topic: _____

Main idea: _____

## Paragraph 2

Ask businesspeople you know about their preferred mode of travel, and no doubt they will say airplane. In any business, time is money. While air travel is not cheap, businesses cannot afford to have their employees away from the office longer than they have to be. That's why, when most businesspeople travel to conferences and meetings, they fly. The destination is the most important part of the business trip, not the journey.

**Topic:** _____

**Main idea:** _____

## Paragraph 3

Do you like to sit back and enjoy the scenery when you travel? How about getting up from your seat and taking a walk? If you enjoy watching the world go by as you have dinner in a moving restaurant or falling asleep to the sound of wheels rolling down the tracks, then train travel is for you. Train travel is not as luxurious as it was in the past, but it offers convenience, relaxation, and the chance to get to know the land that surrounds your destination.

**Topic:** _____

**Main idea:** _____

## ❸ Apply the Strategy

Write a paragraph about your preferred way to travel. First, write your topic and the main idea.

**Topic:** _____

**Main idea:** _____

_____

_____

_____

_____

_____

_____

_____

_____

_____

_____

_____

# LESSON 6

## Using Compound Subjects, Verbs, and Objects

### USING COMPOUND SUBJECTS, VERBS, AND OBJECTS

The word *compound* means having more than one part. A simple sentence might have two or more subjects (a compound subject), verbs (a compound verb), or objects (a compound object).

**EXAMPLES:**
**Compound subject:** The **bus** and the **train** both leave at 9:45.
**Compound verb:** Could I **help** you with your luggage and **show** you to your room?
**Compound object:** The agent said, "Would you mind writing your **driver's license number** and **insurance policy number**?"

## ❶ Practice the Skill

Complete these sentences by adding another subject, verb, or object. Use your own ideas.

1. My sister and _____ her friend _____ got lost on their way to California.
2. He is a good driver but a bad _____.
3. If you have a car accident, you should get the name of the driver of the other car and _____.
4. If you have a car accident, you should stop immediately and _____.
5. Both the bus and _____ leave the city at noon.
6. I like to _____ in the morning and practice the piano in the evening.
7. To get a driver's license, you have to take a written test and _____.
8. You can get to the airport by taxi or _____.
9. The ambulance and _____ arrived at the scene of the accident within minutes.
10. Be careful when you drive in rain or _____.
11. He needed to talk to his mechanic and _____ his insurance company.
12. I have insurance on my car and _____.

**Be careful when you drive in rain or snow.**

> ## WRITING COMPOUND SENTENCES
>
> A compound sentence consists of two or more simple sentences joined by a conjunction (*and, but, or*) or by a semicolon (;).
>
> **EXAMPLES:**
> Traveling by plane can be inexpensive, but you may need to spend a lot of time looking for a cheap fare.
>
> Even numbered interstates run east–west; odd numbered interstates run north–south.

## ❷ Apply the Skill

Join each pair of sentences below to make compound sentences. There is more than one possible answer for some items.

**1.** In many states, it's illegal to drive while talking on a cell phone.

In some states, it's legal to drive while talking on a cell phone.

*In many states, it's illegal to drive while talking on a cell phone, but in some states, it's legal.*

**2.** Taxis are more expensive than most other kinds of public transportation.

Taxis take you exactly where you want to go.

_____

**3.** If you want to travel from Tampa to Miami, you can take the bus.

You can rent a car and drive there.

_____

**4.** You can leave your pet with a neighbor when you travel.

You can find hotels that allow pets.

_____

**5.** Driving across the country takes a lot of time.

Driving across the country allows you to see more than if you fly.

_____

## ❸ Write

Choose a topic from Activity 1 on page 26. Write your ideas in a paragraph. Make sure your paragraph has a main idea. Try to use several compound sentences.

**Target Grammar**

**Requests and offers**  *page 153*

# What Do You Know?

## ❶ Listening Review  017

### Part 1

Listen to what is said. When you hear the question, *Which is correct?*, listen and choose the correct answer: *A*, *B*, or *C*. Use the Answer Sheet.

### Part 2  018

First, you will hear a question. Next, listen carefully to what is said. Then choose the correct answer: *A*, *B*, or *C*. Use the Answer Sheet.

*Answer Sheet*

1 Ⓐ Ⓑ Ⓒ
2 Ⓐ Ⓑ Ⓒ
3 Ⓐ Ⓑ Ⓒ
4 Ⓐ Ⓑ Ⓒ
5 Ⓐ Ⓑ Ⓒ
6 Ⓐ Ⓑ Ⓒ
7 Ⓐ Ⓑ Ⓒ
8 Ⓐ Ⓑ Ⓒ
9 Ⓐ Ⓑ Ⓒ
10 Ⓐ Ⓑ Ⓒ

## ❷ Grammar Review

Circle the correct answer: A, B, or C.

**1.** Jane got _____ new insurance policy today.

 A. Ø
 B. a
 C. the

**2.** Rob moved to _____ San Francisco last year.

 A. Ø
 B. a
 C. the

**3.** We met at _____ intersection of Oak and Pine.

 A. Ø
 B. a
 C. the

**4.** I wonder _____.

 A. is this the right number
 B. this is the right number
 C. if this is the right number

**5.** Ask him _____.

 A. when does the next bus leave
 B. when the next bus leaves
 C. does the next bus leave

**6.** Raul had an accident. He _____ to call the insurance company.

 A. ought
 B. should
 C. might

## ❷ Grammar Review (continued)

**7.** There _____ be an accident ahead, but I'm not sure.
A. ought to
B. might
C. must

**8.** I see an ambulance! Someone _____ be hurt.
A. might
B. ought to
C. must

**9.** I need some directions. _____ me?
A. Would you mind
B. Would you mind help
C. Would you mind helping

**10.** That looks heavy. Could _____ you with that?
A. I help
B. you help
C. helping

---

## LEARNING LOG

### *I know these words:*

**NOUNS**
○ actual cash value
○ boat trailer
○ claim
○ collision
○ comprehensive
○ coverage
○ deductible
○ flares
○ flat tire
○ hazard lights

○ hazard triangle
○ hood
○ limousine
○ motorist
○ overpass
○ policy
○ policyholder
○ premium
○ reimbursement
○ rush hour
○ shoulder of the road

○ side car
○ traffic chopper
○ vehicle

**VERBS**
○ depreciate
○ signal

**ADJECTIVES**
○ cautious
○ uninsured

### *I practiced these skills, strategies, and grammar points:*

○ describing transportation problems
○ understanding insurance terms
○ discussing transportation issues
○ dealing with emergencies
○ sequencing events
○ blending words in questions with *you*
○ identifying topic and main idea

○ writing with compound subjects, verbs, and objects
○ writing compound sentences
○ using articles
○ using indirect questions
○ using modals of possibility, probability, and logical conclusion
○ making polite requests and offers

**Work-Out CD-ROM**

**Unit 2: Plug in and practice!**

## THINGS TO DO

### ❶ Warm Up

Discuss these questions with your classmates.

1. Have you or someone you know ever called 911? What happened?

2. What are five reasons that someone would call 911?

3. What is happening in pictures 1 to 7? Share ideas with classmates.

### ❷ Put in Sequence 🎧 019

Listen. Write the number of the picture that matches the description you hear.

1. ___4___
2. _____
3. _____
4. _____
5. _____
6. _____
7. _____

### ❸ Write

Match the words with the definitions. Then look at the pictures. Write the story in your own words. Use at least three words from the list. Add at least three new details to the story.

| | | |
|---|---|---|
| 1. _____ | frequently | **a.** fell |
| 2. _____ | collapsed | **b.** temperature and blood pressure |
| 3. _____ | wheeled | **c.** took in a wheelchair |
| 4. _____ | vital signs | **d.** machine for delivering medicine into the body |
| 5. _____ | IV | **e.** often |

### ❹ Role-Play

Read the *Tips for Calling 911* on page 33. Then think of an emergency. Role-play a 911 call with a classmate.

**Example:** *A: 9-1-1. Please state your location.*
*B: I'm calling from the corner of 9th and Washington, in Chicago.*
*A: What's your emergency?*
*B: I just saw someone collapse on the sidewalk.*

**wheeled in a wheelchair**

collapsed

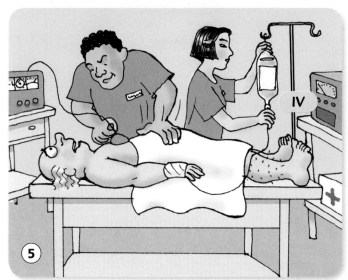

IV

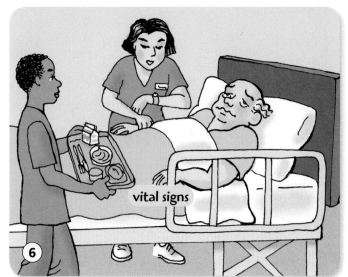

vital signs

## Tips for Calling 911

- Stay calm.
- Be ready to tell the operator your location.
- Wait for the operator to ask questions. Then answer clearly and calmly.
- If you reach a recording, listen carefully to what it says. It might tell you to hang up and call again, or it might ask you to wait on the line.
- Follow all of the directions the operator gives you.
- Do not hang up until the operator tells you to.

**Work-Out CD-ROM**

**Unit 3: Plug in and practice!**

# Identifying Health Care Professionals

## THINGS TO DO

### ❶ Warm Up

Discuss these questions with your classmates.

1. Do you know anyone who works as a health care professional? What does this person do?
2. Circle one of the health professionals on page 35 that you or someone you know has visited. What was the reason for the appointment? What happened at the appointment?

### ❷ Read and Take Notes

Read the information about the nine health care professionals on page 35. Make a chart like this with nine rows. Complete the chart. Then discuss the questions with a classmate.

| Health Care Professional | Specialty |
|---|---|
| 1. Dermatologist | treats skin diseases |
| 2. | |

1. Which of the health care professionals in the chart are medical doctors?
2. What are the similarities and differences between a chiropractor and a physical therapist?

### ❸ Use the Vocabulary

Look at the information with the pictures. Write the missing word forms in the chart.

| Noun | specialist | treatment | diagnosis | prescription |
|---|---|---|---|---|
| Verb | | | | |

### ❹ Match

Match the words to their definitions.

1. _____ treat
2. _____ depressed
3. _____ diagnose
4. _____ vision
5. _____ spine

a. feeling sad for a long period of time
b. sight
c. backbone
d. try to cure
e. decide or say what the problem is

> **Target Grammar**
>
> **Present perfect continuous**
> *pages 154–155*

### ❺ Read and Discuss

Read about the people. Answer the questions with a classmate.

1. Jeb has been feeling depressed for three months. What kind of doctor might be able to help him?
2. Sharon needs to find a doctor for her five-year-old son. What kind of doctor should she look for?
3. Hamid had hip surgery. His doctor wants him to start walking again. Who could help him?

### 1 Cardiologist

Cardiologists are medical doctors who **specialize in** diseases of the heart. They have special training in helping patients with these diseases.

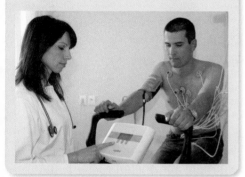

### 2 Primary Care Physician (PCP)

Primary care physicians are medical doctors who **treat** common health problems. They send their patients to a specialist if they need treatment for a specific problem.

### 3 Obstetrician/Gynecologist

Obstetricians and gynecologists are medical doctors who specialize in women's health, pregnancy, and childbirth.

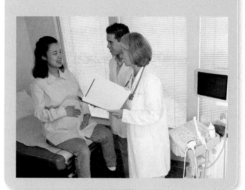

### 4 Physical Therapist (PT)

Physical therapists help patients use a part of the body after an illness or accident. A PT is not a medical doctor, but he or she must have special training.

### 5 Optometrist

An optometrist is a medical doctor who examines people's eyes to **diagnose** eye diseases and **vision** problems.

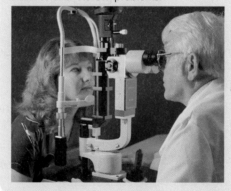

### 6 Chiropractor

Although a chiropractor is not a medical doctor, he or she is a trained health care worker who helps patients who have pain in the neck and **spine**.

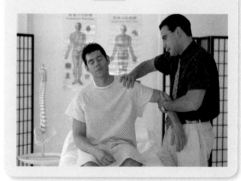

### 7 Pediatrician

A pediatrician is a medical doctor who takes care of children.

### 8 Psychiatrist/Psychologist

Both psychiatrists and psychologists help people with emotional problems and people who are **depressed**. Psychiatrists can prescribe medication, because they are medical doctors. Psychologists cannot.

### 9 Dermatologist

A dermatologist is a medical doctor who treats skin problems and diseases.

## THINGS TO DO

### ❶ Warm Up

Discuss these questions with your classmates.

**1.** Why would someone call a doctor's office? Think of five reasons.

**2.** Look at the photo and the caption on page 37. How do you think the woman feels?

**3.** Look at the bill on page 37. How much does the bill say Mrs. Wong owes?

### ❷ Listen and Take Notes  020

Listen to Conversations 1 through 4. Take notes in the chart.

| | Name of Caller | Purpose for Calling |
|---|---|---|
| 1. | Jeff _____ | make an appointment for annual checkup with Dr. Smith |
| 2. | | |
| 3. | | |
| 4. | | |

Listen to Conversation 1 again. Complete the appointment card on page 37.

### ❸ Listen for Specific Information  021

Listen to the conversation. Look at the doctor's bill on page 37. Write the missing Bill Date, Due Date, Account Number, and Date of Service. Then write the correct Amount Due.

### ❹ Role-Play  022

Listen. Work with a partner. Role-play a telephone conversation between a patient and a receptionist. Replace the underlined words with your own ideas. Use the Communication Strategy.

A: Dr. Smith's office.

B: Hello. This is <u>Jan Li</u>. I need to cancel an appointment. I don't like canceling at the last minute, but I just can't make it.

A: When is your appointment?

B: It's on the <u>5th at 3:00</u>.

A: I don't see your name on the <u>15th</u>.

B: Excuse me, but it's <u>the 5th</u>.

A: Okay. Here it is. I'll cancel it.

B: Thank you.

### COMMUNICATION STRATEGY

#### Interrupting Politely

If someone doesn't understand something you say, use the phrases below to clarify.

Excuse me, but . . .

Excuse me, but I said . . .

That was . . . not . . .

Sorry, but I meant . . . not . . .

 **Target Grammar**

**Gerunds vs. infinitives as objects of verbs** *pages 156–157*

Many medical offices give their patients appointment cards.

### Dr. Smith
### 555-4000

Patient: _____

Date: _____ Time: _____

Mon.    Tues.    Wed.
Thurs.    Fri.

"He's been coughing for a week, and now he has a **fever**."

---

### McCoy Pediatrics
42 Hearst St., Suite 402, Elk Grove, IL 60628
Phone: (847) 555-4001 Fax: (847) 555-4002
Tax ID IL-890-23948

**MAKE CHECK PAYABLE TO:**
**Dr. Alice McCoy**
42 Hearst St., Suite 402
Elk Grove, IL 60628

**PATIENT:** James Wong
806 Marples Ct.
Elk Grove, IL 60628

| BILL DATE | DUE DATE |
|---|---|
| October , 2012 | November , 2012 |
| **AMOUNT DUE**<br>$ | **ACCOUNT NUMBER** |
| **AMOUNT ENCLOSED** | |

☐ Please check box if your address is incorrect or insurance information has changed, and indicate change(s) on back.

- - - - - - - - - - - - - - - - - - - - - - - - - - - - - - - - - - - - - - - - - - -

**PLEASE DETACH AND RETURN TOP PART OF BILL WITH YOUR PAYMENT**

| PATIENT'S NAME | INSURED'S NAME | RELATIONSHIP TO PATIENT | INSURANCE | INSURANCE BILLED |
|---|---|---|---|---|
| Wong, James | Wong, May | Mother | Blue Star | Yes |

| DATE OF SERVICE | TYPE OF SERVICE | TOTAL CHARGES | INSURANCE PAYMENT | AMOUNT DUE |
|---|---|---|---|---|
| 8/ /2012 | Medical Exam | $160.00 | $60.00 | $160.00 |
| | | | | |
| | | | | |
| | | | | |
| | | | | |

**Note:** Your insurance has been billed and made payment on 9/10/2012.
The remaining balance is now due in full.

For questions about this bill, please call (847) 555-4001.

# Interpreting Nutritional Information

## ❶ Warm Up

Discuss these questions with your classmates.

1. What food do you eat while you are at school? While you are at work?

2. Do you read the nutritional information on food labels? Why or why not?

3. Is your diet healthy? What makes it healthy or unhealthy?

## ❷ Read and Respond

Read the Nutrition Facts and the information in the boxes labeled *Serving Size*, *Calories*, and *Percent Daily Value*. Answer the questions in the boxes.

## ❸ Read and Decide

Read the information in the food labels on page 39. Answer the questions.

1. How many servings does a package of peanuts have? _____

2. How many of the calories are from fat? _____

3. What ingredient do the peanuts have the most of? _____

4. What ingredient do the peanuts have the least of? _____

5. Do the peanuts have more fiber or more sugars? _____

6. What percent daily value of iron does the package of peanuts have? _____ %

## ❹ Apply

Work with a classmate to answer these questions. Then compare answers with your classmates.

1. June was too busy to leave the office for lunch, so she ate two packages of peanuts from the vending machine. How many calories did she consume?

_____

2. John takes the stairs to his office instead of the elevator. Climbing stairs for 10 minutes uses 100 calories. How many minutes does John have to climb stairs to burn a serving of peanuts?

_____

3. Paul needs to increase the amount of vitamin A in his diet. Do you think he should eat more peanuts? Why or why not?

_____

### Serving Size

Food labels tell you the size of a serving of that food and the number of servings in the container. For this package, one serving equals 64 peanuts. How many peanuts would be in two servings? _____

### Calories

Calories are a unit of measurement. They tell you how much energy you get from a serving of the food.

How many calories are in 64 peanuts? _____

### Percent Daily Value (%DV)

The percent daily value (%DV) shows you how much of the recommended daily amount of a nutrient (fat, sodium, fiber, etc.) is in a serving of that food.

What is the percent daily value of fat in a package of peanuts? _____

## Nutrition Facts

Serving Size 1 package/About 64 pieces

Servings per container 1

**Amount Per Serving**

**Calories** 260          Calories from Fat 200

| | % Daily Value* |
|---|---|
| **Total Fat** 22g | 34% |
| Saturated Fat 3.5g | 16% |
| Trans Fat 0g | |
| **Cholesterol** 0mg | 0% |
| **Sodium** 190mg | 8% |
| **Potassium** 190mg | 5% |
| **Total Carbohydrate** 8g | 3% |
| Dietary Fiber 4g | 15% |
| Sugars 2g | |
| **Protein** 13g | |

| Vitamin A 0% | • | Vitamin C 0% |
|---|---|---|
| Calcium 4% | • | Iron 4% |

*Percent Daily Values are based on a
 2,000 calorie diet.

**Ingredients:** Peanuts, vegetable oil (contains one or more of the following: peanut, cottonseed, soybean, and/or sunflower oil), and salt.

**Ingredients are listed in order of quantity. The item has the most of the first ingredient listed and the least of the last ingredient.**

## WINDOW ON MATH

### Converting Numbers to Percentages

**A** Read the information.

To convert numerical information to a percentage, divide the part by the whole and multiply by 100.

1. 130 calories (from fat) ÷ 170 calories (total) × 100 = 76.5% total calories from fat
2. 3.5 grams of saturated fat ÷ 22 grams recommended daily amount x 100 = 16% daily value of saturated fat

**B** Calculate the percentages.

1. One package of peanut butter crackers contains 180 calories. Ninety calories come from fat. What percentage of the calories are from fat?
2. A serving of pasta has 42 grams of total carbohydrates. The recommended daily amount of carbohydrates is 300 grams. What percent of the recommended daily amount is the serving of pasta?

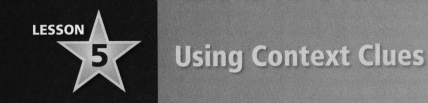
# Using Context Clues

## USING CONTEXT CLUES

When you see a word you don't know, use context (the surrounding words and ideas) to figure out the meaning of the word. Here are some types of context clues you can look for.

**a synonym**

Children need **immunizations** (<u>shots</u>) to protect them from childhood diseases.

**a comparison or a contrast**

She used to get a high **fever** every month, <u>but now her temperature very rarely goes above normal</u>.

**a definition or a description**

It is unusual for a vaccine to have serious **side effects**. However, you might develop <u>a rash or a slight fever</u> after getting vaccinated.

**words in a series**

A **first aid kit** has items you can use for small injuries, such as <u>bandages</u>, <u>alcohol</u>, <u>pain medicine</u>, and <u>ice packs</u>.

**cause and effect**

He is seeing a **cardiologist** because <u>he has heart disease</u>.

## ❶ Practice the Strategy

Use context clues to guess the general meaning of the **boldface** words. Write your ideas on the lines. Then compare ideas with your classmates.

1. **Side effects** can occur with any medicine, including vaccines. Depending on the vaccine, these can include slight fever, rash, or soreness at the site of the injection.

   <u>unwanted effects from a medicine</u>

2. If your child has a **severe** reaction to a vaccine, call your doctor right away.

   _____

3. The percent daily value shows you how much of the recommended daily amount of a **nutrient** (fat, sodium, fiber, etc.) is in a serving of that food.

   _____

4. Many things in your home can be poisonous if they are **swallowed**. These can include cleaning products, medicine, paint, alcohol, and cosmetics.

   _____

5. In its regular form, aspirin is an **analgesic**—a painkilling drug—available without a prescription.

   _____

6. If you need a blood **transfusion** during surgery, you can use your own blood if you get it saved at least a week before surgery.

   _____

**❷ Listen and Read**  023

Listen to the article as you read along.

### Computer Addiction

I think I was **addicted** to the computer when I was in my second year of high school. During that time, the first thing that I did after school was turn on the computer. I used to spend hours on **social networking sites** like Facebook and MySpace. Then I spent a long time just **surfing the Internet.** I would go from site to site, not really looking for anything specific. Though I knew I should stop, I just kept going. I **couldn't help myself.**

This situation lasted for about five months before I **realized** I had a problem. I became aware that I was spending way too much time online. It was not easy to **break the habit,** but I knew I had to stop spending hours in front of the computer. So, I set a time limit for how long I could use the computer: one hour. That small step changed my life. Now when I get home from school, I go online for an hour. Then I turn off my computer and go out for a walk or do my homework. My grades are better, and I feel healthier.

### ❸ Apply the Strategy

Read the paragraph. Then use context clues to write the meanings of the **boldface** words and phrases.

| | |
|---|---|
| addicted | It's when a person has to do something all the time, even when it's not good for him or her. |
| social networking sites | |
| surfing the Internet | |
| couldn't help myself | |
| realized | |
| break the habit | |

### ❹ Write

On another piece of paper, write a paragraph about an unhealthy habit that you have and how you can change it.

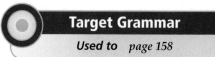

**Target Grammar**

*Used to*   page 158

## IDENTIFYING PUNCTUATION MARKS

Punctuation marks help your reader follow your ideas. Here are the names and symbols for some important punctuation marks.

**In Written Materials**

| | | | | | |
|---|---|---|---|---|---|
| apostrophe | ' | comma | , | hyphen | - |
| quotation marks | " " | period | . | bullet point | • |
| question mark | ? | parentheses | ( ) | colon | : |
| exclamation point | ! | slash | / | semicolon | ; |

**On a Computer** (when talking about a website or an email address)

| | | | | | |
|---|---|---|---|---|---|
| backslash | \ | dash | - | "at" mark | @ |
| forward slash | / | underscore | _ | dot | . |

**On a Phone** (on an automated telephone message)

| | | | |
|---|---|---|---|
| pound | # | star | * |

## ❶ Practice the Skill

Count and identify the punctuation marks in each sentence.

**1.** A first aid kit has items you can use for small injuries or for pain, such as bandages, alcohol, ice packs, and gloves.

   _4 commas and 1 period_

**2.** Since Dr. White is available in the evenings, you can call his office after 5 P.M. at (415) 555-2255.

   _____

**3.** You can get more information at http://www.redcross.org.

   _____

**4.** The recording said, "Using the number keys on your phone, enter your credit card number followed by the pound key."

   _____

**5.** Do not call 911 to do the following:

   • Ask for directions.          • Ask for information about public services.

   _____

## ❷ Write

Write the correct punctuation marks in the sentences.

**1.** The doctor ▢ s patient didn ▢ t arrive on time ▢

**2.** Can you email me at drfranklin ▢ help ▢ net ▢

**3.** My next appointment is on 03 ▢ 20 ▢ 11. That ▢ s the first day of spring ▢

**4.** You can find information about immunizations at http ▢ ▢ ▢ www ▢ cde ▢ gov ▢

**5.** She saw a child run into the street, so she yelled, "Stop ▢ "

## USING COMMAS

Use commas to separate the day of the month from the year. Do not use a comma if only the month and year are given.

> January 10, 2012
> I have lived here since January 2012.

Use a comma before the conjunction in a compound sentence.

> Psychologists help people with emotional problems, but they are not medical doctors.

Use a comma to separate items in a series.

> This food contains a lot of fat, sodium, and potassium.

Use a comma after an introductory word or phrase in a sentence.

> Because so many people wanted flu shots, there weren't enough for everybody.
> There are many kinds of medical specialists. For example, a dermatologist specializes in skin diseases.

Use commas before and after words that interrupt the flow of words in a sentence.

> Today I went to work. Yesterday, however, I stayed at home.

## ❸ Practice the Skill

Add commas where appropriate in each paragraph.

**Target Grammar**

*Because, since,* and
*so*    *page 159*

### Stop Smoking

In 1960 the Surgeon General of the United States announced that smoking was bad for your health. Since then many Americans have stopped using tobacco products. However thousands of teenagers become new smokers every day. Some people think that movies are influencing young people to start smoking.

### Get Moving

According to the U.S. Surgeon General people aren't getting enough exercise and this is causing serious health problems. There are some easy ways to get more exercise. For example you can walk up the stairs instead of taking the elevator. You can also take an exercise class join a gym or play a sport.

## ① Listening Review  024

### Part 1

First, you will hear a question. Next listen carefully to what is said. You will hear the question again. Then choose the correct answer: *A, B,* or *C.* Use the Answer Sheet.

### Part 2  025

You will hear the first part of a conversation. To finish the conversation, listen and choose the correct answer: *A, B,* or *C.* Use the Answer Sheet.

**Answer Sheet**

1 (A) (B) (C)
2 (A) (B) (C)
3 (A) (B) (C)
4 (A) (B) (C)
5 (A) (B) (C)
6 (A) (B) (C)
7 (A) (B) (C)
8 (A) (B) (C)
9 (A) (B) (C)
10 (A) (B) (C)

## ② Grammar Review

Circle the correct answer: A, B, or C.

**1.** Erik _____ since 2009.

A. exercised
B. is exercising
C. has been exercising

**2.** _____ you been feeling depressed for a long time?

A. Have
B. Are
C. Did

**3.** How long _____ he been waiting?

A. does
B. is
C. has

**4.** She needs _____ the doctor.

A. see
B. to see
C. seeing

**5.** Ana dislikes _____ plans at the last minute.

A. changing
B. changes
C. to change

**6.** He _____ seeing the therapist twice a week.

A. promises
B. suggests
C. refuses

## ❷ Grammar Review (continued)

**7.** Chuy _____ spend a lot of time online, but now he does.

    A. didn't use to
    B. didn't used to
    C. wasn't used to

**8.** Where did you _____ to go to school?

    A. used to
    B. use to
    C. went

**9.** He had chest pain, _____ he saw a cardiologist.

    A. because
    B. so
    C. since

**10.** _____ Laura likes babies, she has decided to become an obstetrician.

    A. So
    B. When
    C. Because

# LEARNING LOG

## I know these words:

**NOUNS**
- ○ account
- ○ analgesic
- ○ calories
- ○ cardiologist
- ○ chiropractor
- ○ dermatologist
- ○ fever
- ○ first aid kit
- ○ gynecologist
- ○ insured

- ○ IV
- ○ nutrient
- ○ obstetrician
- ○ optometrist
- ○ pediatrician
- ○ percent daily value
- ○ physical therapist
- ○ primary care physician
- ○ psychiatrist
- ○ psychologist
- ○ serving size

- ○ spine
- ○ transfusion
- ○ vital signs

**VERBS**
- ○ break the habit
- ○ collapse
- ○ diagnose
- ○ realize
- ○ specialize
- ○ swallow
- ○ treat

- ○ wheel in a wheelchair

**ADJECTIVES**
- ○ addicted
- ○ depressed

**ADVERB**
- ○ frequently

**OTHER**
- ○ can't help myself
- ○ social networking sites
- ○ surfing the Internet

## I practiced these skills, strategies, and grammar points:

- ○ describing a health care emergency
- ○ identifying health care professionals
- ○ calling the doctor's office
- ○ interrupting politely
- ○ interpreting nutritional information
- ○ converting numbers into percentages

- ○ using context clues
- ○ identifying punctuation marks
- ○ using the present perfect continuous
- ○ using gerunds and infinitives as objects of verbs
- ○ using *used to*
- ○ using *because*, *since*, and *so*

**Work-Out CD-ROM**

**Unit 3: Plug in and practice!**

## THINGS TO DO

### ❶ Warm Up

Discuss these questions with your classmates.

**1.** What city is in the picture? How do you know?

**2.** What are the people in the picture doing? Describe five things you see happening.

### ❷ True or False

Look at the picture and read the article. Then read the statements and check (✔) *True* or *False*. Write two more true sentences.

|  | True | False |
|---|---|---|
| **1.** Some people in the picture are protesting unpaid overtime work. | ○ | ○ |
| **2.** All of the protesters in the picture are protesting peacefully. | ○ | ○ |
| **3.** The **media** is not **reporting on** the protests. | ○ | ○ |
| **4.** Only young people are involved in protest marches. | ○ | ○ |
| **5.** Protest marches are unusual in the United States. | ○ | ○ |

**6.** _____

_____

**7.** _____

_____

### ❸ Give Opinions

Work with a partner to answer the questions. Discuss your answers with your classmates.

**1.** Why do you think people protest?

**2.** Do you think protesting is useful? Why or why not?

**3.** What are the people in the picture concerned about?

**4.** What are people concerned about in your community or another place you know?

**5.** What should and shouldn't people do during a protest?

### A Tradition of Marches

**Marches** on Washington are an American tradition. In 1894, several hundred unemployed workers marched from Ohio to Washington D.C. because they wanted the government to do something about unemployment. In 1913, thousands of women **marched on** Washington because they wanted women to be able to vote. One of the most famous marches on Washington was in 1963. During this march, Martin Luther King, Jr., gave his famous, "I Have a Dream" speech. Since then, people have marched on Washington to **protest** wars and to express their disagreement with the government.

SUPPORT WORKERS

Washington Monument

mounted police officer

reporter

FAIR PAY for all WORKERS

EQUAL PAY for EQUAL WORK

UNPAID OVERTIME IS UNFAIR

UNPAID OVERTIME IS UN-AMERICAN

EQUAL PAY FOR ALL

UNPAID OVERTIME IS UN-

TOUR THE CITY

**Work-Out CD-ROM**

Unit 4: Plug in and practice!

*Rights and Responsibilities* | **47**

# Identifying Rights and Responsibilities

## THINGS TO DO

### ❶ Warm Up

Discuss these questions with your classmates.

1. What is the difference between a right and a responsibility? Give two examples of each.
2. Are rights and responsibilities in the United States different or the same in your native country? Give two examples.

### ❷ Read and Complete

Read the information on page 49. Then complete these statements using the highlighted words.

1. Every four years, an _____election_____ is held to choose the president of the United States.

2. When you _____ to vote, you fill out a form and mail it to a government office.

3. The right to gather for a protest or political meeting is called freedom of _____.

4. Freedom of religion means that it is legal to have your own religious _____.

5. My boss _____ against me because I am a woman; he said only a man could be manager.

6. After the age of 16, children are not _____ to attend school.

### ❸ Listen 🎧 026

Listen to four conversations. Then find the freedom or right that is discussed. Write the correct letter on the line.

1. _____
2. _____
3. _____
4. _____

    **a.** Right to Vote
    **b.** Free Speech / Freedom of Assembly
    **c.** Right to Education
    **d.** Freedom of Religion

> **Target Grammar**
> Present passive   *pages 160–161*

### ❹ Interview

Talk to some of your classmates. Find someone who answers *yes* to each question. Then ask questions to get the details.

**Example:**  *A: Have you ever voted in an election?*
          *B: Yes, I have.*

         *A: What was the election for?*
         *B: It was for mayor of my town.*

| Find someone who | Person's name | Details |
|---|---|---|
| has voted in an election | | |
| understands basic ideas about the U.S. Constitution | | |
| has a child in school | | |
| knows a lot about current events | | |

# RIGHTS AND RESPONSIBILITIES

## 1. Right to Vote

**Right:** Citizens of the United States who are at least 18 years old have the right to vote in **elections.**

**Responsibility:** It is the responsibility of citizens to **register** to vote. Sometimes you must fill out a form several weeks before an election.

## 2. Right to Education

**Right:** People in the United States have the right to a free education through high school.

**Responsibility:** In most states, students up to age 16 are **required** to attend school. In states where school is required, parents are expected to make sure their children go to school.

## 3. Free Speech / Freedom of Assembly

**Right:** In the United States, people are allowed to speak freely and to **get together** in public to protest.

**Responsibility:** Public **gatherings** and demonstrations must remain peaceful. In addition, it is everyone's responsibility to respect people with different opinions.

## 4. Freedom of Religion

**Right:** People in the United States have the right to have their own **beliefs**. They cannot be legally **discriminated against** because of what they believe. This means no one can treat them differently or unfairly because of their religion.

**Responsibility:** It is the responsibility of all citizens to be **tolerant** of the religious beliefs of others. This means you don't have to agree with everyone, but you have to allow people to have their beliefs.

# Understanding the U.S. Educational System

## THINGS TO DO

### ❶ Warm Up

Discuss these questions with your classmates.

**1.** Read the information on page 51 and answer the questions.

**2.** Study the bar graph on page 51. What is the relationship between level of education and income in the United States?

### ❷ Listen and Take Notes  027

Listen to four people's opinions. Summarize each opinion. Then check (✔) *Agree* if you agree or *Disagree* if you disagree.

| Speaker's opinion | Agree | Disagree |
|---|---|---|
| **1.** Parents should be involved in their child's school and education. | ○ | ○ |
| **2.** | ○ | ○ |
| **3.** | ○ | ○ |
| **4.** | ○ | ○ |

### ❸ Listen and Check Your Answer  028

Listen to five conversations. Check (✔) *They agree* if the people agree or *They disagree* if the people disagree.

| | 1 | 2 | 3 | 4 | 5 |
|---|---|---|---|---|---|
| They agree. | ✔ | ○ | ○ | ○ | ○ |
| They disagree. | ○ | ○ | ○ | ○ | ○ |

### ❹ Role-Play  029

Listen. Work with a partner. Ask for opinions about three things that interest you. Agree or disagree. Use the Communication Strategy.

A: Do you think <u>students should speak only English in school</u>?

B: <u>No, I don't.</u>

A: I don't either.

B: Do you think <u>high school should be required</u>?

A. <u>Yes, I do.</u>

B: I do, too . <u>I think high school is very important</u>.

## COMMUNICATION STRATEGY

### Agreeing and Disagreeing

**Agreeing with a Positive Statement**

**A:** I think children should start school at four years old.

**B:** I do, too. / So do I. / Me too.

**Agreeing with a Negative Statement**

**A:** I don't think religion should be taught in public schools.

**B:** I don't either. / Neither do I.

**Disagreeing Politely**

**A:** I think all children should be taught at home.

**B:** Hmm, I don't know about that. / Really? I'm not sure I agree.

 **Target Grammar**

**Past passive** *pages 162–163*

# Public Schools in the United States

**1.** In the United States, parents are encouraged to **take an active role in** their children's education. Teachers want parents to make sure their kids do their homework and to ask them about their studies. Why is this important?

**2.** Many students participate in **extracurricular activities** such as sports, drama, or publishing a school newspaper. Were you encouraged to participate in extracurricular activities? What extracurricular activities did you participate in?

**3.** Classes in most public schools are **coeducational**; girls and boys study together. Do you think schools should be coeducational?

**4.** Students take required classes, such as math and history. In high school, students can also take **electives** such as photography, music, or cooking. Did you take any electives in high school?

## EDUCATION AND INCOME

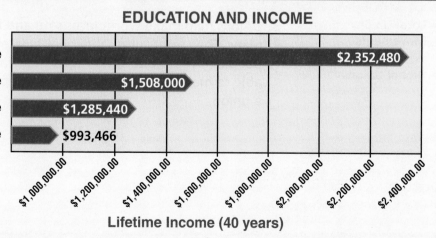

Highest Education Level Achieved

| | Lifetime Income (40 years) |
|---|---|
| Bachelor's Degree | $2,352,480 |
| Associate's Degree | $1,508,000 |
| High School Graduate | $1,285,440 |
| Not a High School Graduate | $993,466 |

$1,000,000.00  $1,200,000.00  $1,400,000.00  $1,600,000.00  $1,800,000.00  $2,000,000.00  $2,200,000.00  $2,400,000.00

**Lifetime Income (40 years)**

# Understanding Workers' Rights

## ❶ Warm Up

Answer these questions with a partner.

**1.** Do you know what a union is?  What does a union do?

**2.** Do you belong to a union? Does anybody you know belong to one?

## ❷ Read and Respond

Read the information on the website. Answer the questions.

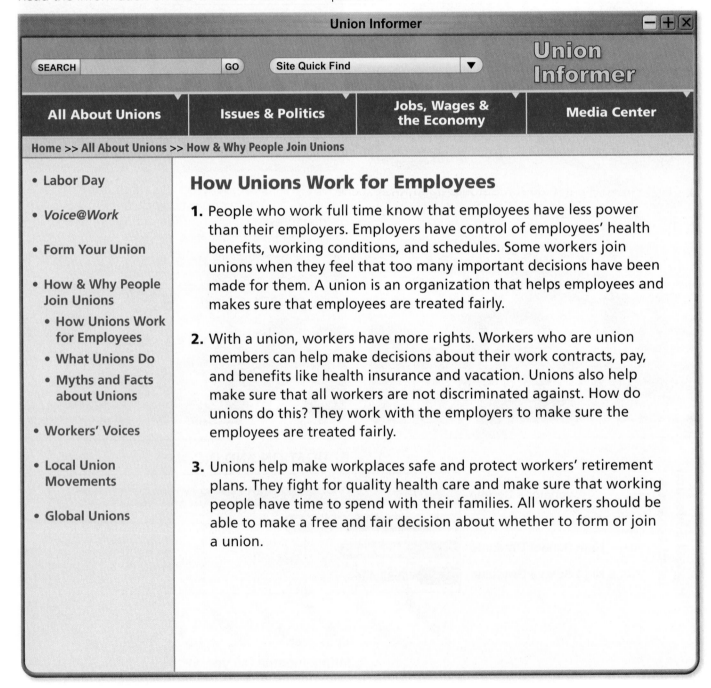

**Union Informer**

| SEARCH | GO | Site Quick Find ▼ |

**Union Informer**

| **All About Unions** | **Issues & Politics** | **Jobs, Wages & the Economy** | **Media Center** |

Home >> All About Unions >> How & Why People Join Unions

- Labor Day
- *Voice@Work*
- Form Your Union
- How & Why People Join Unions
  - How Unions Work for Employees
  - What Unions Do
  - Myths and Facts about Unions
- Workers' Voices
- Local Union Movements
- Global Unions

### How Unions Work for Employees

**1.** People who work full time know that employees have less power than their employers. Employers have control of employees' health benefits, working conditions, and schedules. Some workers join unions when they feel that too many important decisions have been made for them. A union is an organization that helps employees and makes sure that employees are treated fairly.

**2.** With a union, workers have more rights. Workers who are union members can help make decisions about their work contracts, pay, and benefits like health insurance and vacation. Unions also help make sure that all workers are not discriminated against. How do unions do this? They work with the employers to make sure the employees are treated fairly.

**3.** Unions help make workplaces safe and protect workers' retirement plans. They fight for quality health care and make sure that working people have time to spend with their families. All workers should be able to make a free and fair decision about whether to form or join a union.

**QUESTIONS**

**1.** What is the purpose of a union?

_____

_____

**2.** What rights can a union help workers win?

_____

_____

## ❸ Apply

Work with a classmate to answer the questions.

**1.** Pat heard that union members earn more money than nonunion workers. Where on this website could she find out about this topic?

**2.** Ira wants to find out about unions in his city. Where on this website could he find this information?

**3.** Shirin would like to read some stories about the experiences of other workers. Where might she find this information on the website?

**4.** Read the information in the website again. Which workers' issue is most important to you? Discuss why.

**Target Grammar**

**Passive with present perfect**   *page 164*

---

## WINDOW ON MATH

### Understanding Bar Graphs

**A** Read the information.

> Bar graphs contain a vertical axis (*y*-axis) and a horizontal axis (*x*-axis). Each axis presents different information. Numbers along an axis are called the scale. (See page 51 for an example.)

**B** Look at the bar graph on page 51. Answer the questions.

   **1.** What's the highest educational level included in the bar graph?

   **2.** How many types of educational backgrounds are being compared in the bar graph?

   **3.** How much money do people with an associate's degree (a two-year college degree) usually earn during their lifetime?

# Adjusting Your Reading Speed

## Adjusting Your Reading Speed

Good readers are flexible. They change the way they read to match their reading goals.

| Ways to read | Goals |
|---|---|
| **Skim**<br>When you skim a text, you move your eyes quickly across the words. | Learn the topic or the general meaning of the text, maybe decide if you want to read it in more detail |
| **Scan**<br>When you scan a text, you move your eyes quickly across the text to look for specific words or information. | Quickly find specific information in the text, such as names, numbers, or dates |
| **Read quickly**<br>When you read quickly, you try to read groups of words together. You don't read each word separately. | Understand the basic idea of what you're reading and some important facts, or read for fun |
| **Read slowly**<br>When you read slowly, you make sure you understand everything that you're reading, sometimes visualizing the ideas. | Deeply understand and remember every detail of what you're reading |

## ❶ Practice the Strategy

How would you read each item? Check (✔) your answer. Answers will depend on your reading goals. Then compare ideas with your classmates. Give your reasons.

|  | Skim | Scan | Read Quickly | Read Slowly |
|---|---|---|---|---|
| **1.** a chart with tonight's TV programs | ○ | ○ | ○ | ○ |
| **2.** a letter from your boss | ○ | ○ | ○ | ○ |
| **3.** a paycheck | ○ | ○ | ○ | ○ |
| **4.** instructions for taking a test | ○ | ○ | ○ | ○ |
| **5.** a funny story | ○ | ○ | ○ | ○ |
| **6.** a movie review | ○ | ○ | ○ | ○ |
| **7.** a very big bill | ○ | ○ | ○ | ○ |
| **8.** a newspaper article about you | ○ | ○ | ○ | ○ |

## ❷ Preview 🎧 030

Follow the steps to read the article on page 55.

**Step 1:** How interesting does the article look to you? Skim it and circle your answer.

Very interesting          Somewhat interesting          Not very interesting

**Step 2:** What is the topic of the article? Skim it again and write your answer. _____

**Step 3:** What numbers appear in the article? Scan to find them. _____

**Step 4:** What is the writer's main idea? Read the article quickly without the audio. Write your idea. _____

_____

**Step 5:** Which paragraph in the article was the most interesting to you? _____

Read this paragraph again slowly while you listen to the audio. Then summarize it in your own words.

### Rights at Work for Immigrant Workers

1   Many immigrant workers think that employees' rights should be protected better. Seventy-eight percent of Latino immigrants and 73 percent of Asian immigrants—compared with 68 percent of workers overall—say "much more" or "somewhat more" protection is necessary.

2   Sixty-five percent of black workers, 66 percent of Asians, and 74 percent of Latinos think that employers **take advantage of** recent immigrants. And 85 percent of black workers, 83 percent of Asians, and 86 percent of Latinos say immigrants are more likely than others to be treated unfairly by employers.

3   Immigrants also are more likely than workers overall to say they have experienced discrimination at work. Thirty-one percent of Latino immigrants and 25 percent of Asian immigrants say they have experienced discrimination based on race or ethnicity.

4   The survey shows differences between immigrants and workers overall in employer-provided workplace benefits. Only 31 percent of Latino immigrants and 42 percent of Asian immigrants say they have retirement plans to which their employers contribute, compared with 51 percent of all workers. Forty-four percent of Latino immigrants and 51 percent of Asian immigrants say they are covered by their employer's health plans, compared with 60 percent of workers overall.

> **Target Grammar**
> Passive with modals   *page 165*

## ❸ Understand the Reading

Use information from the article to complete the bar graph.

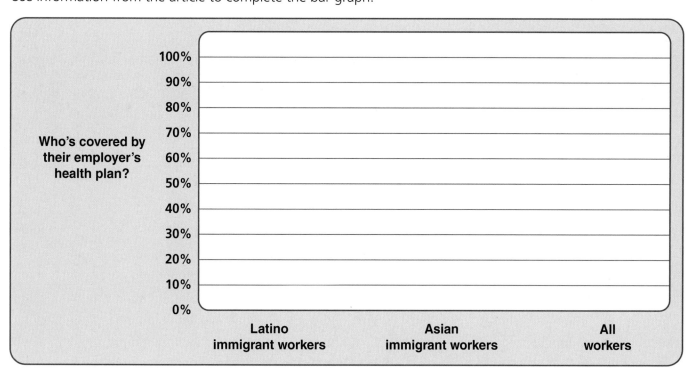

**Who's covered by their employer's health plan?**

| | 100% |
| | 90% |
| | 80% |
| | 70% |
| | 60% |
| | 50% |
| | 40% |
| | 30% |
| | 20% |
| | 10% |
| | 0% |

Latino immigrant workers          Asian immigrant workers          All workers

# Identifying Your Purpose for Writing

> ## IDENTIFYING YOUR PURPOSE FOR WRITING
>
> There are many different reasons for writing. For example, you might want to:
>
> - give your opinion about something
> - ask for information
> - ask for help
> - inform someone about something
> - identify a community problem
>
> - persuade someone
> - invite someone to an event
> - entertain someone
> - thank someone
>
> In a business letter, it is especially important to make your purpose for writing clear.

## ❶ Practice the Skill

Read letters 1 to 3. Identify the writer's purpose for writing each letter.

**Letter 1**

244 SW 15th Street, Apt. 23
Miami, Florida 33129

July 23, 2012

Senator Bill Nelson
United States Senate
317 Hart Senate Office Building
Washington, D.C. 20510

Dear Senator Nelson:

I am writing to you to voice my opinion about the President's energy plan. I hope that you will support this plan. I believe that every American has the right to affordable, safe energy. I hope you will consider this when the President needs your support for his energy plan.

Sincerely,

*Gerald Santiago*

Gerald Santiago

Writer's purpose: _____

_____

## Letter 2

4536 Santini Street
Jersey City, NJ 07306

April 12, 2012

Representative Albio Sires
United States House of Representatives
2238 Rayburn House Office Building
Washington, D.C. 20515

Dear Representative Sires:

I am writing to ask for help in getting my social security checks. I have written to the proper authorities several times, but I have not yet received a response. Please find enclosed copies of this correspondence.

I thank you in advance for your help.

Sincerely,

*Sonya Bluvosky*

Sonya Bluvosky

Writer's purpose: _____
_____

## Letter 3

642 South Beverly Dr.
Palm Springs, CA 92264

August 21, 2012

Congresswoman Mary Bono Mack
404 Canon House Office Building
Washington, D.C. 20515

Dear Congresswoman Mack:

I am writing to invite you to speak at a meeting of the Durham Voter's Network. The Voter's Network is a group that is interested in many of the environmental issues that you have supported in the past. Our members would especially be interested in hearing about the environmental issues you are currently working on in the House. If you are available on any of the dates on the attached sheet, we would be honored to have you speak to our group.

I look forward to hearing from you.

Sincerely,

*Dora Lasky*

Dora Lasky

Writer's purpose: _____
_____

## ❷ Write

Think of an issue or problem in your community. Imagine that you are going to write a letter to your town's mayor about it. Write the purpose of your letter in the box. Then write the letter. Explain the problem and suggest a solution.

My purpose: _____
_____

# What Do You Know?

## ① Listening Review 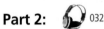 031

**Part 1:**

Listen to what is said. When you hear the question, *Which is correct?*, listen and choose the correct answer: *A, B,* or *C.* Use the Answer Sheet.

**Part 2:**  032

First, you will hear a question. Next, listen carefully to what is said. You will hear the question again. Then choose the correct answer: *A, B,* or *C.* Use the Answer Sheet.

### *Answer Sheet*

1. Ⓐ Ⓑ Ⓒ
2. Ⓐ Ⓑ Ⓒ
3. Ⓐ Ⓑ Ⓒ
4. Ⓐ Ⓑ Ⓒ
5. Ⓐ Ⓑ Ⓒ
6. Ⓐ Ⓑ Ⓒ
7. Ⓐ Ⓑ Ⓒ
8. Ⓐ Ⓑ Ⓒ
9. Ⓐ Ⓑ Ⓒ
10. Ⓐ Ⓑ Ⓒ

## ② Grammar Review

Circle the correct answer: *A, B,* or *C.*

**1.** Parents _____ to attend the PTA meeting.

   A. request
   B. are requested
   C. requesting

**2.** She _____ to attend school every day.

   A. be expected
   B. been expected
   C. is expected

**3.** Chinese _____ at my school.

   A. not taught
   B. isn't taught
   C. been taught

**4.** A computer was _____from the classroom.

   A. stolen
   B. stole
   C. stealing

**5.** Physical education _____ at my school.

   A. required
   B. were required
   C. was required

**6.** She _____ at home because she was sick.

   A. is kept
   B. were kept
   C. was kept

## ❷ Grammar Review (continued)

**7.** We haven't _____ paid this month.
   A. being
   B. been
   C. be

**8.** _____ a union representative been elected yet?
   A. Has
   B. Have
   C. Is

**9.** The workers should _____ better.
   A. treat
   B. be treated
   C. be treating

**10.** Immigrants must _____ discriminated against.
   A. not be
   B. not have
   C. not been

## LEARNING LOG

### *I know these words:*

**NOUNS**
- belief
- election
- elective
- extracurricular activity
- freedom of assembly
- gathering
- march
- media
- mounted police officer
- reporter
- responsibility
- right

**VERBS**
- discriminate against (someone)
- get together
- march on
- protest
- register
- require
- report on
- take advantage of (someone)
- take an active role in

**ADJECTIVES**
- coeducational
- tolerant

### *I practiced these skills, strategies, and grammar points:*

- describing an event
- identifying rights and responsibilities
- understanding the U.S. educational system
- agreeing and disagreeing
- understanding workers' rights
- understanding bar graphs

- adjusting reading speed
- identifying a purpose for writing
- using the present passive
- using the past passive
- using the passive with the present perfect
- using the passive with modals

**Work-Out CD-ROM**

**Unit 4: Plug in and practice!**

## THINGS TO DO

### ❶ Warm Up

Discuss these questions with your classmates.

**1.** What do you like about shopping?

**2.** What do you dislike about shopping?

**3.** Have you ever bought something you didn't really need? Why did you buy it?

**4.** What things are being advertised in the picture?

### ❷ Discuss

Discuss the questions with a partner. Then report your answers to the class.

**1.** Why do you think there are so many people going into May's?

**2.** Are there any advertisements on pages 60 and 61 that don't seem honest? Why do you think so?

**3.** Which advertisements on pages 60 and 61 are most effective? Why?

**4.** The average person sees and hears hundreds of advertisements a day. What effect do you think this has on people?

### ❸ Analyze

Work with a partner. Choose one of the advertisements from pages 60 and 61. Change the ad to make it more effective. Then present the ad to the class. Explain how your changes make the ad more effective.

Example:  A: *The Carl's Cafe ad would be better if it listed the lunch specials.*
B: *Why?*
A: *The list of specials might make people hungry, and then they would want to come into the restaurant.*
B: *That's a good idea.*

## THINGS TO DO

### ❶ Warm Up

Discuss these questions with your classmates.

**1.** Do you shop when you need to buy something specific, or do you shop for fun?

**2.** How often do you buy things that you don't need?

**3.** How does shopping make you feel? Tired? Excited? Bored?

### ❷ Use Context Clues

Read *Tips for Consumers* on page 63. Use context clues to guess the meaning of the highlighted words. Write your answers in a chart like this. Then compare ideas with your classmates.

| Word or phrase | Meaning |
|---|---|
| purchases | *the things you buy* |
| impulse buyer | |
| refund policy | |

### ❸ Listen and Write  033

Listen to each conversation. Then complete each statement about what you heard. Use the highlighted words from page 63.

**1.** The salesperson is trying to _____*pressure her into*_____ buying a sweater.

**2.** The shopper is asking about the store's _____.

**3.** Ann's friend is an _____.

**4.** The store sells rice _____.

### ❹ Use the Vocabulary

Read *Tips for Consumers* again. Answer the question in each box. Check (✔) *Yes* or *No*. Then talk to different classmates. Find someone who answers *Yes* to each question. Then ask another question to get more information.

**Example:**　*A: Are you an impulse buyer?*
　　　　　　*B: Yes.*
　　　　　　*A: What was the last thing you bought that you didn't need?*
　　　　　　*B: I bought a tennis racket because it was on sale, but I don't play tennis!*

**Target Grammar**

**Adjectives ending in –*ed***
**and –*ing*** *pages 166–167*

## TIPS FOR CONSUMERS

**1**

Plan your **purchases** before you go shopping so that you buy only things you need. Don't be an **impulse buyer**. Impulse buyers buy things without thinking and usually spend more than they want to.

Are you an impulse buyer?

○ Yes    ○ No

**2**

When you buy something, be sure to keep your receipt and make sure you understand the store's **refund policy**. Find out if the store gives a cash refund or **store credit** if you return the item. You should also ask if there is a **time limit** for returning a purchase.

Have you ever gotten a store credit for something you bought?

○ Yes    ○ No

**3**

You can buy used clothes and other things at **thrift stores** and **yard sales**. You can also buy and sell used clothes at **consignment shops**. Consignment shops will sell your items for you and give you a percentage of the money.

Have you ever bought something at a thrift store, consignment shop, or yard sale?

○ Yes    ○ No

**4**

You can save money by **buy**ing food or other items **in bulk**. Many stores sell loose grains, pasta, cereal, and nuts out of large containers. Customers can pour the amount they want into a bag or bottle, weigh it, and buy it.

Did you buy anything in bulk last month?

○ Yes    ○ No

**5**

Don't let a salesperson **pressure you into** buying **merchandise** you don't want. Salespeople often try to **convince** you to buy things you don't really want. If you don't want help from a salesperson, you can say, "I'm just looking, thank you."

Do you like to have salespeople help you when you shop?

○ Yes    ○ No

**6**

One-Year Limited Warranty

Some products come with a written **warranty**. The warranty says that the company that made the product will fix or replace the product for a certain period of time. Before you buy something, it's a good idea to look at the warranty.

Do you usually look at the warranty before you buy something expensive?

○ Yes    ○ No

## THINGS TO DO

### ❶ Warm Up

Discuss these questions with your classmates.

1. What are four common questions that customers ask salespeople?

2. What do you think the people in each picture are saying?

### ❷ Listen and Match  034

Listen to five conversations. Match each conversation to a picture on page 65. Write the number of the conversation in the circle.

### ❸ Listen for Specific Information  035

Listen to the conversations again. What does each customer want? Take notes in the chart.

| What does the customer want? |
|---|
| 1.    She wants to pay with a check. |
| 2. |
| 3. |
| 4. |
| 5. |

### ❹ Role-Play 🎧 036

Listen. Then work with a partner. Role-play a conversation between a customer and a salesperson. Use the Communication Strategy.

A: Could you tell me <u>if this comes with a warranty</u>?

B: I think it does, but I'm not positive.

A: Could you check for me?

B: Yes, of course. Just give me a minute. I'll be right back.

A: Thanks.

**Target Grammar**

Tag questions   *pages 168–169*

## COMMUNICATION STRATEGY

### Expressing Doubt

If you aren't certain your answer to a question is 100 percent correct, it's important to explain that. Use these sentences:

- I think _____, but I'm not positive.

- It's possible that _____, but I'm not sure.

- It seems to me that _____, but I'm not sure.

- I'm pretty sure that _____, but I'm not absolutely certain.

## WINDOW ON PRONUNCIATION

### Intonation in Tag Questions  037

**A** Read the information.

When tag questions give an opinion or confirm something, they have rising and then falling intonation. When tag questions are used like *yes/no* questions, they have rising intonation.

**B** Listen to the questions. Then listen and repeat.

| Question | Confirmation | Yes/No |
|---|:---:|:---:|
| **1.** That's a really good price, isn't it? | ○ | ✔ |
| **2.** You didn't bring your credit card, did you? | ○ | ○ |
| **3.** We paid that bill last month, didn't we? | ○ | ○ |
| **4.** They can't cancel our Internet service without notice, can they? | ○ | ○ |
| **5.** These cookies aren't very fresh, are they? | ○ | ○ |

**C** Listen to the questions again and check the appropriate column.

**D** Write two tag questions. Ask a classmate your questions.

**1.** _____

**2.** _____

## ❶ Warm Up

Discuss these questions with your classmates.

**1.** In addition to the newspaper, where can you find information about houses or apartments for rent?

**2.** What do you think is the best way to find a house or an apartment for rent?

**3.** What advice would you give to someone looking for a house or an apartment for rent?

## ❷ Read and Respond

Read the information. Answer the questions on page 67.

### Houses for Rent    453

North End. 2 BR, 2 baths. $1000/mo. + sec. dep. Call Karen 555-3590

2BR, newly remodeled, W/D hkup, 1.5 BA, no pets/smoking, $1200/mo. Patty or Sam 555-8998

2BR house. Stove, refrigerator, dishwasher, W/D included. Large backyard. $1200/mo. + utils. 555-5827

3 BR house, large deck $900/mo. 555-3325

3 BR, 2.5 bath, short term, no lease $1200/mo. Cell 555-0949

New 3 BR, 2 baths, garage, pets ok. $1100/mo. Call Peter 555-3356

Nice 2 BR home w/porch & garage, $1100. No pets. Call Dick 555-2113

### Condominium Rentals    457

2 BR, Includes utils. $900/mo. Call Jennifer 555-7867

Brand NEW condo. 6 rms, 2BR, central air. $1200/mo. Call Kathleen after 8 P.M. 555-3354

WEST SIDE Lg 1 BR, new paint/carpet, pets ok, parking, a/c, ht & hw included, $850/mo. 555-0878

### Unfurnished Apartments    459

WEST SIDE. Lg 1 BR, include garage, nice yard, small dog ok. $800/mo. 555-9984

EAST SIDE. 2 BR completely new, parking, no utils. $900/mo. 555-6657

DOWNTOWN Lg 2 BR, new windows, laundry. $675/mo. 555-9068

South Beach. Safe neighborhood, 1 BR, new windows/paint/floor. No smoking/pets. Available 2/1. $900/mo. 555-3256

EAST SIDE 2BR, nice area, nice building, storage room, no dogs, $800/mo. 555-3657

### Furnished Apartments    461

South Beach. 1st flr, 1 BR/LR, kitchen, bath, prkg, deposit, $200/wk, includes all utils. 555-6584

2 1/2 rms, 1 bath, furnished, no pets/smokers, prkg & all utils included. $750/mo. 555-4463

**KEY**
BR = bedroom(s)
LR = living room
sec dep = security deposit
W/D = washer and dryer
hkup = hookup
utils = utilities
a/c = air conditioning
ht = heat
hw = hot water
mo = month
wk = week
rms = rooms
lg = large
prkg = parking

**Questions**

**1.** You are looking for a condo to rent. Which section of the want ads should you look at?

_section 457, Condominium Rentals._

**2.** You want to rent an apartment that you will **furnish** . Which section would you look at?

**3.** You are looking for a house with three bedrooms to rent. Which numbers would you call?

**4.** You are looking for an apartment that **allows** pets. Which number would you call?

**5.** Choose two of the one-bedroom apartments for rent. How are they similar and different?

**6.** Which ad looks the most interesting to you? Why?

## ❸ Write

Write a classified ad for your own house or apartment.

## ❹ Apply 038

Listen. Check (✔) the correct boxes for each message. Write the number of bedrooms and the amount of rent in the last two boxes.

| Message | House | Condo | Apartment | Furnished | Pets allowed | Number of bedrooms | Rent |
|---------|-------|-------|-----------|-----------|--------------|--------------------|------|
| 1 | | | ✔ | | | 3 | $1,500 |
| 2 | | | | | | | |
| 3 | | | | | | | |
| 4 | | | | | | | |
| 5 | | | | | | | |
| 6 | | | | | | | |

## USING A DICTIONARY

There is a lot of interesting and useful information in an English language learner's dictionary. In addition to finding the definition of a word, you can:

- learn how to pronounce a word.
- learn the part of speech of a word.
- learn the number of syllables in a word.
- learn irregular forms of nouns and verbs.
- find a synonym for a word.
- read sample sentences with the word.
- learn phrasal verbs such as *look into* and *find out*.
- learn cultural information about the word.

Words in English often have more than one meaning. When you look up a word in a dictionary, make sure you choose the correct definition. The first definition is usually the most common, but it might not be the one you are looking for.

## ❶ Practice the Strategy

Read the dictionary definitions. Answer the questions.

> **bulk**/ bûlk/ *n.* **1.** large size: *Big animals, such as elephants and whales, have huge bulk.*
> **2.** the most of, (syn.) majority: *The bulk of the students passed the exam.* **3. in bulk:**
> large amount: *You can save money by buying things in bulk.*
>
> —*adj.* a bulk shipment: a large quantity: *The bulk shipment was 500 boxes of shoes.*
>
> **bulk·y**/ bûlki / *adj.* –ier, –iest, large and difficult to handle, (syn.) unwieldy:
> *A mattress is too bulky for one person to carry.*

**1.** What is the most common meaning of the word *bulk*?

_____

**2.** What is the superlative form of the word *bulky*?

_____

**3.** What is a synonym for one definition of *bulk*?

_____

**4.** What is a synonym for the adjective *bulky*?

_____

## ❷ Read and Discuss

Read the dictionary definitions and the usage note. Discuss the questions with a partner.

> **garage sale** *n.* a sale of used household items (old lamps, tables, etc.) inside or near a person's garage: *When my parents moved to a smaller house, they held a garage sale one weekend.*
>
> ──────────────────────────────
>
> USAGE NOTE: Also known as yard sales, rummage sales, tag sales, or sidewalk sales, *garage sales* are popular in both cities and suburbs. Homeowners may post signs around their neighborhood to advertise a sale. People who live in apartments usually just put things out on the sidewalk and wait for passersby: *I need some bookshelves. Let's drive around the university area and look for a garage sale.*
>
> ──────────────────────────────
>
> **yard sale** *n.* the sale of unwanted household items, such as old lamps and tables, in a person's yard: *We bought a beautiful old table at a yard sale for $10! See*: garage sale, USAGE NOTE.

**1.** What is the difference between a yard sale and a garage sale?

_____

**2.** This dictionary provides sample sentences in italics. Do the sample sentences help you to understand the meanings of the words? How?

_____

**3.** What is the purpose of a usage note?

_____

**4.** How helpful is this usage note to you? Why?

_____

## ❸ Apply

Read the sentences. Choose the correct definition for the word *yard* in each context. Circle *1* or *2*.

> **yard** /yard/ *n.* **1.** a length of three feet or 36 inches (0.91 meter): *She bought a yard of cloth.* **2.** an area usually behind or in front of a house: *The children went outside to play in the yard.*

| | | |
|---|---|---|
| **1.** I spent an hour yesterday cleaning the yard. | 1 | 2 |
| **2.** I need three yards to make a new dress. | 1 | 2 |
| **3.** I found a yard of rope downstairs. | 1 | 2 |
| **4.** My new tie is a yard long. | 1 | 2 |
| **5.** My yard is about 20 yards wide. | 1 | 2 |

# Writing a Letter of Complaint

## WRITING A LETTER OF COMPLAINT

Writing a letter of complaint is often the best way for a consumer to correct a problem. Be concise and clear in a letter of complaint and include the following information:

- the date and place of the purchase
- a description of the purchase
- an explanation of the problem
- the length of time you are willing to wait
- a copy of the receipt
- what you want

## ❶ Practice the Skill

Read the written complaints and check (✔) the information each one provides.

|  | Email | Letter |
|---|:---:|:---:|
| 1. the date the complaint was written | ○ | ✅ |
| 2. the date of the purchase | ○ | ○ |
| 3. the recipient's name and address | ○ | ○ |
| 4. the recipient's title | ○ | ○ |
| 5. a description of the purchase | ○ | ○ |
| 6. an explanation of the problem | ○ | ○ |
| 7. what the writer wants | ○ | ○ |
| 8. how long the writer will wait | ○ | ○ |
| 9. the writer's name and address | ○ | ○ |
| 10. a copy of the receipt | ○ | ○ |

**Email**

Dear Sir or Madam:

In February, I went to the Lucky Sam's toy store in Oyster, New Jersey, to buy a Sander's Outdoor Play Set (product #2678). This product was advertised as being on sale in the store's flyer, but when I got to the store, they did not have any in stock. The salesperson said that I could have a rain check to redeem when they got more in the store. But now I have waited more than 10 weeks, and I still don't have a Sander's gym.

I feel strongly that the company needs to do something soon to resolve this problem. I look forward to your reply.

Sincerely,
Frank Muller

5677 Torrence Avenue
Millville, New Jersey 08332
FMuller@freeemail.net

## Letter

4567 Melody Avenue, Apt 4A
San Carlos, CA 94070

May 6, 2012

Lisa Jones
Consumer Service Manager
Dyno Electronics
432 Southwest Avenue
Modesto, CA 95350

Dear Ms. Jones:

On April 15, I bought a Dyno MP3 player (serial number 45605048844) at your store in San Carlos. Unfortunately, the player has not worked properly since the day I bought it. I called the store the day after I purchased it to report the problem, but the store manager refuses to repair or exchange the MP3 player. Enclosed you will find a copy of my receipt.

To resolve the problem, I feel strongly that I should be able to exchange this MP3 player for one that works properly.

I look forward to your reply and a resolution to my problem. I will wait until June 1 before seeking help from a consumer protection agency or the Better Business Bureau. Please contact me at the address above or by phone at (650) 555-4993.

Sincerely,

*Jon Phillips*

Jon Phillips

## ❷ Write

Think of something you bought but weren't satisfied with. Write a letter of complaint explaining the situation. Then read a classmate's letter and identify the information in Activity 1 that the letter provides.

**Target Grammar**

**Reported speech** *pages 170–171*

# What Do You Know?

## ❶ Listening Review  039

**Part 1:**

You will hear the first part of a conversation. To finish the conversation, listen and choose the correct answer: *A*, *B*, or *C*. Use the Answer Sheet.

**Part 2:** 🎧 040

Listen to what is said. When you hear the question, *Which is correct?*, listen and choose the correct answer: *A*, *B*, or *C*. Use the Answer Sheet.

*Answer Sheet*

1  Ⓐ  Ⓑ  Ⓒ
2  Ⓐ  Ⓑ  Ⓒ
3  Ⓐ  Ⓑ  Ⓒ
4  Ⓐ  Ⓑ  Ⓒ
5  Ⓐ  Ⓑ  Ⓒ
6  Ⓐ  Ⓑ  Ⓒ
7  Ⓐ  Ⓑ  Ⓒ
8  Ⓐ  Ⓑ  Ⓒ
9  Ⓐ  Ⓑ  Ⓒ
10  Ⓐ  Ⓑ  Ⓒ

## ❷ Grammar Review

Circle the correct answer: *A*, *B*, or *C*.

**1.** I don't like shopping. I think it's _____

A. bored
B. boring
C. bore

**2.** Mary was very _____ when she saw the receipt.

A. surprising
B. surprises
C. surprised

**3.** Buying things that I don't need make me feel _____.

A. depressed
B. depressing
C. depress

**4.** I can't understand these directions. They're too _____.

A. confused
B. confusing
C. confuses

**5.** They don't take checks here, _____?

A. don't they
B. do they
C. did they

**6.** She's a good shopper, _____?

A. isn't she
B. doesn't she
C. isn't it

## ❷ Grammar Review (continued)

**7.** You returned those shoes, _____?

    A. don't you
    B. didn't you
    C. did you

**8.** A: This is nice, isn't it? B: Yes, _____.

    A. it isn't
    B. is it
    C. it is

**9.** Wei: I need a rain check.
Wei said that _____.

    A. I needed a rain check
    B. he needed a rain check
    C. you needed a rain check

**10.** The salesperson told _____.

    A. me I could have a refund
    B. you can have a refund
    C. to me I could have a refund

## LEARNING LOG

### *I know these words:*

**NOUNS**
- ○ consignment shops
- ○ garage sale
- ○ impulse buyer
- ○ merchandise
- ○ purchases

- ○ refund policy
- ○ store credit
- ○ thrift stores
- ○ time limit
- ○ warranty
- ○ yard sale

**VERBS**
- ○ allow
- ○ convince
- ○ furnish

**ADJECTIVE**
- ○ furnished

**OTHER**
- ○ buy in bulk
- ○ pressure (someone) into

### *I practiced these skills, strategies, and grammar points:*

- ○ interpreting advertisements
- ○ understanding shopping terms
- ○ talking to salespeople
- ○ using correct intonation in tag questions
- ○ using resources to find housing
- ○ using a dictionary
- ○ writing a letter of complaint

- ○ using adjectives with –ed and –ing
- ○ using tag questions
- ○ using reported speech

**Work-Out CD-ROM**

**Unit 5: Plug in and practice!**

# UNIT 6 RULES AND LAWS

**LESSON 1 Describing a Court of Law**

## THINGS TO DO

### ❶ Warm Up

Discuss these questions with your classmates.

1. Have you ever seen a courtroom in real life or in a movie? Describe what happened.
2. What are the people in this courtroom doing?
3. What should the woman talking on the cell phone do?

### ❷ Identify

Who in this courtroom does each thing? Write your guesses. Then compare ideas with a classmate.

__The jury__ discusses whether the defendant is **guilty** or not guilty of a crime.

_____ records what people say.

_____ tries to prove that the **defendant** is guilty.

_____ is in charge of security in the courtroom.

_____ tries to prove the defendant is not guilty.

### ❸ Put in Sequence

Read the journal entries on this page. Put the events in order from first (1) to last (8).

_____ The **jury** went into a special room.

_____ She went to court for the first time.

_____ She became a member of the jury.

_____ A **judge** and two lawyers interviewed her.

___1___ She received a summons for jury duty in her mailbox.

_____ She received a check from the court.

_____ The jury made a decision.

_____ She listened to the testimony of many **witnesses**.

Compare ideas with a classmate. Then take turns telling the story in your own words.

**Target Grammar**

*Could, should, and ought to for advice* *pages 172–173*

### My Journal

<u>May 21</u>: Today I found a **summons** for jury duty in my mailbox. It was an official notice from the county. It said that I should go to the courthouse at 9 A.M. on June 22.

<u>June 22</u>: I arrived at court at 9 A.M. A lot of other people were there, too. A judge and two **lawyers** interviewed each person. The lawyers are the same people who will try to prove that the defendant is guilty or **innocent** Some people were **dismissed**. They left immediately. Some were asked to stay and be on the jury. When it was my turn, I answered all their questions. They told me to come back tomorrow to be a member of the jury.

<u>June 23</u>: My first day on a jury. It's a **criminal** case! The **prosecutor** says that the defendant did something that was against the law. He is accused of **battery**. That means he was arrested for hurting someone. We listened to witnesses talk about what they saw. Their **testimony** was very interesting. They all said that they saw the defendant beat up another man.

<u>July 9</u>: I've been listening to testimonies for over two weeks, and today the trial ended. In the afternoon, all of us—the jury members— went into a special room to make a decision. It didn't take us very long to make our final decision. We **found him guilty** of battery.

<u>Aug. 2</u>: There was a check from the court in my mailbox today. They paid me $20 a day to serve on the jury.

Judge

Court Reporter

Witness

Bailiff

Jury

Defense Attorney

Defendant

Prosecutor

# Identifying Infractions and Crimes

## THINGS TO DO

### ❶ Warm Up

Discuss these questions with your classmates.

**1.** Have you ever seen anyone get arrested in real life or on television? What happens?

**2.** What are some examples of minor and major crimes?

### ❷ Use the Vocabulary

Use the chart on pages 76–77 to answer these questions.

**1.** Which is the most serious—an **infraction**, a **misdemeanor**, or a **felony**? Give an example of each.

**2.** What type of crime is **punishable** by a year or less in prison?

**3.** For what crimes can a person go to **prison** for more than a year?

**4.** Which is more serious—shoplifting or burglary?

### ❸ Write

Complete each sentence with a highlighted word on pages 76–77.

**1.** Amy has to _____ of $200 for jaywalking.

**2.** If you _____ a misdemeanor in Greenville, you may have to do community service.

**3.** In some places, a misdemeanor is punishable by _____ only, especially if the person has never broken the law before.

**4.** A serious felony, such as aggravated assault, can be punishable by _____ for 30 to 90 years in the United States.

**5.** Littering is a minor _____; vandalism is more serious.

### ❹ Listen and Identify 🎧 041

Listen to the conversations. Check (✔) the type of crime you hear about.

|   | Infraction | Misdemeanor | Felony |
|---|---|---|---|
| **1** |  |  |  |
| **2** |  |  |  |
| **3** |  |  |  |

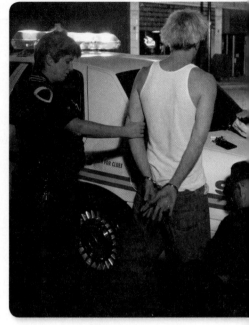

"You're under arrest."

| Types of Illegal Action |
|---|
|  Infraction |
|  Misdemeano |
|  Felony |

**Target Grammar**

*Should have, could have,* and *must have* pages 174–175

## WINDOW ON PRONUNCIATION

### Reduction of Past Modals  042

Sometimes we say words quickly and the pronunciation changes. These are **reductions.** People use reductions in informal speaking situations. People use the long forms in formal speaking situations and in writing.

**A** Listen to the words. Then listen and repeat.

| | |
|---|---|
| should have (sounds like *shuduv*) | shouldn't have (sounds like *shudnuv*) |
| could have (sounds like *cuduv*) | couldn't have (sounds like *cudnuv*) |

**B** Listen to the sentences. Write the missing words. Use the correct spelling.

1. I _____ turned off my cell phone before I went into the courtroom.
2. He _____ crossed the street in the middle of the block.
3. They _____ paid the fine earlier.
4. She _____ slowed down at the intersection.
5. You _____ worn your seat belt.
6. We _____ gotten a better lawyer.

**C** Work with a partner. Ask the questions. Write your partner's answers.

What could you have done to help someone last week? What did you do to help someone last week?

_____

_____

| Definitions | Examples | Consequences |
|---|---|---|
| infraction is a minor **fense**. It is the least serious e of offense. | <ul><li>littering</li><li>**jaywalking**</li><li>minor traffic **violations**</li></ul> | People who **commit** an infraction usually have to **pay a fine**. Jaywalking fines vary from city to city, ranging from under $50 to $700. |
| misdemeanor is more serious n an infraction but less ous than a felony. In general, demeanors are crimes nishable by less than one year prison. | <ul><li>petty theft (in many states, this includes shoplifting)</li><li>trespassing</li><li>vandalism</li></ul> | People who commit misdemeanors may be punished with a fine, **probation**, community service, or **imprisonment** for one year or less. |
| elony is a very serious crime. many states, a felony is any ne punishable by more than year in prison. | <ul><li>arson</li><li>burglary</li><li>murder</li><li>rape</li><li>**aggravated assault**</li></ul> | Felony crimes are punishable by imprisonment for more than a year. The most serious felonies can be punishable by death. |

# Interpreting Permit and License Requirements

## THINGS TO DO

### ❶ Warm Up

Discuss these questions with your classmates.

**1.** What do you need a permit or license for in your community?

☐ to get married    ☐ to vote    ☐ to build a house

☐ to ride a bicycle    ☐ to ride a motorcycle    ☐ other: _____

**2.** What do you have to do to get a marriage license and a driver's license? Read questions 1 and 2 on page 79. Check (✔) your ideas in the *Before listening* column.

### ❷ Listen and Match  043

Listen. Write the number you press for the information.

___ business license    ___ ceremony    _1_ office hours    ___ passport

### ❸ Listen for Specific Information  044

Listen to recorded messages about getting a marriage license and a driver's license. Check (✔) the things you have to do in the *After listening* column on page 79.

### ❹ Listen and Take Notes  045

Read the questions in the *Note-Taking Chart* on page 79. Then listen again for the answers to the questions and take notes. After you listen, work with a classmate. Take turns asking and answering the questions.

### ❺ Role-Play 🎧 046

Listen. Then work with a partner. Role-play a conversation about each question. Use the Communication Strategy.

**Example:**   ***A: Do I need to have a blood test to get a marriage license?***
                  ***B: No, it's not necessary.***
                  ***A: So a blood test is not required?***
                  ***B: That's right.***

**Questions**

**1.** Is it expensive to get a marriage license?

**2.** How long does a marriage license last?

**3.** Where do I go to get a driver's license?

**4.** How many times can I take the written test?

**Couples must get a marriage license before getting married.**

**A vision test is required to get a driver's license.**

### COMMUNICATION STRATEGY

#### Paraphrasing to Check Understanding

When you paraphrase, you put information into your own words. Paraphrasing is a good way to check your understanding of something.

A: It usually takes about 30 minutes to issue a marriage license.

B: So I can get a license in about half an hour?

A: That's right.

### 1. What do you have to do to get a marriage license?

Before listening | | After listening
--- | --- | ---
☐ | a. You have to get a blood test. | ☐
☐ | b. You have to complete an application. | ☐
☐ | c. You have to make an appointment. | ☐
☐ | d. You have to go to the County Clerk's office. | ☐
☐ | e. You have to show a picture ID. | ☐
☐ | f. You have to show your Social Security card. | ☐
☐ | g. You have to take a test. | ☐
☐ | h. You have to have your picture taken. | ☐
☐ | i. You have to pay a fee. | ☐
☐ | j. You have to be fingerprinted. | ☐

### 2. What do you have to do to get a driver's license?

Before listening | | After listening
--- | --- | ---
☐ | a. You have to get a blood test. | ☐
☐ | b. You have to complete an application. | ☐
☐ | c. You have to make an appointment. | ☐
☐ | d. You have to go to the County Clerk's office. | ☐
☐ | e. You have to show a picture ID. | ☐
☐ | f. You have to show your Social Security card. | ☐
☐ | g. You have to take a test. | ☐
☐ | h. You have to have your picture taken. | ☐
☐ | i. You have to pay a fee. | ☐
☐ | j. You have to be fingerprinted. | ☐

| Note-Taking Chart | |
| --- | --- |
| **Marriage License Questions** | **Notes** |
| **1.** What forms of identification can you use to get a marriage license? | 1. |
| **2.** How much does a marriage license cost in this county? | 2. |
| **3.** How long does the marriage license last? | 3. |
| **Driver's License Questions** | **Notes** |
| **1.** In this state, what forms of identification can you use to get a driver's license? | 1. |
| **2.** How much does it cost to get a driver's license in this state? | 2. |
| **3.** How many questions are there on the test? | 3. |

## ❶ Warm Up

Discuss these questions with your classmates.

**1.** What are the biggest problems in your neighborhood?

**2.** How safe is your neighborhood?

**3.** What can people do to make their neighborhoods safer?

## ❷ Read and Respond

Read about Neighborhood Watch. Answer the questions on page 81.

### Neighborhood Watch

Do you want to get rid of problems such as drugs and violence in your neighborhood? Start a Neighborhood Watch group. It's the most effective and inexpensive way to reduce crime in your neighborhood. To start a Neighborhood Watch group, invite your neighbors to a meeting at your community center. See who's interested. Be sure to involve senior citizens and teens.

**What Do Neighborhood Watch Members Do?**

- **Have Community Meetings.** Members meet on a regular basis, for example, once a month or every other month.
- **Patrol the Community.** Neighborhood Watch volunteers walk or drive through the neighborhood and contact the police if they see **suspicious** behavior such as strange cars or people taking things from houses when no one is home.
- **Have Special Events.** Neighborhood Watch groups invite speakers to present information on safety and crime issues. They also have social activities, such as block parties, to get to know each other.

**What Are Neighborhood Watch Members Supposed to Look Out For?**

- Someone shouting for help.
- Someone looking into windows of houses or parked cars.
- People taking things from houses when no one is home.
- Strange cars moving slowly through the neighborhood.
- A person forcing someone into a car or van.
- Strangers in cars talking to young children.

**If You See a Problem in Your Neighborhood:**

- Call 9-1-1.
- Give your name and address.
- Explain what happened.
- Briefly describe the suspicious person: sex, race, age, height, weight, hair color, clothing, and other characteristics such as facial hair or scars.
- Describe the vehicle if one was involved: color, make, model, year, and license plate.

Source: National Crime Prevention Council.

**Target Grammar**

*Be supposed to*    *page 176*

**QUESTIONS**

**1.** What is a reason to start a Neighborhood Watch group?

_____

**2.** What do Neighborhood Watch members do?

_____

**3.** What do you think *patrol* means?

_____

**4.** Give an example of *suspicious* behavior.

_____

**5.** Do you think the Neighborhood Watch program is a good idea? Why or why not?

_____

_____

## ❸ Listen and Write 🎧 047

Listen to the conversations. Write the problem.

| | Problem |
|---|---|
| 1 | A suspicious van was driving up and down Grand Street. |
| 2 | |
| 3 | |
| 4 | |

## ❹ Apply

Write a paragraph about your community. What problems do you and your neighbors have? Would an organization like Neighborhood Watch help? Why or why not?

_____

_____

_____

_____

_____

_____

_____

---

### RECOGNIZING CAUSE AND EFFECT

A **cause** is an event or action that makes something else happen. An **effect** is what happens because of a certain event or action.

EXAMPLES:

Cause | Effect
If you don't pay your parking ticket, | you won't be able to register your car.

Effect | Cause
She took time off from work | because she had jury duty.

When you are reading, it's important to recognize any cause and effect relationships. You may see the words below when you are reading about a cause and effect relationship.

| if | because | since |
| as a result | for this reason | consequently |

It's also important to recognize false cause and effect relationships. Just because one event follows another does not mean there is a cause and effect relationship. The following have no cause and effect relationship. They are false cause and effect relationships.

Examples: *Jane had jury duty ~~since~~ I went to work.*
*We were talking on the phone ~~because~~ she fainted.*

---

## ❶ Practice the Strategy

Read the paragraph. What are the possible effects of running a red light? Take notes in the chart.

     If you think running a red light is a minor thing, you'd better think again. If you get just one traffic ticket for breaking this law, the cost of your car insurance can go up. And this price increase can last for five years or more. That makes running a red light a very expensive offense. Running a red light could also cause a horrific accident. I once witnessed a fatal car crash that was caused by a car that didn't stop for a red light.

| Cause | Effects |
|---|---|
| Running a red light | |

## ❷ Preview

Look at the title of the article on page 83. Then scan the paragraphs. Answer the questions.

**1.** What cause and effect do you think the article will be about?

Cause: _____ Effect: _____

**2.** What ideas do you already have about this cause and effect relationship?

_____

## ❸ Listen and Read  048

Listen to the article as you read along. Then complete the chart.

### Effects of Drunk Driving

Is it wise to drive under the influence of alcohol? Not at all. Drunk driving is a serious offense. If you drink and drive, you can hurt yourself, damage property, or worse, injure or even kill another person.

Driving while drunk is against the law. If you drive while drunk, you can lose your driver's license. This can cause serious problems. For example, you may lose your job. In some cases, if you drive while you are drunk, you can go to jail. Consequently, you can get a criminal record.

Driving while drunk can also cause property damage. Over $1 billion of property damage occurs yearly because of alcohol abuse. If you drive while drunk and lose control of your car, you can destroy your own car. You may also destroy public property.

Finally, if you drive while drunk, you can kill yourself and other people. More than 50 percent of all fatal car accidents in the United States every year are alcohol-related. About 115 people die every day in vehicle crashes in the United States. This adds up to one death every 13 minutes.

Face it. You *had better not* drink and drive. It's not a smart thing to do.

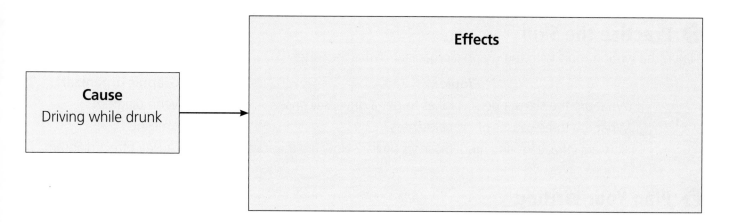

**Effects**

**Cause**
Driving while drunk

## ❹ Talk About It

Discuss this question with your classmates: What effects can alcohol abuse have on relationships, jobs, and schoolwork?

**Target Grammar**

*Had better / had better not*
*page 177*

## USING GRAPHIC ORGANIZERS

It is good to organize your ideas before you start writing. Organizing your ideas is really a way to "think on paper." Taking notes in a graphic organizer is one good way to collect and organize your ideas.

- If you want to compare or contrast two things, use a Venn diagram. In the overlapping area of the two circles, identify how the two things are similar. In the outer part of each circle, write how each thing is different.

- If you want to identify a sequence of events, use a time line.

- If you want to identify a cause and effect relationship, use a cause / effect diagram.

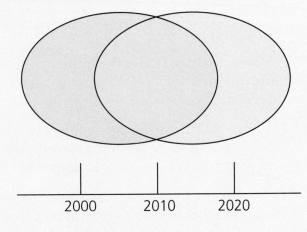

2000    2010    2020

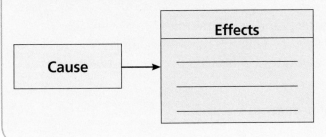

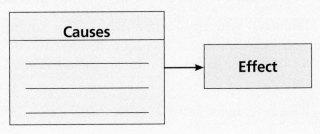

## ❶ Practice the Skill

Match the writing topic with the graphic organizer. Write the letter.

| Topic | Graphic organizer |
|---|---|
| _____ What are the steps a person takes to get a driver's license? | **a.** Venn diagram |
| _____ What are three causes of homelessness? | **b.** timeline |
| _____ How are infractions and misdemeanors similar? How are they different? | **c.** cause / effect diagram |

## ❷ Plan Your Writing

Use a graphic organizer to answer the questions.

**1.** What do you think are three causes of crime in the United States? Write them in the Causes box.

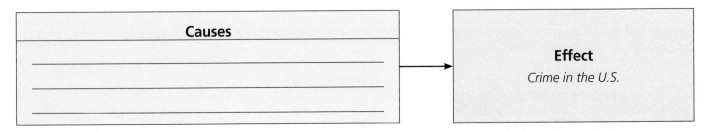

**2.** How are traffic laws in the United States and in another country that you know similar? How are they different?

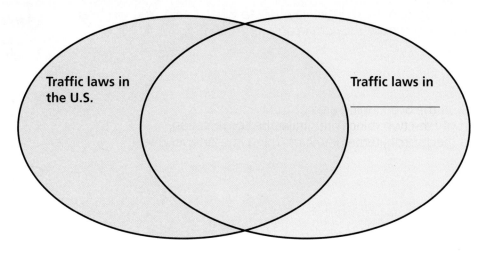

Traffic laws in the U.S.

Traffic laws in _____

**3.** What are the steps a person takes to get married?

## ❸ Write

Now write one paragraph to answer each question in Activity 2.

**Paragraph 1**

_____

_____

_____

_____

**Paragraph 2**

_____

_____

_____

_____

**Paragraph 3**

_____

_____

_____

_____

# What Do You Know?

## ❶ Listening Review  049

### Part 1:

First, you will hear a question. Next, listen carefully to what is said. You will hear the question again. Then choose the correct answer: *A, B,* or *C.*
Use the Answer Sheet.

### Part 2: 🎧 050

You will hear part of the conversation. To finish the conversation, listen and choose the correct answer: *A, B,* or *C.* Use the Answer Sheet.

*Answer Sheet*

| | | | |
|---|---|---|---|
| 1 | Ⓐ | Ⓑ | Ⓒ |
| 2 | Ⓐ | Ⓑ | Ⓒ |
| 3 | Ⓐ | Ⓑ | Ⓒ |
| 4 | Ⓐ | Ⓑ | Ⓒ |
| 5 | Ⓐ | Ⓑ | Ⓒ |
| 6 | Ⓐ | Ⓑ | Ⓒ |
| 7 | Ⓐ | Ⓑ | Ⓒ |
| 8 | Ⓐ | Ⓑ | Ⓒ |
| 9 | Ⓐ | Ⓑ | Ⓒ |
| 10 | Ⓐ | Ⓑ | Ⓒ |

## ❷ Grammar Review

Circle the correct answer: *A, B,* or *C.*

**1.** You _____ to get to the courthouse ten minutes early.
   A. ought
   B. could
   C. must

**2.** You shouldn't _____ late.
   A. to arrive
   B. arriving
   C. arrive

**3.** When _____ leave?
   A. should I
   B. I should
   C. should

**4.** He could _____ called the police.
   A. have
   B. has
   C. been

**5.** You should have _____ at the red light.

   A. stop
   B. stops
   C. stopped

**6.** A: Jack got a ticket while he was crossing the street.
   B: He _____ jaywalked.
   A. could have
   B. should have
   C. must have

## ❷ Grammar Review (continued)

**7.** The neighbors _____ organize a watch group.

   A. is supposed to
   B. are supposed
   C. are supposed to

**8.** How often _____ to meet?

   A. we are supposed
   B. are we supposed
   C. are we suppose

**9.** A: Ana is driving too fast.
   B: She _____ slow down.

   A. better
   B. ought
   C. 'd better

**10.** If you don't want to pay a fine, you'd better _____ the law.

   A. not to break
   B. not break
   C. don't break

# LEARNING LOG

## *I know these words:*

**NOUNS**
- ○ aggravated assault
- ○ bailiff
- ○ battery
- ○ court reporter
- ○ defendant
- ○ defense attorney
- ○ felony
- ○ imprisonment
- ○ infraction
- ○ jaywalking
- ○ judge

- ○ jury
- ○ lawyer
- ○ misdemeanor
- ○ offense
- ○ prison
- ○ probation
- ○ prosecutor
- ○ summons
- ○ testimony
- ○ violation
- ○ witness

**VERBS**
- ○ commit
- ○ dismiss
- ○ patrol

**ADJECTIVES**
- ○ criminal
- ○ guilty
- ○ innocent
- ○ punishable
- ○ suspicious

**OTHER**
- ○ find someone guilty
- ○ pay a fine

## *I practiced these skills, strategies, and grammar points:*

- ○ describing a court of law
- ○ identifying infractions and crimes
- ○ interpreting permit and license requirements
- ○ paraphrasing to check understanding
- ○ participating in your community
- ○ recognizing cause and effect
- ○ using graphic organizers for writing

- ○ reducing past modals
- ○ using *could, should,* and *ought to* for advice
- ○ using *should have, could have,* and *must have*
- ○ *Be supposed to*
- ○ *Had better* and *had better not*

**Work-Out CD-ROM**

**Unit 6: Plug in and practice!**

## THINGS TO DO

### ❶ Warm Up

Discuss these questions with your classmates.

**1.** What are the characteristics of a good job? List five things.

**2.** Would you like to work in the store in the picture? Why or why not?

**3.** What are the employees in the picture doing?

### ❷ Match

Match the words with the definitions.

1. ___d___ unacceptable    **a.** to punish someone

2. _____ discipline    **b.** missing a lot of work or school

3. _____ reprimand    **c.** to fire someone from a job

4. _____ dismiss    **d.** wrong or bad, not okay

5. _____ disorderly    **e.** to do something against the rules

6. _____ excessive absenteeism    **f.** not to do something that you are supposed to do

7. _____ ignore    **g.** to pay no attention to something

8. _____ violate    **h.** causing trouble

9. _____ fail to    **i.** to tell someone that they did something wrong

### ❸ Analyze

Study the picture and read the work rules. Then answer the questions.

**1.** Which work rule is the most serious to break?

**2.** What are three other types of inappropriate workplace behavior?

**3.** Find five people in the picture who are breaking a work rule. What are they doing?

**4.** Imagine that the five people from item 3 are your co-workers. What should you do?

### ❹ Listen and Match  051

Listen to the conversations and look at the picture. Match each conversation to the correct person.

1. ___c___    4. _____    **a.** Tim    **d.** Tom

2. _____    5. _____    **b.** Nina    **e.** Ken

3. _____    6. _____    **c.** Stu    **f.** Pete

**Target Grammar**

Past perfect    *pages 178–179*

## WORK RULES

The company considers the following behaviors **unacceptable**. Any employee who engages in these behaviors will be **disciplined**; for example, they may be **reprimanded**, warned, or **dismissed** from work.

1. Fighting, playing games, or engaging in **disorderly** behavior.
2. Unexcused or **excessive absenteeism**.
3. **Ignoring** work duties or sitting or lying down during working hours.
4. **Failing to** wear appropriate clothing.
5. **Violating** safety or health regulations.
6. Improper use of company equipment and tools.
7. Failing to observe time limits for lunch and other breaks.

**Work-Out CD-ROM**

**Unit 7: Plug in and practice!**

# Identifying Job Responsibilities

## THINGS TO DO

### ❶ Warm Up

Scan the job posting information on page 91. Find the answers to the questions. Discuss your answers with a partner.

**1.** What job is described in each of the job postings on page 91?

**2.** Which job requires more direct contact with customers?

**3.** Of these two jobs, which would you prefer? Why?

### ❷ Find the Synonym

Find a synonym on page 91 for these words.

**1.** hires _____recruits_____

**2.** deals with _____

**3.** deliveries _____

**4.** makes sure _____

**5.** polite _____

**6.** wanted _____

**7.** sets up _____

**8.** helps _____

**9.** manages _____

**10.** selling _____

**11.** before _____

### ❸ Listen  052

Listen to the conversations. Which job is each person interviewing for? Check (✔) the correct position.

|  | Shift Supervisor | Store Manager |
|---|---|---|
| **1.** | ◯ | ◯ |
| **2.** | ◯ | ◯ |
| **3.** | ◯ | ◯ |
| **4.** | ◯ | ◯ |

### ❹ Write

Imagine that you want to hire someone to help you with something at home or work. Write a job description for that position.

SAYERS

HOME

SAYERS

HOME

---

www.sayersstores.com

## *Welcome to Our Company*  SEARCH OUR SITE [_____] GO

| WHAT'S IN OUR STORE | OUR COMPANY | ABOUT US | CAREERS | COMMUNITY |

## Career Opportunities

**Job Title:** Shift Supervisor

**Job Description**
The Shift Supervisor has the following responsibilities, in addition to other duties as assigned:

- provides excellent customer service (**handles** refunds and exchanges, **assists** customers, and resolves customer complaints)
- counts and balances money, and **prepares** deposits
- **ensures** that **shipments** are taken care of correctly
- ensures that the store appearance is pleasing to the customer

**Skills**
Six months of **retail** experience. **Previous** supervisory experience is **preferred**.

**Education**
High school diploma or General Education Degree (GED).

---

www.sayersstores.com

## *Welcome to Our Company*  SEARCH OUR SITE [_____] GO

| WHAT'S IN OUR STORE | OUR COMPANY | ABOUT US | CAREERS | COMMUNITY |

## Career Opportunities

**Job Title:** Store Manager

**Job Description**
The Store Manager has the following responsibilities, in addition to other duties as assigned:

- ensures that prompt and **courteous** service is given to all customers
- **oversees** the daily activities of the store to ensure its smooth operation
- orders merchandise
- reviews profit and loss (P&L) reports
- provides leadership and development opportunities for sales associates
- **recruits** and trains sales associates

**Skills**
Two or more years supervisory experience in a retail setting. Hands-on leadership skills. The ability to work varied shifts (including evenings/weekends).

**Education**
High school diploma or General Education Degree (GED) or higher. College degree is desired.

## THINGS TO DO

### ❶ Warm Up

Discuss these questions with your classmates.

**1.** When was the last time you interviewed for a job? How did it go?

**2.** What should and shouldn't you do at a job interview? How can you be **businesslike**?

**3.** What are five things you know about Roberta from her job application on page 93?

### ❷ Listen for Specific Information  053

Listen to Roberta's interview and add the missing information to her job application on page 93.

### ❸ Listen and Evaluate 🎧 054

Read the questions. Then look at the pictures and listen to the interview again. Check (✔) your answers about Roberta.

| Do you think Roberta / Richard _____ ? | Roberta | | Richard | |
|---|---|---|---|---|
| | **Yes** | **No** | **Yes** | **No** |
| **1.** was dressed appropriately | ○ | ○ | ○ | ○ |
| **2.** was prepared for the interview | ○ | ○ | ○ | ○ |
| **3.** spoke clearly | ○ | ○ | ○ | ○ |
| **4.** was businesslike | ○ | ○ | ○ | ○ |
| **5.** was polite | ○ | ○ | ○ | ○ |
| **6.** had a friendly tone of voice | ○ | ○ | ○ | ○ |
| **7.** had a positive attitude | ○ | ○ | ○ | ○ |

Now listen to Richard's interview. Answer questions 1–7 about him. Then compare the two interviews.

### ❹ Role-Play

Role-play a conversation between an interviewer and a job applicant. Take turns asking and answering the questions. Write two new questions. Use the Communication Strategy.

**1.** Do you like your school?

**2.** Do you have a job now?

**3.** Have you lived here for a long time?

**4.** _____ ?

**5.** _____ ?

Roberta submits her résumé.

Richard fills out his application.

## COMMUNICATION STRATEGY

### Expanding Your Answers 🎧 055

It can seem rude or unfriendly if you give very short answers to questions. Expanding your answers helps to show that you want to have a conversation.

A: Do you like your school?

B: Yes, I do. The people are very friendly.

A: Did you go to school here last year?

B: No, I didn't. I wasn't here last year. I was in Haiti.

A: Where in Haiti did you live?

B: In Port-au-Prince. That's where I was born.

# SAYERS

## Welcome to Our Company

## Job Application

| Name | Madera | Roberta | S |
|------|--------|---------|---|
| | Last | First | MI |

| Address | 245 Longwood Blvd. | Hayworth | |
|---------|--------------------|----------| |
| | Street | City | |

| | Florida | 33000 | 123-45-6789 |
|-|---------|-------|-------------|
| | State | Zip Code | Social Security |

| Telephone | (786) 555-4959 | (786) 555-5467 | rsm@metrocast.net |
|-----------|----------------|----------------|-------------------|
| | Primary | Secondary | Email |

Do you have the legal right to work in the United States?  ☒ Yes  ☐ No

Are you under the age of 18?  ☐ Yes  ☒ No

**Position Applied For:**

| Assistant Manager | Hayworth Store | |
|-------------------|----------------|-|
| Position | Location | Start Date |

**Education:**

| Northeast Community College | | | |
|-----------------------------|--|--|--|
| Name of School | Years Completed | Diploma/Degree | Major |
| Sanchez High School | 4 | H. S. Degree | N/A |
| Name of School | Years Completed | Diploma/Degree | Major |

**General Information:**

Have you ever been convicted of a felony or misdemeanor?  ☐ Yes  ☒ No

*(A Yes answer is not an automatic bar to employment.)*

Have you ever been dismissed or forced to resign from any employment?  ☐ Yes  ☒ No

**1. Employer and Complete Address:**

| 06/09 | Floormart | | Miguel Sandor |
|-------|-----------|--|---------------|
| From Mo/Yr | Name of Employer | Your Title | Your Supervisor |
| 04/12 | 13600 Industrial Rd. Hayworth, FL 33000 | | |
| To Mo/Yr | Address | | |

| | | |
|-|-|-|
| Reason for Leaving | | |

**2. Employer and Complete Address:**

| 05/07 | Reiko's | | Jean Phillips |
|-------|---------|--|---------------|
| From Mo/Yr | Name of Employer | Your Title | Your Supervisor |
| 05/09 | 1220 Bayside Dr. Bayview, FL 33003 | | |
| To Mo/Yr | Address | | |

| | | |
|-|-|-|
| Reason for Leaving | | |

## ❶ Warm Up

Discuss these questions with your classmates.

**1.** Some companies and businesses are called family-friendly companies. What do you think that means?

**2.** What are three ways that work can interfere with your family life?

**3.** What do you think it means to balance work and family?

**4.** In what ways do you think a company can help workers balance work and family?

## ❷ Read and Circle

Scan the reading. Find and circle the following words.

| | | | |
|---|---|---|---|
| on-site training | flextime | personal days | dental insurance |
| telecommute | on-site child care | paid family leave | 401(k) |

## New Employee Benefits Package Information

At Wendall Corporation, we know that our employees are the reason for our success. We value the people who work for us and want to ensure that they are happy working here and have well-balanced lives. For that reason, we offer a very competitive benefits package to all our employees. If you have questions, our human resources manager will be happy to go over these benefits with you.

- **Retirement Benefits:** We offer a 401(k) plan to assist our employees in planning for retirement.

- **Medical and Dental:** All our employees receive full health and dental insurance.

- **Day Care:** Any employee can drop off his or her children at our on-site child care center, located on the first floor. Parents can drop in to check on their children at any time of the work day. Wendall Corporation will pay for 50 percent of on-site child care costs.

- **Paid Time Off:** All employees are allowed 10 paid personal days per year of employment. Expectant mothers are permitted up to 12 weeks of paid family leave at 75 percent pay. Expectant fathers are allowed up to 8 weeks of paid leave at 75 percent pay.

- **Flexibility:** We offer flextime to all employees. Talk to your manager to work out a schedule that best fits your needs. We can adjust the hours that you start and end work, and we also offer a four-day, 10-hour-a-day workweek.

- **Working from Home:** Employees are permitted to telecommute up to one day per week, as their duties allow. They can communicate with co-workers via email or phone.

- **Growth:** We encourage employees to look into possibilities for growth within the company. At Wendall Corporation, hard work pays off. For this reason, managers may request that their star employees receive on-site training in order to be promoted to higher positions within the company.

## ❸ Read and Discuss

Read the *Benefits Package Information* on page 94. Discuss your answers to these questions with a partner.

**1.** Employees at Wendall Corporation rarely leave the company. What inference can you make from this fact?

**2.** What benefits does Wendall Corporation offer its employees?

**3.** Which of Wendall's benefits would be the most useful to you? Why?

**4.** What are some other things that companies could do to help employees balance work and family?

## ❹ Apply

Read the list of family-friendly job benefits that some companies offer. Which are most important to you? Least important? Number them from most important (1) to least important (9).

**a.** _____ Paid vacation of two weeks or more

**b.** _____ Health and dental insurance for all family members

**c.** _____ Tuition assistance

**d.** _____ Merchandise discount: the ability to buy the company's products at a special price

**e.** _____ Flexible schedules: the ability to adjust work schedules to fit school or child care schedules

**f.** _____ Telecommuting: the ability to work from home, when appropriate

**g.** _____ On-site day care

**h.** _____ Sixteen weeks of unpaid leave to take care of a sick family member, give birth, or adopt a child

**i.** _____ Job sharing: two half-time employees work to meet the demands of one full-time position

---

## WINDOW ON MATH

### Computing Averages

**Ⓐ** Read the information.

You can find the average of a set of numbers by adding all the numbers and dividing by the number of items in the sample.

Daily classroom attendance for the week of January 8:

| Mon. | | Tues. | | Wed. | | Thurs. | | Fri. |
|------|---|-------|---|------|---|--------|---|------|
| 17 | + | 15 | + | 13 | + | 14 | + | 16 |

Average daily attendance

$17 + 15 + 13 + 14 + 16 = 75 \div 5$ (number of days) $= 15$

**Ⓑ** Compute the average.

**1.** Six people work at Speedy Copy. Their hourly wages are as follows: Jim ($10), Cindy ($12), Ken ($11), Ivan ($15), Lucy ($13), and Chang ($14). What is the average hourly pay at Speedy Copy?

**2.** In one department at South Wood, there are eight full-time employees. Look at the number of sick days taken in one year by each employee. What is the average number of sick days taken by employees in that department?

| Ming | 7 | Oliveira | 5 | Grant | 1 |
|------|---|----------|---|-------|---|
| Park | 3 | Mahmoud | 2 | Lopez | 8 |
| Sanders | 2 | Thomas | 6 | | |

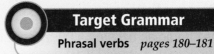

**Target Grammar**

**Phrasal verbs** *pages 180–181*

# Identifying a Sequence of Events

## IDENTIFYING A SEQUENCE OF EVENTS

When you are reading about a sequence of events, it's important to keep track of what happened and in what order. Below are some words that can help you follow a sequence of events.

| after | before | later | previously | after that | first |
|---|---|---|---|---|---|
| meanwhile | today | afterward | in + (year) | now | then |

## ❶ Practice the Strategy

Number the sentences in the correct order.

_____1_____ Working part time can be a good way to get your foot in the door, says Nancy Lin.

_____ Immediately after graduating, she began working full time at the store.

_____ Today, she is a successful general manager of the Mill's store in San Bernardo.

_____ Meanwhile, she continued studying full time to get her degree.

_____ Her first job was as a part-time sales associate with Mill's Hardware while she was in school.

_____ Soon after that, she became an assistant store manager.

## ❷ Preview

Scan the article on page 97. Circle the words that help you follow the sequence of events.

## ❸ Listen and Read  056

Listen to the article as you read along. List some of the important events in Chez Raginiak's life in the boxes. Sequence them from the beginning.

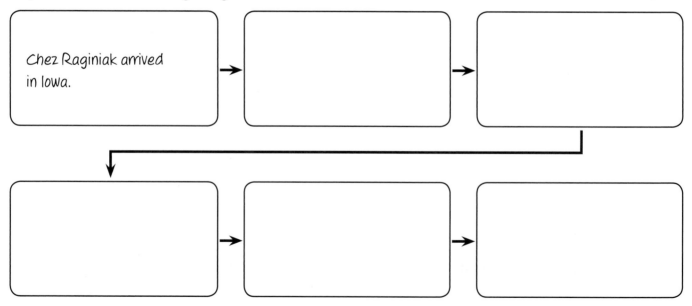

Chez Raginiak arrived in Iowa.

## ❹ Analyze

Chez Raginiak became a businessman after his friend asked him to start a company with her. What do you think Raginiak would have done if he hadn't started a company with his friend? Give your reasons.

# Education and Language Learning:
## A Recipe for Success

Chez Raginiak is a successful American businessman. He owns a company, speaks fluent English, and lives a comfortable life with his two daughters. But life wasn't always so good for this Polish immigrant.

Before Raginiak came to America from Poland, he had no money and no possibility of a better job. When he first arrived in Iowa in 1985, he was an uneducated 25-year-old with a few dollars in his pocket and only a few words of English. He began working hard to earn money and improve his life, but he found that he was able to get only low-paying jobs. When he saw that college graduates were earning twice as much as he was, he became motivated to get a college degree.

Raginiak had been living in America for 13 years when he decided to learn about computer programming at a technical college. He took classes in computer programming in the evenings and on weekends when he wasn't working. After he finished that program, he transferred to a four-year university where he earned a bachelor's degree in Information Technology Management and graduated with a 4.0 grade point average.

After he earned his degree, a friend of Raginiak's approached him with a business idea. She wanted to create and sell CDs to help children develop their speech and language skills. She had a background in language development and she knew that Raginiak had the skills to create and operate an online company. Raginiak agreed to work with her, and now the two partners are the proud owners of a successful company called Kids' Express Train.

The Kids' Express Train CDs help children with learning difficulties such as dyslexia, autism, and Down syndrome. The songs on the CDs use repetition and common words and phrases like *go, bye,* and *let's eat* to encourage the children to imitate the sounds they hear. The company has been so successful and helpful to children that it has been named one of the most valuable products in the country.

Today, Raginiak is not only a business owner. He is also a motivational speaker. He tells his story to large groups of people to help them improve their own lives. Raginiak has a lot of advice for people, but his most important piece of advice for immigrants is to learn English and speak it every day. According to Raginiak, the ability to speak English well is the key to a good life in America.■

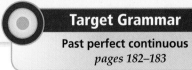

**Target Grammar**

**Past perfect continuous**
*pages 182–183*

# Writing a Résumé

## Writing a Résumé

When you apply for a job, you will often be required to submit a résumé. A résumé is a one- to two-page document about your education and work experience. It can contain several different types of information:

| | |
|---|---|
| **Contact Information:** | Include your name, address, email address, and phone number. |
| **Education:** | List any certifications or degrees you have earned. For example, you can include a nursing certification, a GED, a high school diploma, an associate's degree, or a bachelor's degree. |
| **Work Experience:** | List your previous jobs and the skills you used at each one. List jobs from the most recent to the least recent. Try to list skills that are important to the company that you want to work for. |
| **Special Skills:** | List any skills you have that might help you perform well at the job that you are applying for. For example, if you are applying for a job as an office manager, you might list computer and office equipment skills. If you are applying to work for a company that does international business, you might list the languages that you can speak. |

## ❶ Practice the Skill

Make a list of the jobs that you have had. Start with your most recent job.

| Job Title | Company | Dates of Employment |
|---|---|---|
| _____ | _____ | _____ |
| _____ | _____ | _____ |
| _____ | _____ | _____ |
| _____ | _____ | _____ |

## ❷ Brainstorm

Think of the last job that you had. List three tasks that you did at that job.

_____

_____

_____

_____

_____

## ❸ Read and Respond

Scan the résumé on page 99. Then answer the questions.

## Anna Chen
117 14th Street, Apt. 4
San Francisco, CA 94114
(415) 555 7001 • annachen@bmail.com

### EDUCATION
Associate's Degree in Computer Science, San Francisco City College, 2008

### EXPERIENCE

**Right Now Technical Services**
Technical support associate, 2008 to present
- Assist callers with computer hardware and software problems
- Install computer equipment for customers in their homes
- Write a report about each caller and how the caller's problem was resolved
- Attend weekly staff meetings to discuss frequent computer problems and how to resolve them

**San Francisco City College**
Computer lab assistant, 2006 to 2008
- Signed students in to use computers in the lab
- Assisted students when they had trouble using the lab's computer equipment
- Taught a workshop once a week on basic computer skills

### SPECIAL SKILLS
- Knowledge of Microsoft Operating Systems, Apple Operating Systems
- Fluent in Cantonese

**1.** What is the résumé writer's name? _____

**2.** What is her most recent job title? _____

**3.** When did she start that job? _____

**4.** What certifications or degrees does she have? _____

**5.** What special skills does she have? _____

**6.** Look at the verbs used in the résumé. Circle the verbs that are in the simple present. Underline the verbs in the simple past.

Which verb form did she use for her most recent job? _____

Why do you think the writer used that verb form? _____

## ❹ Plan Your Writing
Read the information about a job. List this kind of information for at least two jobs you have had.

Company: _____ B & C Industries _____

Job title: _____ office manager _____ Dates: _____ 2005–2009 _____

Skills: _____ ordered supplies for the whole office _____ managed four assistants _____

_____ used Microsoft Excel to keep track of schedules _____

## ❺ Write
Use the information from Activity 4 to write a résumé.

## ❶ Listening Review  057

**Part 1**

You will hear the first part of a conversation. To finish the conversation, listen and choose the correct answer: *A, B,* or *C.* Use the Answer Sheet.

**Part 2**  058

Listen to what is said. When you hear the question, *Which is correct?*, listen and choose the correct answer: *A, B,* or *C.* Use the Answer Sheet.

### Answer Sheet

| | A | B | C |
|---|---|---|---|
| **1** | Ⓐ | Ⓑ | Ⓒ |
| **2** | Ⓐ | Ⓑ | Ⓒ |
| **3** | Ⓐ | Ⓑ | Ⓒ |
| **4** | Ⓐ | Ⓑ | Ⓒ |
| **5** | Ⓐ | Ⓑ | Ⓒ |
| **6** | Ⓐ | Ⓑ | Ⓒ |
| **7** | Ⓐ | Ⓑ | Ⓒ |
| **8** | Ⓐ | Ⓑ | Ⓒ |
| **9** | Ⓐ | Ⓑ | Ⓒ |
| **10** | Ⓐ | Ⓑ | Ⓒ |

## ❷ Grammar Review

Circle the correct answer: *A, B,* or *C.*

**1.** I had already _____ to work when she called.

  A. went
  B. go
  C. gone

**2.** Tom _____ just started working here when Ann was dismissed.

  A. had
  B. have
  C. was

**3.** At 7:30, the interview _____.

  A. just begun
  B. just had begun
  C. had just begun

**4.** I have to drop my children _____ at the day care center.

  A. on
  B. off
  C. in

**5.** Will you _____ information with me?

  A. go over this
  B. go this over
  C. go it over this

**6.** Jim _____ late this morning. He arrived at 10:00.

  A. followed through
  B. ran into
  C. showed up

## ❷ Grammar Review (continued)

**7.** Don't worry. I'll _____ the problem for you.
   A. look into
   B. play around
   C. put away

**8.** I _____ to Alan when Brian called.
   A. talked
   B. have talked
   C. had been talking

**9.** Lin and Chan _____ in America long when Lin _____ to go back to school.
   A. hadn't been living / decided
   B. haven't been living / decided
   C. didn't live / had been deciding

**10.** You _____ here for a month when you _____ a promotion.
   A. worked / got
   B. worked / had been getting
   C. had been working / got

---

## LEARNING LOG

### *I know these words:*

**NOUNS**
- ○ absenteeism
- ○ shipment

**VERBS**
- ○ assist
- ○ discipline
- ○ dismiss
- ○ ensure
- ○ fail

- ○ handle
- ○ ignore
- ○ oversee
- ○ prefer
- ○ prepare
- ○ recruit
- ○ reprimand
- ○ violate

**ADJECTIVES**
- ○ businesslike
- ○ courteous
- ○ disorderly
- ○ excessive
- ○ previous
- ○ retail
- ○ unacceptable

### *I practiced these skills, strategies, and grammar points:*

- ○ solving problems
- ○ identifying job responsibilities
- ○ understanding job applications
- ○ expanding your answers
- ○ exploring job benefits
- ○ computing averages

- ○ identifying a sequence of events
- ○ writing a résumé
- ○ using the past perfect
- ○ using phrasal verbs
- ○ using the past perfect continuous

**Work-Out CD-ROM**

**Unit 7: Plug in and practice!**

## THINGS TO DO

### ❶ Warm Up

Discuss these questions with your classmates.

**1.** Do you have a monthly **budget**, or spending plan? How closely do you follow it?

**2.** What is your biggest **expense** each month?

**3.** Look at the pictures. Fill in the missing amounts on page 103.

### ❷ Match

Match the words with the definitions.

**1.** ___c___ budget

**2.** _____ expense

**3.** _____ miscellaneous

**4.** _____ debt

**5.** _____ investment

**6.** _____ entertainment

**a.** a group of different unrelated items

**b.** money that you owe

**c.** a plan for spending money

**d.** money that earns interest

**e.** things that people do for fun

**f.** something that you spend money on

### ❸ Decide

Study the monthly budget goals and actual spending of the Lee family. Then answer the questions.

**1.** In which categories did the Lees spend more than their goal?

**2.** Which of their budget goals did the Lees meet?

**3.** What could the Lees do to meet all of their budget goals? For example, in what categories could they try to spend less money? How?

**4.** How much will the Lees save this month for their vacation?

### ❹ Listen 🎧 059

Check (✔) *True* or *False*.

| | True | False | | | True | False |
|---|---|---|---|---|---|---|
| **1.** | ○ | ✔ | | **4.** | ○ | ○ |
| **2.** | ○ | ○ | | **5.** | ○ | ○ |
| **3.** | ○ | ○ | | **6.** | ○ | ○ |

**1** Housing
Actual Spending: $900

**9** Transportation
Actual Spending: $325

**8** Food
Actual Spending: $850

# The Lee Family's Monthly Budget: March

**2** **Savings & Investments**
Actual Spending: $300

**3** **Entertainment**
Actual Spending: $175

## Monthly Budget Goals
### (Lee Family)
### Income after taxes   $3,500

| | Goals | Actual Spending | Amount Over | Amount Under |
|---|---|---|---|---|
| 1. Housing | $900 | $900 | | |
| 2. Savings/Investments | $300 | $300 | | |
| 3. Entertainment | $150 | | | |
| 4. Utilities | $150 | | | |
| 5. Debts | $100 | | | |
| 6. Clothing | $150 | | | |
| 7. Miscellaneous | $400 | | | |
| 8. Food | $800 | | | |
| 9. Transportation | $300 | | | |
| 10. (Extra) Vacation Savings | | | | |

**4** **Utilities**
Actual Spending: $190

**5** **Debts**
Actual Spending: $120

**7** **Miscellaneous**
Actual Spending: $300

**Work-Out CD-ROM**
**Unit 8: Plug in and practice!**

**6** **Clothing**
Actual Spending: $130

## THINGS TO DO

### ❶ Warm Up

Discuss these questions with your classmates.

**1.** Read questions 1 to 9 on pages 104–105. Which question is the most interesting to you? Which is the least interesting?

**2.** What do you see in each picture?

### ❷ Use the Vocabulary

Complete each sentence with a highlighted word from pages 104–105.

**1.** Because of _____, we are paying $25.00 a month more for our groceries than last year.

**2.** I think that it's important to save money for retirement. I plan on _____ 10 percent of my income every year.

**3.** Don't rely on credit too much. It's easy to _____ your credit cards by using them for daily purchases.

**4.** My monthly spending _____ from month to month. It's never the same two months in a row.

**5.** The United States has a large _____. We spend much more than we make.

**6.** I had to pay a _____ on my credit card last month because I paid my bill late.

**7.** I pay a $25 _____ every year to have a credit card.

**8.** I called a _____ because I had too much debt.

### ❸ Summarize

Take turns asking and answering the questions on pages 104–105 with a partner. Use your own words to answer.

**Example:**  *Q: Are all credit cards the same?*
*A: No, they aren't. Credit cards have different annual fees and interest rates.*

### ❹ Evaluate

Work with a partner. Read about each person and answer the questions. Then share ideas with your classmates.

**1.** Carla always pays her credit card bill in full. Should she choose a no-fee card with 18 percent interest or a card with an annual fee of $50 and a 15 percent interest rate? Why?

**2.** You are saving money to buy a house. Should you put your money in an IRA, a savings account, or a CD? Why?

---

**1**

**Q:** Are all credit cards the same?

**A:** Absolutely not. Some credit cards charge an **annual fee** while others do not. Some credit cards offer things like frequent flier miles. In addition, the interest rates **vary** from one card to another.

**4**

**Q:** What happens if you pay your credit card bill late?

**A:** You will be charged a **penalty fee**, which could be $35 or more. In addition, your interest rate can go up even when you are late in paying other bills such as your utility bill.

**7**

**Q:** Where can I get help with credit problems?

**A:** A **credit counselor** will talk to you about ways to pay off your debt and lower the interest rates on your credit cards. You can find a counselor near you at the website for the National Foundation for Credit Counseling.

---

**Target Grammar**

**Present real conditionals**
*pages 184–185*

**2**

**Q:** If you make the minimum $100 monthly payment on a $5,000 credit card bill at 18 percent interest, how long will it take to pay off?

**A:** If you **carry** a $5,000 **balance** and make the minimum payment, it will take more than 46 years to pay off your debt! You will also pay $13,931 in interest. However, if you pay $200 a month, you can pay off your debt in fewer than three years and pay $1,314 in interest. If you **pay** your bill **in full**, you won't pay any interest at all.

**Paying Off a $5,000 Credit Card Bill**

Pay $100/month = 46 years = $13,931 in interest

Pay $200/month = 3 years = $1,314 in interest

**3**

**Q:** What types of credit card problems do people have?

**A:** Credit card problems occur when you **max out** your credit card, or reach your spending limit. They also happen when you make a late payment or don't have enough money to pay your bill for a few months.

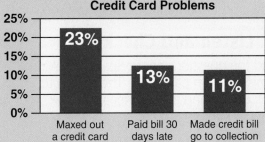

**Americans with Credit Card Problems**

| | | |
|---|---|---|
| 23% | 13% | 11% |
| Maxed out a credit card | Paid bill 30 days late | Made credit bill go to collection |

**5**

**Q:** Is it better to put your money in a savings account or to buy a **certificate of deposit (CD)**?

**A:** That depends on your needs. A CD is a special kind of savings account. It earns a fixed interest rate over a specific period of time. The interest rate is higher than a savings account, but you cannot use the money for a certain amount of time.

**6**

**Q:** What are the advantages of **investing** in an **individual retirement account (IRA)**?

**A:** The money you invest in an IRA doesn't count as part of your income, so you don't have to pay taxes on it until you withdraw it. The purpose is to save it so you can use it after you retire.

**8**

**Q:** What is **inflation**?

**A:** Inflation is a continuous increase in the price of goods and services. As prices increase, the value of money goes down. For example, a coat that cost $10 in 1914 would cost $219 in 2010.

**9**

**Q:** What is a **budget deficit**, and why do governments sometimes have them?

**A:** If you spend more than you earn, you have a budget deficit. Governments have budget deficits when they spend more money than they collect in taxes.

# Comparing Banking Services

## THINGS TO DO

### ❶ Warm Up

Discuss these questions with your classmates.

**1.** What banking services do you see in the pictures?

**2.** What other banking services can you think of?

### ❷ Listen and Check 🎧 060

Read the questions about Seattle Banking checking accounts and home loans on page 107. Then listen to a conversation between a bank officer and a customer. Check (✔) four questions the customer asks.

### ❸ Listen and Take Notes 🎧 061

Listen again. Add the missing information to the chart on page 107.

### ❹ True or False

Read each sentence. Check (✔) *True* or *False*. Use the information in the chart on page 107.

|  | True | False |
|---|---|---|
| **1.** The Circle Account earns interest. | ○ | ○ |
| **2.** The Basic Account provides free checks. | ○ | ○ |
| **3.** If Sylvia has $5,000 in her Circle Account, she won't have to pay a maintenance fee. | ○ | ○ |
| **4.** Only the Circle Account provides a free ATM card. | ○ | ○ |
| **5.** All three accounts provide free online banking. | ○ | ○ |
| **6.** Sylvia needs $50 to open a Green Checking Account. | ○ | ○ |

### ❺ Role-Play 🎧 062

Listen. Role-play a conversation between a bank officer and a customer. Take turns asking and answering questions about banking services. Use the Communication Strategy in your conversation.

A: If I open a savings account, how much interest will I earn?

B: Was that a savings account?

A: Yes, that's right.

B: Two percent.

A: Did you say two percent?

B: Yes, that's correct.

**Target Grammar**

**Future real conditionals**
*pages 186–187*

## COMMUNICATION STRATEGY

### Repeating to Confirm

Misunderstandings can cause a lot of problems. To avoid this, it's important to confirm what you hear.

Did you say twenty-five dollars?

You said twenty-five dollars?

That was twenty-five dollars?

Was that twenty-five dollars?

I'd like to open a checking account.

| Seattle Banking: Checking Accounts | Circle Checking Account | Green Checking Account | Basic Checking Account |
|---|---|---|---|
| **1.** How much money do I need to open a checking account? ☑ | $50 | | |
| **2.** Does this account earn interest? ○ | | No | |
| **3.** Will I be charged to use the ATM at other banks? ○ | | | |
| **4.** Does this account provide free checks? ○ | | | |
| **5.** How much is the monthly maintenance fee? ○ | | | |
| **6.** How much do I have to keep in my account to avoid a monthly maintenance fee? ○ | | N/A | N/A |
| **7.** Does a free ATM or debit card come with this account? ○ | Yes | | |
| **8.** Does this account provide free online banking? ○ | | | |
| **9.** Can I pay my bills online free of charge? ○ | | | |

| Seattle Banking: Home Loans | 20-Year Mortgage | 30-Year Mortgage |
|---|---|---|
| **1.** What is the interest rate? | | |
| **2.** How much would the interest be per year? | | |
| **3.** How much is the monthly mortgage payment? | | |

# LESSON 4 — Interpreting Pay Stubs

## ❶ Warm Up

Discuss these questions with your classmates.

**1.** What kinds of information appear on a pay stub?

**2.** What kinds of things are often deducted from a paycheck?

## ❷ Check *True* or *False*  063

Listen to the statements about Osvaldo's pay stub. Check (✔) *True* or *False*.

|  | True | False |  | | True | False |
|---|:---:|:---:|---|---|:---:|:---:|
| **1.** | ✔ | ○ | | **5.** | ○ | ○ |
| **2.** | ○ | ○ | | **6.** | ○ | ○ |
| **3.** | ○ | ○ | | **7.** | ○ | ○ |
| **4.** | ○ | ○ | | **8.** | ○ | ○ |

### ATWOOD INDUSTRIES

Employee: Osvaldo Vargas  
Social Security Number: 123-45-6789  
Pay Period Date: 3/1/12 to 3/15/12  
Check Date: 3/20/12  

Check Number: **947930**

**PAY STUB**

| EARNINGS | Rate | Hours | This Period | Year-to-Date |
|---|---|---|---|---|
| | 20.00 | 80 | $1,600.00 | $8,000.00 |
| **GROSS PAY** | | | 1,600.00 | 8,000.00 |
| **DEDUCTIONS** | | | | |
| | Federal Income Tax | | $208.00 | $1,040.00 |
| | Social Security | | 176.00 | 880.00 |
| | Medicare | | 41.60 | 208.00 |
| | CA Income Tax | | 48.22 | 241.10 |
| | CA State Disability Ins. | | 22.40 | 112.00 |
| **Total Deductions** | | | $496.22 | $2,481.10 |
| **NET PAY** | | | $1,103.78 | $5,518.90 |

## ❸ Apply

When you get a paycheck, it's important to check it carefully. Look at Osvaldo's pay stub on page 109. Fill in the missing numbers. You can look at the pay stub in Activity 2 to help you. Then compare ideas with your classmates.

**PAY STUB**

## ATWOOD INDUSTRIES

| | | |
|---|---|---|
| Employee: | Osvaldo Vargas | Check Number: **947941** |
| Social Security Number: | 123-45-6789 | |
| Pay Period Date: | 3/16/12 to 3/31/12 | |
| Check Date: | 4/5/12 | |

| EARNINGS | Rate | Hours | This Period | Year-to-Date |
|---|---|---|---|---|
| | 20.00 | 40 | $ _____ | $ _____ |
| **GROSS PAY** | | | _____ | _____ |
| **DEDUCTIONS** | | | | |
| | Federal Income Tax | | $104.00 | $1,144.00 |
| | Social Security | | 88.00 | _____ |
| | Medicare | | 20.80 | 228.80 |
| | CA Income Tax | | 24.11 | _____ |
| | CA State Disability Ins. | | 11.20 | 123.20 |
| **Total Deductions** | | | $ _____ | $2,729.21 |
| **NET PAY** | | | $ _____ | $6,070.79 |

## WINDOW ON MATH

### Understanding Rates

**A** Read the information.

A **rate** is a comparison of two measurements that is expressed as a fraction, where the two measurements have different units, such as: $30/5 hours.

A **unit rate** is the rate in which the bottom number (denominator) is 1: $6/1 hour. You can convert a rate to a unit rate if you divide the top number (numerator) by the denominator: $30 divided by 5 hours, or $6 for 1 hour.

> **Example:** *Tina was charged $40 in bank fees on her checking account for the first four months of 2012. The rate was $40/4 months. The unit rate was $10 per month.*

**B** Change the following rates to unit rates.

**1.** $5 for two hours: _____ per hour    **3.** $30 for six months: _____ per month

**2.** 12 sick days per year: _____ per month    **4.** $9 for three pounds: _____ per pound

**C** Read the information. Then answer the questions.

**1.** Henry is thinking of changing jobs. At his current job, he works 40 hours and earns $500 a week. At his new job, Henry would work 40 hours a week and earn $15 an hour. At which job would Henry make more money?

**2.** Paula drives to work every day. She notices that she can go about 500 miles on a tank of gas. Her tank holds 20 gallons. What is the unit rate?

# Identifying the Elements of a Story

## IDENTIFYING THE ELEMENTS OF A STORY

There are six elements that are necessary to make a good story. These are:

**Character:** the actors in the story and what they are like

**Setting:** the place or places where the story happens

**Plot:** the events that happen in the story

**Conflict:** the problem

**Climax:** the turning point in the story when the reader wonders whether or not the conflict will be resolved

**Resolution:** the point at which the conflict is resolved

## ❶ Practice the Strategy 🎧 064

Listen as you read the story on page 111. Then answer the questions.

**1.** Who are the two main characters in the story? _____

**2.** Write three adjectives to describe each of the two main characters.

| Character | Adjectives |
|---|---|
| _____ | _____ _____ _____ |
| _____ | _____ _____ _____ |

**3.** Where does the story take place? _____

**4.** Write four sentences to describe the main events of the story.

_____

_____

_____

_____

**5.** Which sentence describes the conflict of the story? Circle the correct answer.

   **a.** A mother and father die, and their sons find out that there is a bag of gold hidden in the house.

   **b.** When two brothers become wealthy, one brother gets greedy and wants to take his brother's gold.

   **c.** A mother and father die, and their sons have to steal gold because they can't afford to buy food.

**6.** In which paragraph does the climax happen? _____

**7.** Which sentence describes the resolution of the story? Circle the correct answer.

   **a.** An tricks Bao into giving away his gold.

   **b.** An and Bao beat up the kidnappers and keep the gold for themselves.

   **c.** An understands that his brother's love is more valuable than gold.

# Two Brothers

**(1)**　Once, a family lived in a small village near the woods—brothers An and Bao, their mother Lan, and their father Trung. One very cold winter, Lan and Trung became very sick, and they both died. The brothers were sad to lose their parents, and they cried for a month. But at the end of that month, their uncle came to see them.

**(2)**　"An and Bao, your mother and father wanted you to value family and friendship more than wealth, so they lived a simple life without a lot of money," the uncle said. "But they had a large bag of gold hidden under the fireplace. Now they're gone, and the gold is yours—half for each of you."

**(3)**　The brothers were very surprised. Bao sat staring at his uncle, but An ran to the fireplace and began digging up the dirt floor. After a few minutes, he found what he was looking for. The old and dirty bag was very large and very heavy.

**(4)**　"We're rich!" he cried, his eyes as round as coins.

**(5)**　The uncle sighed. "Good luck to you both," he said. Then he patted Bao's shoulder, gave An a worried look, and left.

**(6)**　After that day, An could think about nothing but the gold. "If I had Bao's gold too, I would be the richest man in the village," he thought. So he made a plan to get his brother's gold. He hid for two days in a neighboring village and asked a boy from the village to take a note to Bao. The note said that kidnappers had taken An and that they wanted both brothers' gold.

**(7)**　When Bao received the note, he walked to the neighboring village with the gold. While An was waiting for Bao, he ate some berries he found in the woods. The berries made him feel ill. When Bao arrived, he saw that his brother was very sick. Bao knew that he had to get his brother back home quickly to take care of him. He couldn't carry both his brother and the gold, so he left the gold and carried his brother 20 miles to their house.

**(8)**　After several weeks, An recovered. When he understood what had happened, he realized that his brother's love was more important than any amount of money. After that day, the brothers went back to their simple way of life, and An never thought of the gold again.

**Target Grammar**

**Present unreal conditionals**
*pages 188–189*

# Using Transition Words and Phrases

## USING TRANSITION WORDS AND PHRASES

Writers use transition words and phrases to show how the ideas in a paragraph are related. Below are some common transition words and phrases.

| To add information | also | further | moreover |
| | and | furthermore | too |
| | besides | in addition | |
| **To show the order of events or of importance** | first | the most important | |
| | second | the second most important | |
| | third | the third most important | |
| **To show cause and effect** | as a result | due to | so |
| | because | for this reason | therefore |
| | consequently | since | thus |
| **To give an example** | for example | like | |
| | for instance | such as | |
| **To show a contrast** | although | even though | nevertheless |
| | but | however | on the other hand |
| | conversely | in spite of | whereas |
| | despite | instead of | yet |

## ❶ Practice the Skill

Circle the transition words and phrases in the paragraphs. In the chart, write the purpose of each transition word or phrase.

**1.** Early Greek coins were both useful and beautiful, (and) many cities competed to produce the most beautiful coins. The city of Corinth, for example, made silver coins with a picture of the winged horse Pegasus. Athens, on the other hand, made coins with gold and silver decorated with a picture of the Athenian owl.

| Word/Phrase | Purpose |
| --- | --- |
| and | to add information |
| | |
| | |
| | |

**2.** The rulers of countries quickly learned that having their faces on coins was a good form of advertising. The first ruler to do so was probably Ptolemy I of Egypt. Having their faces on coins, however, did not stop rulers from making the coins less valuable. The Roman emperor Nero, for instance, reduced the amount of silver in Roman coins and kept the money he saved for himself.

| Word/Phrase | Purpose |
| --- | --- |
| | |
| | |
| | |
| | |

3. Coins became impractical for trading because in large quantities they were very heavy. For this reason, paper money became common.

| Word/Phrase | Purpose |
|---|---|
|  |  |

4. Credit cards are useful for a number of reasons. Perhaps the most important reason is their convenience. When you have a credit card, you don't have to carry around cash. Despite their usefulness, credit cards can also cause problems. If you carry a balance on your credit card bill, you end up paying a lot of interest.

| Word/Phrase | Purpose |
|---|---|
|  |  |

## ❷ Read and Respond

Complete the sentences with a transition word or phrase. More than one answer may be possible.

1. The most important thing you can do is pay off your debts. _The second most important thing_ is to start saving your money.

2. You should put your money in a savings account _____ not touch it.

3. _____ putting money into my bank account, I'm going to buy some stocks.

4. We stopped driving so much _____ the increase in gasoline prices.

5. When I was a teenager, I spent a lot of money on clothes. Nowadays, _____, I never buy expensive clothes.

6. My wife started investing her money when she was in her 20s, and _____ she'll be able to retire by the time she is 50.

7. _____ eating out a lot, I try to save money by eating at home.

8. I never had any money when I was a child, and _____ I worry a lot about money now.

9. I spend a lot of my money on entertainment every month. _____, I spend about $60 a month on movies and $50 on CDs.

10. _____ I earn a good salary, I have a hard time saving money.

11. I'm trying to save a lot of money for retirement. I put $200 in a savings account every month. _____, I take advantage of the 401(k) provided by my company.

12. _____ my sister is single and pays rent for a small apartment, I have three children and pay rent for a four-bedroom house. That's why my sister's monthly expenses are much lower than mine.

## ❸ Write

Describe your spending habits in the past and today. Remember to collect ideas before writing and to write several drafts. Use transition words and phrases where appropriate.

## LESSON 7 — What Do You Know?

### ❶ Listening Review  065

**Part 1**

Listen to what is said. When you hear the question, *Which is correct?*, listen and choose the correct answer: *A*, *B*, or *C*. Use the Answer Sheet.

**Part 2**  066

First, you will hear a question. Next, listen carefully to what is said. You will hear the question again. Then, choose the correct answer: *A*, *B*, or *C*. Use the Answer Sheet.

*Answer Sheet*

1. Ⓐ Ⓑ Ⓒ
2. Ⓐ Ⓑ Ⓒ
3. Ⓐ Ⓑ Ⓒ
4. Ⓐ Ⓑ Ⓒ
5. Ⓐ Ⓑ Ⓒ
6. Ⓐ Ⓑ Ⓒ
7. Ⓐ Ⓑ Ⓒ
8. Ⓐ Ⓑ Ⓒ
9. Ⓐ Ⓑ Ⓒ
10. Ⓐ Ⓑ Ⓒ

### ❷ Grammar Review

Circle the correct answer: *A, B,* or *C*.

**1.** If Mary pays her credit card bill late, the bank _____ a late fee.
A. will charge
B. is charging
C. charged

**2.** You _____ interest if you pay off your credit card bill.
A. aren't paying
B. won't pay
C. doesn't pay

**3.** If we _____, we _____ late.
A. won't hurry / don't be
B. will hurry / don't be
C. don't hurry / will be

**4.** If I save enough money, I _____ a vacation.
A. take
B. taking
C. am going to take

**5.** If he _____ late this morning, I'll talk to him.
A. be
B. is
C. were

**6.** Eric _____ the check if he goes to the bank today.
A. will deposit
B. deposits
C. is depositing

114 | **UNIT 8**

## ❷ Grammar Review (continued)

**7.** We _____ you if we _____ your help.

A. will call / need

B. will call / will need

C. call / are going to need

**8.** If I _____ twenty thousand dollars, I would buy a new car.

A. have

B. had

C. would have

**9.** Jack _____ a computer class if his company paid for it.

A. would take

B. took

C. takes

**10.** We _____ a new house if home prices _____ lower.

A. buy / would be

B. would buy / was

C. would buy / were

# LEARNING LOG

## *I know these words:*

**NOUNS**

○ annual fee

○ budget

○ budget deficit

○ certificate of deposit (CD)

○ credit counselor

○ debt

○ entertainment

○ expense

○ individual retirement account (IRA)

○ inflation

○ investment

○ penalty fee

**VERBS**

○ carry a balance

○ invest

○ max out

○ pay in full

○ vary

**ADJECTIVES**

○ miscellaneous

## *I practiced these skills, strategies, and grammar points:*

○ budget planning

○ understanding financial terms

○ comparing banking services

○ repeating to confirm

○ interpreting pay stubs

○ understanding rates

○ identifying the elements in a story

○ using transition words and phrases

○ using present real conditionals

○ using future real conditionals

○ using present unreal conditionals

**Work-Out CD-ROM**

**Unit 8: Plug in and practice!**

**LESSON 1**

# Reporting a Problem with Workplace Equipment

## THINGS TO DO

### ❶ Warm Up

Discuss these questions with your classmates.

1. What kind of equipment do you use or have you used at work?
2. What kinds of problems have you or your co-workers had with workplace equipment?

### ❷ Use the Vocabulary

Complete each sentence with a highlighted word or phrase from pages 116–117.

1. This building has _____. We need more fresh air.
2. The _____ that we use to clean the machines is _____. We shouldn't use poisonous products.
3. Our safety gear is _____. The _____ for our eye protection are supposed to be ¼ inch thick.
4. This machine is _____. Someone might run into it and get hurt.
5. I wish we had a better photocopier. This one has a _____ again.
6. I have to _____ our scheduling software. The software we have is five years old.

### ❸ Listen and Write 🎧 067

Listen to the conversation. Then complete the Hazard Report Form.

update

Softwa Expre

paper j

| **Workplace Hazard Report Form** |

**Details of the problem:**

Name the piece of equipment. _____

Describe the specific problem. _____

_____

| Check an answer for each question. | Not Likely | Likely | Very Likely |
|---|---|---|---|
| 1. Is the problem likely to delay work? | ☐ | ☐ | ☐ |
| 2. Is it likely to cause injury? | ☐ | ☐ | ☐ |
| 3. Is it likely to make someone ill? | ☐ | ☐ | ☐ |
| 4. Is it likely to kill someone? | ☐ | ☐ | ☐ |

**Work-Out CD-ROM**

**Unit 9: Plug in and practice!**

### Target Grammar
*Wish*   page 190

# Discussing a Work Schedule

## THINGS TO DO

### ❶ Warm Up

Discuss these questions with your classmates.

**1.** Have you ever asked to change your work schedule?

**2.** What are some reasons that you might want to change your work schedule?

### ❷ Write

Complete each sentence. Write the word from the box.

| closed for a holiday | early shift | switch shifts | the day off | work for |
|---|---|---|---|---|

**1.** Can you _____ with me on Tuesday?

**2.** I'm going to _____ Julie on the 8th.

**3.** I have to work the _____ on Friday.

**4.** Can I have _____ next Wednesday?

**5.** The store is _____ on Friday.

### ❸ Role-Play 🎧 068

Listen. Role-play a conversation between two co-workers. Take turns playing each role.

A: Do you have to work next Saturday?

B: No, I have Saturday off .

A: Can you work for me ? My sister's going to have surgery next Saturday.

B: Sure, I'll work for you .

| **1** Yes, I work the morning shift. | **2** No, I'm off on Tuesday. | **3** No, but I have to work on Monday. | **4** No, I have the day off. |
|---|---|---|---|
| switch shifts with me | work the early shift | switch days with me | work for me |

### ❹ Check *True* or *False* 🎧 069

Look at the schedule on page 119. Then listen. Check (✔) *True* or *False*.

|  | True | False |  | True | False |
|---|---|---|---|---|---|
| **1.** | ✔ | ○ | **4.** | ○ | ○ |
| **2.** | ○ | ○ | **5.** | ○ | ○ |
| **3.** | ○ | ○ | **6.** | ○ | ○ |

**Target Grammar**

*Be going to* and *will*
*pages 191–192*

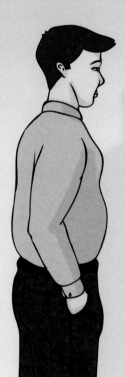

| Day | Morning Shift | Afternoon Shift | Evening Shift |
|---|---|---|---|
| **Monday** July 4 | Closed for Independence Day ① | | |
| **Tuesday** July 5 | ~~Joe~~ Ann<br>Alan | ~~Ann~~ Joe ②<br>Mia | Jack<br>Kim |
| **Wednesday** July 6 | Joe<br>Jack | Mia<br>Eric | Alan<br>Pete |
| **Thursday** July 7 | Joe<br>~~Pete~~ Kim | Jack<br>Mia | ~~Kim~~ Pete<br>Eric |
| **Friday** July 8 | ~~Pete~~ Joe ③<br>Ann | Kim<br>Pete | Ken ④<br>~~Mia~~ Jack |
| **Saturday** July 9 | ~~Alan~~ Jack<br>Ann | Kim<br>~~Jack~~ Alan | Mia<br>Pete ⑤ |

1. The business is **closed for a holiday** on Monday.
2. Ann **switched shifts with** Joe on Tuesday.
3. Joe is going to **work for** Pete on Friday.
4. Ken is working **the late shift** on Friday.
5. Joe **has the day off** on Saturday.

## THINGS TO DO

### ❶ Warm Up

Discuss these questions with your classmates.

**1.** What job do you think you will have in two years?

**2.** What job do you hope you will be doing in five years?

### ❷ Listen for General Information 🎧 070

Listen to the conversation. Look at pictures 1–3 on pages 120–121. Write the number of the picture that shows Sue. _____

Listen to the conversation Look at pictures 4–6 on pages 120–121. Write the number of the picture that shows Dave. _____

### ❸ Listen for Specific Information 🎧 071

Listen to the conversations again. Then complete the sentences.

**1.** I (**think / don't think**) Sue will get a promotion because _____

_____.

**2.** If Sue wants a promotion, she should _____

_____.

**3.** I (**think / don't think**) Dave will get a raise because _____

_____.

**4.** If Dave wants a raise, he should _____

_____.

### ❹ Role-Play 🎧 072

Listen. Role-play a conversation between an employee and a supervisor. Take turns playing each role. Use the Communication Strategy.

A: Thanks for meeting with me today, Rick.

B: Of course. What did you want to discuss with me today?

A: I'd like to discuss the possibility of getting a promotion.

B: Can you tell me why you feel you deserve a promotion?

A: Well, I work hard, and I'm reliable.

### ❺ Write

What job do you want to have in ten years? What do you need to do to get that job? Write two sentences on a piece of paper.

## COMMUNICATION STRATEGY

### Asking Someone What They Want to Talk About

What did you want to discuss with me today?

What can I help you with?

What's on your mind?

**Target Grammar**

**Future continuous**   *page 193*

## WINDOW ON PRONUNCIATION

### Stressing Important Words in Sentences  073

**A** We stress the most important words in a sentence. The words you stress can change the meaning of your sentence. Listen to the sentences. Then listen and repeat.

**1.** I'm very <u>organized</u>.
**2.** <u>I'm</u> very organized.
**3.** You <u>haven't been</u> here very <u>long</u>.
**4.** You haven't been <u>here</u> very long.
**5.** Mark enjoys working <u>here</u>.
**6.** <u>Mark</u> enjoys working here.

**B** Listen to the sentences. Underline the stressed words.

**1.** I'm happy to hear that.
**2.** What's on your mind?
**3.** I have good interpersonal skills.
**4.** I've been carrying out some managerial duties.
**5.** I've trained three of the new employees.
**6.** Is there anything else I can do?

# Analyzing Performance Evaluations

## THINGS TO DO

### ❶ Warm Up

Discuss these questions with your classmates.

**1.** What are five characteristics of the ideal employee and the ideal employer? List your ideas in a chart like this one. Then share ideas with your classmates.

| The ideal employee | The ideal employer |
|---|---|
| is always on time | is fair |

**2.** Look at the chart you made in 1. How many of the characteristics describe you? How many describe your current or your last employer?

### ❷ Make Inferences

Match each comment to one or more possible inferences.

**Comments**

**1.** Petra completes her work on time. She ___c, e___ .

**2.** Max prepares deposits accurately. He _____ .

**3.** Tim often comes in early to work. He _____ .

**4.** Paul helped to train three new employees without being asked. He _____ .

**5.** Mei is very friendly with everyone. She _____ .

**6.** Yoshiko does what her employer asks. She _____ .

**7.** Hiro always has wonderful new ideas. He _____ .

**8.** Patricia delivers her work on time. She _____ .

**9.** Tony shows respect to everyone. He _____ .

**Inferences**

**a.** shows **independence**

**b.** is **creative**

**c.** is **dependable**

**d.** is **punctual**

**e.** is **productive**

**f.** is **cooperative**

**g.** shows **initiative**

**h.** has good **interpersonal skills**

**i.** other: _____

Sarah Wang relies on public transportation to get to work.

### ❸ Read and Respond

Read the employee performance evaluation on page 123. Answer the questions.

**1.** What do you know about Sarah Wang from her performance evaluation?

**2.** What are Sarah's greatest strengths on the job?

**3.** What is Sarah's greatest weakness on the job?

**4.** What are three things Sarah could do to improve her job performance?

**Target Grammar**

*So . . . that* and *such . . . that*
*page 194*

Sarah Wang's manager discusses her performance evaluation with her.

# Employee Performance Evaluation

| EMPLOYEE | TITLE |
|---|---|
| Sarah Wang | Store Associate |
| **DEPARTMENT** | **EMPLOYEE NO.** |
| Housewares | 214 |

**TYPE OF EVALUATION**

☒ ANNUAL    ☐ PROMOTION    ☐ MERIT    ☐ OTHER

**DIRECTIONS:** Evaluate the employee's work **performance** as it relates to the requirements of the job. Write the number that best describes the employee's performance since the last evaluation.

**1** = Excellent    **2** = Very Good    **3** = Satisfactory    **4** = Decreased Performance    **5** = Unsatisfactory

| Job Responsibilities | Rating | Comments |
|---|---|---|
| **PUNCTUALITY** The employee is on time and follows the rules for breaks and **attendance**. | 4 | Ms. Wang is not always punctual. She was late to work more than ten times in the past three months due to transportation problems. |
| **BEHAVIOR** The employee is polite on the job. | 3 | There have been no customer complaints about Ms. Wang's behavior. |
| **CREATIVITY** The employee suggests ideas and better ways of accomplishing goals. | 1 | Ms. Wang thinks of such creative ways to solve problems that both the store and the customers benefit. |
| **RELIABILITY** The employee can be **relied on** to efficiently complete a job. | 4 | Ms. Wang is so often late to work that we cannot always rely on her to do her share of the work. |
| **INDEPENDENCE** The employee accomplishes work with little or no supervision. | 2 | Ms. Wang rarely requires assistance from her supervisor or co-workers. She knows what she has to do and she usually does it without being asked. |
| **INITIATIVE** The employee looks for new tasks and expands abilities professionally. | 1 | Ms. Wang is taking a design course because she would like to be more involved in improving the appearance of the store. She set up an attractive display for the holiday season without being asked to do so. |
| **INTERPERSONAL SKILLS** The employee is willing and able to communicate, cooperate, and work with co-workers, supervisors, and customers. | 3 | Ms. Wang works well with her co-workers. She's cooperative, and she listens well. She had a conflict with a co-worker and because she was able to communicate well, they resolved the problem. |
| **JOB SKILLS** The employee has the appropriate skills to do the job well. | 3 | Ms. Wang has carefully and correctly completed the tasks assigned to her. |

# Highlighting Important Information

## Highlighting

One way to improve your reading skills is to practice highlighting important information. In order to decide what is important, consider these questions:

- What is my purpose for reading this passage?
- What do I want to remember after reading this passage?

In the highlighted passage below, the reader's purpose was to find out what he needs to register for a class at City College.

At City College, we offer over 100 evening courses for working students. It's easy to register. All you need is a form of I.D., such as a driver's license or a state-issued I.D. card; proof of address, such as a utility bill; and a method of payment. We accept cash, checks, and all major credit cards. If you have any questions, come to the Administration Office in Building A or call the number on your registration form.

## ❶ Practice the Strategy

Imagine that you have just gotten a new job. You want to have a management role at the company within the next five years. Read the passage. Highlight or underline the ideas that are important to you.

Are you ambitious? Are you hoping to receive a promotion at your current job? If so, there are a few things that you can do to ensure your boss considers you the next time a management position becomes available. First of all, whatever your job is now, be sure to do your best at every task. Create a reputation as a reliable and responsible employee. Next, get to know the people you work with and treat everyone with respect. The person you talk to today may help you get a promotion a year from now. Another important thing to do is share your opinions and ideas with your colleagues. Don't stay silent during company meetings. Also, be sure to show initiative and volunteer to do work that you haven't been asked to do. Your boss will see that you take your job seriously. And finally, when the time comes, ask for a promotion if your boss doesn't offer one first. You are responsible for your own success!

## ❷ Listen and Read  074

Listen to the article on page 125 as you read along. Highlight or underline the important ideas.

## ❸ Understand the Reading

Use the highlighted or underlined information to answer the questions.

**1.** What are some things you can do before you formally discuss a promotion with your boss? _____

_____

_____

_____

**2.** What are some things you can do when you are almost ready to formally discuss a promotion with your boss?

_____

**3.** When should you approach your boss to discuss a promotion? _____

_____

# Tips for Asking for a Promotion

At several points in your working life, you may have the opportunity to ask your boss for a promotion. When these opportunities arise, you should be prepared to negotiate for what you want. Negotiation skills are important for anyone who is interested in developing his or her career path. If you follow these negotiating tips, you'll have a better chance of getting the promotion that you want.

There are a few things that you can do before you have a formal discussion with your boss about a promotion. First of all, you can casually let him or her know that you're interested in moving up in the company. You could mention the idea after a meeting or during an informal conversation with your boss in the break room. Another thing you can do before you have a meeting with your boss is to prepare yourself to do the job that you want to get. Find out exactly what skills the job requires and make sure you have those skills. For example, if the job requires the use of computers, take a course in basic computer skills. If the job includes hiring new employees, take an interviewing skills class. You should also let your boss see that you are ready to take on more responsibility. Volunteer for challenging projects, but make sure that you have the skills and the time to complete the projects before you take them on.

When you are almost ready to approach your boss about a promotion, prepare a list of accomplishments that you can give to your boss during your meeting. For example, if you successfully finished a difficult project or you took on extra responsibilities, include them in your list. If you work in a large company, your boss might not be aware of all of the exceptional things that you have done at work. He or she will want to know why you feel you deserve a promotion.

Finally, when you are ready to talk to your boss about a promotion, be sure to choose a good time for your discussion. Wait for a time when your boss is not too busy and there isn't a lot going on at work. Your boss will be more relaxed and willing to listen to what you have to say.

## Creating a Job Advertisement

When you post a job advertisement online or in a newspaper, you should include:

- **Job Title:** What is the job?
- **Skills:** What skills does the position require?
- **Education/Experience:** Is there a minimum education requirement or minimum experience requirement for the job?
- **Tasks:** What kinds of things will an employee do in this job?
- **Hours/Days:** How many hours a week will the employee work? What days?
- **Contact Information:** How can a person contact you? By phone? By email? By mail? Should they send a résumé?
- **Salary/Benefits:** You can include the amount if the pay rate is set. You can also say "Salary Negotiable" or "Depends on Experience."

## ❶ Practice the Skill

Read the job descriptions on page 127. Check (✔) the categories below that each advertisement includes. Then underline the information for each category in the advertisements.

**Job 1**
- ○ Job Title
- ○ Skills
- ○ Education/Experience
- ○ Tasks
- ○ Hours/Days
- ○ Contact Information
- ○ Salary/Benefits

**Job 2**
- ○ Job Title
- ○ Skills
- ○ Education/Experience
- ○ Tasks
- ○ Hours/Days
- ○ Contact Information
- ○ Salary/Benefits

## ❷ Plan Your Writing

Think about the job that you want to have. If you are a small-business owner, think of a job that you need to fill. Write notes for each category. Don't write complete sentences.

**Job Title:** _____

**Skills:** _____

**Education/Experience:** _____

**Tasks:** _____

**Hours/Days:** _____

**Contact Information:** _____

**Salary/Benefits:** _____

## ❸ Write

Write a job description on a separate piece of paper. Use your notes from Activity 2. Write complete sentences.

## Job 1

**WWW.GETJOBS.COM**

**WWW.GETJOBS.COM/SHOPMANAGER**

HOME     FEATURED JOBS     NEW LISTINGS     SEARCH

**Shop Manager at HHH Sheet Metal**

We currently have an opening for a full-time Sheet Metal Shop Manager.

**Qualifications:**

Candidates must have at least five years sheet metal construction experience and be bilingual in Spanish and English. Candidates must also have basic computer skills and good team skills.

**Duties:**

The Shop Manager will:

- manage 10 to 12 employees.
- be responsible for worker safety.
- hire and train new employees.
- schedule delivery of products to customers.

**Hours:** 7:00 A.M. to 4:00 P.M. Monday through Friday.

Interested candidates should send their résumés to jobs@hhhsheetmetal.com

## Job 2

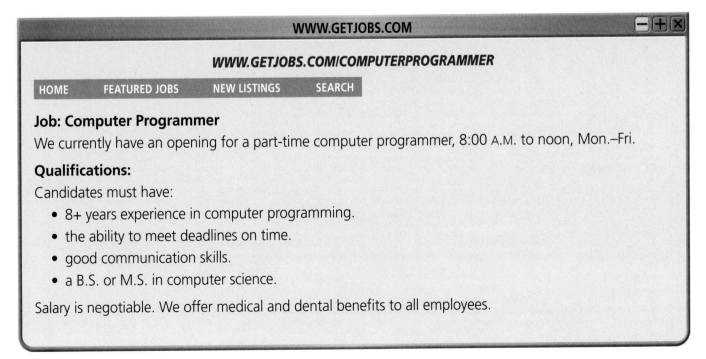

**WWW.GETJOBS.COM**

**WWW.GETJOBS.COM/COMPUTERPROGRAMMER**

HOME     FEATURED JOBS     NEW LISTINGS     SEARCH

**Job: Computer Programmer**

We currently have an opening for a part-time computer programmer, 8:00 A.M. to noon, Mon.–Fri.

**Qualifications:**

Candidates must have:

- 8+ years experience in computer programming.
- the ability to meet deadlines on time.
- good communication skills.
- a B.S. or M.S. in computer science.

Salary is negotiable. We offer medical and dental benefits to all employees.

# What Do You Know?

## ❶ Listening Review  075

**Part 1:**

First, you will hear a question. Next, listen carefully to what is said. You will hear the question again. Then choose the correct answer: *A, B,* or *C.* Use the Answer Sheet.

**Part 2:**  076

You will hear the first part of a conversation. To finish the conversation, listen and choose the correct answer: *A, B,* or *C.* Use the Answer Sheet.

*Answer Sheet*

1 Ⓐ Ⓑ Ⓒ
2 Ⓐ Ⓑ Ⓒ
3 Ⓐ Ⓑ Ⓒ
4 Ⓐ Ⓑ Ⓒ
5 Ⓐ Ⓑ Ⓒ
6 Ⓐ Ⓑ Ⓒ
7 Ⓐ Ⓑ Ⓒ
8 Ⓐ Ⓑ Ⓒ
9 Ⓐ Ⓑ Ⓒ
10 Ⓐ Ⓑ Ⓒ

## ❷ Grammar Review

Circle the correct answer: *A, B,* or *C.*

**1.** I wish I _____ a supervisor.
   A. am
   B. were
   C. was

**2.** Jim _____ he _____ a better-paying job.
   A. wished / has
   B. wishes / has
   C. wishes / had

**3.** Alan _____ for me next Tuesday. We talked about it last week.
   A. will work
   B. going to work
   C. is going to work

**4.** _____ switch shifts with me tomorrow? I just remembered that I have a doctor's appointment in the morning.
   A. You will
   B. Are you going to
   C. Will you

**5.** I _____ go to Sarah's party on Saturday.
   A. won't
   B. am not
   C. am not going to

**6.** Tomorrow, Martin _____ checking the ventilation systems from noon to 5:00 P.M.
   A. will
   B. will be
   C. be

## ❷ Grammar Review (continued)

**7.** _____ Jan and Tom _____ working all afternoon?

  A. Will / are
  B. Will / be
  B. Are / be

**8.** I _____ from 8:00 A.M. to noon tomorrow. I have the morning off.

  A. won't be working
  B. won't work
  C. will be working

**9.** My manager was _____ happy with my work that he gave me a raise.

  A. so
  B. such
  C. such a

**10.** This is _____ great company that most people stay here for years.

  A. so
  B. such
  C. such a

---

## LEARNING LOG

### *I know these words:*

**NOUNS**
- ○ attendance
- ○ cleanser
- ○ creativity
- ○ early shift
- ○ goggles
- ○ independence
- ○ initiative
- ○ interpersonal skills
- ○ late shift
- ○ paper jam
- ○ performance
- ○ reliability
- ○ ventilation

**VERBS**
- ○ rely on
- ○ update
- ○ work for (someone)

**ADJECTIVE**
- ○ closed for a holiday
- ○ cooperative
- ○ creative
- ○ dependable
- ○ hazardous
- ○ inadequate
- ○ productive
- ○ punctual
- ○ toxic
- ○ (not) up to code

**OTHER**
- ○ have the day off
- ○ switch shifts

### *I practiced these skills, strategies, and grammar points:*

- ○ reporting a problem with workplace equipment
- ○ discussing a work schedule
- ○ discussing your career path
- ○ asking someone what they want to talk about
- ○ stressing important words in a sentence
- ○ analyzing performance evaluations
- ○ highlighting important information
- ○ creating a job advertisement
- ○ using *wish*
- ○ using *be going to* and *will*
- ○ using the future continuous
- ○ using *so . . . that* and *such . . . that*

**Work-Out CD-ROM**

**Unit 9: Plug in and practice!**

## THINGS TO DO

### ❶ Warm Up

Discuss these questions with your classmates.

**1.** What is your favorite holiday?

**2.** What do you do on this holiday?

**3.** What U.S. holidays do you know? How are they celebrated?

### ❷ Match

Look at the pictures on page 131. Write the letter of the picture next to the correct description.

_____ **1.** This Chinese festival occurs on the 15th day of the eighth **lunar** month when the moon looks larger than it does at other times of the year. Families **celebrate** by enjoying fruits and moon cakes while looking at the moon.

_____ **2.** This holiday **commemorates** an Irish saint. According to **legend**, he chased all the snakes out of the country. People all over the world celebrate this holiday by wearing green. The city of Chicago puts dye in the Chicago River to make it green!

_____ **3.** On this three-day summer festival in Japan, people **honor** their family members who have died. They visit the graves of their **ancestors** and float lanterns down rivers.

_____ **4.** It is a common **misconception** that this holiday celebrates Mexico's independence day. It **actually** is a celebration of Mexico's victory over the French army at the Battle of Puebla on May 5, 1862.

_____ **5.** This Thai holiday is on the full moon of the 12th lunar month. It is **customary** to float boats that are shaped like lotus flowers down rivers to carry away bad luck.

_____ **6.** This celebration occurs in January or February each year. People often celebrate by participating in or watching a **parade** and by dressing up in **costumes**. This holiday is celebrated all over the world, but the biggest celebration is in Brazil.

### ❸ Write

Write a highlighted vocabulary word from Activity 2 for each definition.

**1.** _____ : do something special to show that a day is important

**2.** _____ : members of your family who lived before you

**3.** _____ : really; truly

**4.** _____ : an event in which performers move down a street while they perform

**5.** _____ : show respect for someone

**6.** _____ : relating to the moon

**7.** _____ : special clothes that can make you look like someone or something else

**8.** _____ : an old, famous story about a special person, place, event, or thing

**9.** _____ : do something special to show that you remember a person or an event

**10.** _____ : an incorrect idea or belief

**11.** _____ : traditional or usual

> **Target Grammar**
>
> Adjective clauses—*who* or *that* as subject   *pages 195–196*

**A**    Obon Festival

**B**    Cinco de Mayo

**C**    Carnival

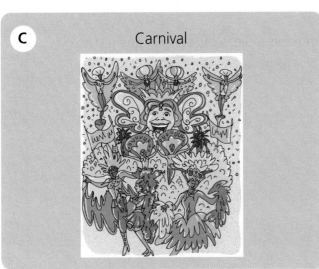

**D**    St. Patrick's Day

**E**    Loy Krathong

**F**    Mid-Autumn Festival

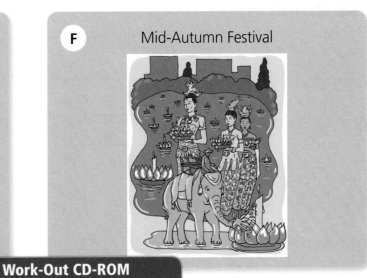

**Work-Out CD-ROM**

**Unit 10: Plug in and practice!**

## THINGS TO DO

### ❶ Warm Up

Discuss these questions with your classmates.

**1.** How many hours do you spend at work and at school per week? With family and friends?

**2.** How much vacation time do you get every year, not including national holidays?

### ❷ Match

Match each word or phrase with its definition.

**1.** statistics      **a.** someone who receives an income

**2.** service      **b.** time that a woman does not have to work because she has just had a baby

**3.** conclude      **c.** decide that something is true

**4.** balance      **d.** numbers that show facts or measurements

**5.** wage earner      **e.** the people who live together in one house or apartment

**6.** household      **f.** a situation in which two or more things have equal importance

**7.** maternity leave      **g.** typical

**8.** mandatory      **h.** work

**9.** average      **i.** required

### ❸ Listen  077

Look at the information on page 133. Listen. Check (✔) *True* or *False*.

|  | True | False |  | True | False |  | True | False |
|---|---|---|---|---|---|---|---|---|
| **1.** | ○ | ✔ | **3.** | ○ | ○ | **5.** | ○ | ○ |
| **2.** | ○ | ○ | **4.** | ○ | ○ | **6.** | ○ | ○ |

### ❹ Write

Choose one of the charts or graphs on page 133. Make a similar chart or graph about yourself and four classmates.

Example:

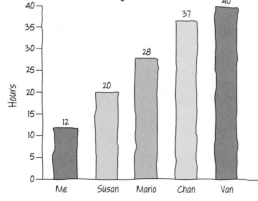

Average Work Week

## Average Vacation Days After 10 Years of Service

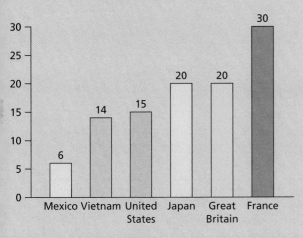

According to some **statistics**, workers in the United States have half as many paid vacation days after 10 years of **service** as French workers do. Workers in Mexico have one-fifth as much paid vacation as French workers do. Based on this information, you might **conclude** that the French have a better **balance** between work life and home life.

## Mandatory Maternity Leave Rights by Country

| Country | Paid maternity leave (in weeks) | Percentage of salary paid | Unpaid maternity leave (in weeks) |
|---|---|---|---|
| China | 12 | 100% | 0 |
| France | 16 | 100 | 104 (shared with father) |
| Great Britain | 39 | 90 for 6 weeks | 26 |
| Japan | 14 | 60 | 0 |
| Mexico | 12 | 100 | 0 |
| United States | 0 | N/A | 12 |

United States law does not require businesses to offer any paid **maternity leave** to their employees. However, many companies do give their employees 4 to 12 weeks of paid maternity leave. In other countries, such as China and France, some paid leave is **mandatory**.

## Average Work Week by Country

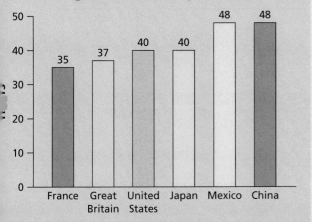

The **average** number of working hours per week varies from country to country. In both Japan and the United States, an average full-time worker spends 40 hours per week at work. In Mexico and China, the average full-time work week is 48 hours.

## Mandatory Paternity Leave Rights by Country

| Country | Paid paternity leave (in weeks) | Percentage of salary paid | Unpaid paternity leave (in weeks) |
|---|---|---|---|
| China | 0 | N/A | 0 |
| France | 2 | 100 | 104 (shared with mother) |
| Great Britain | 2 | 90 or a maximum of £123.06 | 0 |
| Japan | 0 | N/A | 0 |
| Mexico | 0 | N/A | 0 |
| United States | 0 | N/A | 12 |

In many families, the father is an important **wage earner**. As a result, fathers in many **households** are not able to spend a lot of time with their children. In most countries, fathers do not receive any **paternity leave** when a child is born. In recent years, more men have expressed a wish to spend more time with their children.

## THINGS TO DO

### ❶ Warm Up

Discuss these questions with your classmates.

**1.** In your culture, what do you say and do when you meet someone for the first time?

**2.** In the United States, do you behave the same way or differently? Explain.

### ❷ Listen for General Information  078

Read the article on page 135. Listen to the conversations. Then check (✔) whether Joe's behavior was appropriate or inappropriate. Don't complete the third column yet.

| Category | Appropriate behavior ✓ | Inappropriate behavior ✓ | What happened? |
|---|---|---|---|
| **Conversation 1** | | | |
| Bringing gifts | | ✓ | Joe brought a cake to the dinner party. |
| Bringing guests | | | |
| Saying thanks | | | |
| **Conversation 2** | | | |
| Sitting down to dinner | | | |
| Making small talk | | | |

### ❸ Listen for Specific Information  079

Listen to the conversations again. Then complete the third column in the chart in Activity 2.

### ❹ Role-Play  080

Listen. Then role-play a conversation. Replace the underlined words with your own ideas. Use the Communication Strategy.

A: Can I ask your advice about something?

B: Sure.

A: <u>A co-worker invited me to her house for dinner</u>, and I'm not sure what I should do.

B: What do you mean?

A: Well, is it okay if I <u>bring a gift</u>?

B: Sure, that would be fine. <u>You can bring something inexpensive, like flowers or a box of candy.</u>

### COMMUNICATION STRATEGY

#### Asking if Something Is Appropriate

| | |
|---|---|
| Is it okay if I …? | Sure, that would be fine. |
| Is it all right if I …? | It's not necessary, but it would be okay. |
| Is it appropriate to …? | No, that wouldn't really be appropriate. |

**Target Grammar**

Adjective clauses—*who* or *that* as object   *pages 197–198*

## Dinner Party Etiquette 101

These days, shortcuts like emails and text messages might make people feel they can be a bit more relaxed and casual than they used to be. However, there are still a few rules of etiquette that we should follow in certain situations. For example, say someone with whom you work or someone whom you don't know very well has invited you to a dinner party. Would you know what to bring? Would you know how to behave? Follow these rules and you'll be sure to get through the evening without embarrassing yourself (or your date!).

### Bringing Gifts

When you're invited to someone's home for dinner, it's customary to bring a small gift, such as chocolates or flowers or a beverage to share. Don't bring an expensive gift. In addition, avoid bringing a dish for the other guests to eat unless the host asks you to do so.

### Bringing Guests

A spouse, a boyfriend, or a girlfriend can come along if your host includes him or her in the invitation. It's not appropriate to bring someone that your host isn't expecting.

### Sitting Down to Dinner

You should not begin eating until everyone has been served and the host begins to eat. If there is food that you don't want to eat or can't eat for dietary or religious reasons, it's perfectly appropriate not to have it. Just say, "No, thank you," when your host offers it, or if you are serving yourself, don't put any of it on your plate.

### Making Small Talk

Conversations about what people do for a living, what they like to do for fun, or movies or books that they've enjoyed recently are appropriate topics for people who don't know each other well. But it's best not to start conversations about religion, politics, or money.

### Saying Thanks

A polite "Thank you for inviting me" at the end of the evening is appropriate. A thank-you card isn't necessary. However, you may send the host a note of thanks if you would like to.

## WINDOW ON PRONUNCIATION

### Changing Stress with *That*  081

**A** Read the information.

The word *that* is often stressed when it is a demonstrative adjective or pronoun.

> He needs **that** book, not this one.
> We don't want **that**.

*That* is not usually stressed when it is at the beginning of an adjective clause.

> I can't find the book that I left on the desk.

**B** Listen to the statements and questions. Circle *that* each time it is stressed.

1. That's the man that was on TV.
2. Remember the movie that I told you about? It's at that theater over there.
3. Did you meet the girl that Matt likes? That's her.
4. Not that book. I want the one that I gave you last week.
5. The neighbor that had an accident last week lives in that house.

# LESSON 4

# Recognizing Bias and Stereotyping

## ❶ Warm Up

**1.** Read the definitions of the word *stereotype*. Make a list of some common stereotypes about men or women.

> **stereotype**[1] *n* [C] an oversimplified belief that one group of people has about another group of people based on general, often incorrect ideas
>
> **stereotype**[2] *v* [T] to decide unfairly and often incorrectly what a person is like based on their race, sex, religion, or social class

**2.** Think about someone you know. Compare that person's traits with your list of stereotypes from item 1.

## ❷ Read and Respond

Read the information. Answer the questions on page 137.

> **Target Grammar**
>
> Indefinite pronouns: *You, one, we,* and *some*    *page 199*

Many of us are probably guilty of making **unconscious** **assumptions** about people all the time. The reason we do it is because we want to be able to organize everyone and everything we see into nice, neat **categories**, and it's easier to stereotype people than to really get to know them.

It's easy to find stereotypes in the media. For example, in the TV show *The Simpsons*, most of the characters fit into a stereotype. Homer fits many people's idea of the **stereotypical** American father. He is fat, lazy, not very smart, and likes football so much that he even listens to it while he's in church. As the mother, Marge is a **homemaker** who takes care of her children and doesn't seek a life outside of her family. Lisa is well-behaved, gets good grades, and wears a pretty little dress all the time—we think she is a stereotypical young girl. Bart is a 10-year-old boy who gets bad grades and causes **mischief**.

*The Simpsons* is a funny show, and often, the stereotypes can be the reason for some of the humor. But stereotyping, which is based on assumptions and **ignorance**, can be harmful in real life. When you stereotype, you don't consider the individual. You may assume someone is not intelligent or doesn't have certain skills before they have a chance to prove themselves. For example, you might believe that all little boys are mischievous and bad at school. An assumption like that might keep you from noticing a young boy's good behavior and achievements. On the other hand, you might assume that someone does have characteristics that they don't have. You might believe that all little girls get good grades. This might set you up for disappointment when a little girl you know has trouble at school. And it might make the little girl feel that there is something wrong with her.

Pay attention to the assumptions that you make about people. The next time you find yourself assuming that you know what someone is like, pause for a moment and take a closer look. You may find that all your assumptions are wrong.

## QUESTIONS

**1.** What are some common stereotypes listed in the article?

**2.** According to the article, why is it harmful to stereotype people?

**3.** What examples of stereotyping have you experienced?

**4.** What can you do to stop stereotyping in your community?

## ❸ Identify

Read the sentences. Check (✔) the statements that show evidence of stereotyping.

_____ **1.** Women are better than men at taking care of children.

_____ **2.** I know several women who like to watch football.

_____ **3.** Bill is probably a good basketball player because he's very tall.

_____ **4.** Everyone from the South drives a pickup truck.

_____ **5.** Everyone who lives in California is a vegetarian.

_____ **6.** My friend Teri, who is from San Francisco, is a vegetarian.

_____ **7.** Women aren't good drivers.

_____ **8.** My sister is a terrible driver.

## ❹ Listen  082

Listen to the conversations. Complete the chart.

| | Are the speakers using stereotypes? | If the speakers are using stereotypes, what assumptions do they make? |
|---|---|---|
| **1.** | (Yes) / No | Assumption: Tom can fix computers. <br> Reason: He wears glasses and likes science fiction movies. |
| **2.** | Yes / No | Assumption: <br> Reason: |
| **3.** | Yes / No | Assumption: <br> Reason: |
| **4.** | Yes / No | Assumption: <br> Reason: |

# Comparing and Contrasting

## Comparing and Contrasting

Writers often describe or explain something by comparing or contrasting it to something else. When writers compare two things, they emphasize the similarities. When they contrast two things, they emphasize the differences.

**Examples:** Both of my brothers are tall and thin. (comparing)

CDs have higher interest rates than savings accounts. (contrasting)

Writers often use these words to show that they are comparing or contrasting two things.

| Comparing | | Contrasting | |
|---|---|---|---|
| both | similar to | but | in contrast |
| in common | similarly | different from | neither…nor |
| like | | however | unlike |

## ❶ Practice the Strategy

Look at the Venn diagram. Then complete the sentences with comparing and contrasting words above.

**American Public High Schools**
- For students age 13–18
- Free
- Most courses are mandatory
- Students don't usually choose specialty
- Students live with parents

**Both**
- 4 years
- Students get a degree
- Some courses are optional

**American Universities**
- For high school graduates or people with GEDs
- Students pay tuition
- Some courses are mandatory
- Students choose majors
- Students sometimes live in dormitories

1. Students typically spend four years in _____ a high school and a university.

2. _____ students in high school, students in university choose majors.

3. Public high school is free in the United States. _____, students must pay tuition to go to a university.

4. Students receive a degree when they graduate from high school. _____, students receive a degree when they finish college.

5. Most students in high school live with their parents, _____ many college students live in dormitories.

**Target Grammar**

**Future passive** *page 200*

## ❷ Listen and Read  083

Listen to the article as you read along. Find words that describe the different education systems. Write them in the chart.

| United States | China |
|---|---|
| most children attend for 13 years | school is mandatory for 9 years |

## Education in the United States and China

The American and Chinese education systems share many similarities, but there are a few differences. In the United States, children are required to go to school. Most children attend school for 13 years. These 13 years include primary school, middle school or junior high school, and high school. Students can attend free public schools, or they can pay tuition to attend private schools. State governments are usually responsible for making decisions regarding education standards for each grade.

Typically, American students enter kindergarten (followed by first grade) at age four or five and remain in primary school until the fifth or sixth grade. Then students move on to either middle school or junior high school. Middle school begins with sixth grade, and junior high school begins with seventh grade. After that, students enter high school either in eighth or ninth grade. Students typically graduate from high school at age 17 or 18.

Similarly, China also has a mandatory education policy. However, children in China are only required to attend primary school for five or six years and junior middle school for three or four years, for a total of nine years. After nine years, education is optional. After junior middle school, students must take examinations that determine whether they will move on to academic senior middle schools or vocational schools.

After graduating from high school, American students may choose to attend a college or university. In order to do so, students must take one or more entrance exams, and their acceptance will be based on their exam scores, their high school grades, their activities outside of school, and their completion of an application. Each college or university makes its own admissions decisions, and students must pay tuition to attend.

In contrast, university and college admissions decisions in China are made by the Ministry of Education. Students who have completed senior middle school and want to attend a college or university take the National College Entrance Exam, and admission will be based mainly on the students' scores on that exam. However, a student's admission might also include an investigation into the student's moral character and social behavior. Like American college and university students, students in China must also pay tuition to get a higher education.

## ❸ Understand the Reading

Read the article again. How are the educational systems in the United States and China similar and different? Make a Venn diagram. Then share ideas with your classmates.

# Communicating by Email

## Communicating by Email

Writers are often very informal when writing emails to friends and family members. However, for emails to co-workers, there are some basic rules to follow.

**Responding Quickly:** Reply to a business email within 24 hours.

**Capitalization:** Be careful not to use all capital letters. It indicates that you are shouting.

**Length and Content:** Get to the point quickly and keep your emails brief. If your email is a reply to someone else's email, answer all the questions included in that email.

**Subject Lines:** Always include something on the subject line so the recipient of your email knows what your message is about.

**Editing:** Use proper grammar and punctuation. After you've written an email, check it for mistakes at least once before you send it.

**Topics:** Don't use email to discuss confidential information or to complain about a co-worker. Emails can easily be sent or forwarded to the wrong person.

**Jokes:** Don't forward jokes or chain letters to your co-workers or to your boss.

**Abbreviations:** Avoid abbreviations such as *CU* (see you) and *TTYL* (talk to you later) in your business emails. They are very informal, and your recipient might not understand them.

**Email Addresses:** If you use a personal email account for business purposes, include your name in your email address so recipients know who you are.

## ❶ Practice the Skill

Read the email. Then look at 1-9 on page 141. Check (✔) the mistakes that the writer made.

---

FROM: dogowner@speedymail.com
SUBJECT:
DATE: January 10, 2011
TO: may.chang@shopmart.com

---

Hi May,

I received your email about computer training last week. I'm sorry I didn't get back to you sooner. I've been really busy. My daughter has been sick for the past two weeks and my brother-in-law has been visiting.

Anyway, in your email you asked when I would be able to attend the computer training class on Tuesday, February 15. I'm working the evening shift that day, so I can attend the class in the morning or the afternoon. Let me know what time I should be there.

Also, can I talk to you on Monday about Roger? He hasn't been doing his share of the work lately. He takes long breaks and leaves early almost every night.

TTYL,

Cindy

---

_____ **1.** used all capital letters

✔ **2.** didn't respond within 24 hours

_____ **3.** didn't get to the point quickly

_____ **4.** didn't include a subject line

_____ **5.** made grammar and punctuation errors

_____ **6.** discussed inappropriate topics

_____ **7.** forwarded a joke

_____ **8.** used abbreviations

_____ **9.** used an inappropriate email address

## ❷ Plan Your Writing

Read the email. Underline the questions that you need to reply to. Then write answers to the questions.

| | |
|---|---|
| FROM: | may.chang@shopmart.com |
| SUBJECT: | personnel update |
| DATE: | February 10, 2011 |
| TO: | kimstanley@speedymail.com |

Kim,

We're updating all of our personnel files and I realize that I don't have all of your information. Can you please send me the month and day of your birthday? I have the year. Also, I need to know what city you live in, whether you have a high school or a college degree, and whether you are attending school right now.

Please send this information by next Friday at the latest. If you have any questions, come by my office or give me a call.

Thanks,

May

**Answers:**

1. _____

2. _____

3. _____

4. _____

## ❸ Write

Use your notes from Activity 2 to write a reply email.

| | |
|---|---|
| FROM: | |
| SUBJECT: | |
| DATE: | |
| TO: | |

# What Do You Know?

## ① Listening Review  084

**Part 1:**

Listen to what is said. When you hear the question, *Which is correct?*, listen and choose the correct answer: *A, B,* or *C.* Use the Answer Sheet.

**Part 2:** 🎧 085

You will hear the first part of a conversation. To finish the conversation, listen and choose the correct answer: *A, B,* or *C.* Use the Answer Sheet.

### Answer Sheet

1. Ⓐ Ⓑ Ⓒ
2. Ⓐ Ⓑ Ⓒ
3. Ⓐ Ⓑ Ⓒ
4. Ⓐ Ⓑ Ⓒ
5. Ⓐ Ⓑ Ⓒ
6. Ⓐ Ⓑ Ⓒ
7. Ⓐ Ⓑ Ⓒ
8. Ⓐ Ⓑ Ⓒ
9. Ⓐ Ⓑ Ⓒ
10. Ⓐ Ⓑ Ⓒ

## ② Grammar Review

Circle the correct answer: *A, B,* or *C.*

**1.** I know someone _____ celebrates the Mid-Autumn Festival every year.

A. what
B. who
C. is

**2.** My children like holidays _____ involve costumes.

A. what
B. who
C. that

**3.** The holiday _____ I like the best is New Year's Day.

A. what
B. that
C. who

**4.** I had dinner at a restaurant _____ read about last week.

A. who I
B. that
C. I

**5.** The people _____ at dinner had never met before.

A. who were
B. they were
C. were

**6.** We _____ because we _____ to put things into neat categories.

A. stereotypes / likes
B. stereotyping / liking
C. stereotype / like

142 | UNIT 10

## 2 Grammar Review (continued)

**7.** When one _____ an assumption about someone, one might be guilty of stereotyping.

  A. make

  B. made

  C. makes

**8.** The exams _____ in one week.

  A. will be given

  B. will give

  C. be given

**9.** You _____ a school official next Monday.

  A. be called

  B. will call by

  C. will be called by

**10.** The food for the celebration _____ Marla and Tom.

  A. will prepare

  B. will be prepared

  C. will be prepared by

## LEARNING LOG

### I know these words:

**NOUNS**

- ancestors
- assumptions
- balance
- categories
- costumes
- homemaker
- household
- ignorance
- legend
- maternity leave
- mischief
- misconception
- parade
- paternity leave
- service
- statistics
- stereotype
- wage earner

**VERBS**

- celebrate
- commemorate
- conclude
- honor
- stereotype

**ADJECTIVES**

- appropriate
- average
- customary
- inappropriate
- lunar
- mandatory
- stereotypical
- unconscious

**ADVERB**

- actually

### I practiced these skills, strategies, and grammar points:

- comparing international celebrations
- discussing work and family balance around the world
- understanding cultural behavior
- asking if something is appropriate
- changing stress with *that*
- recognizing bias and stereotyping
- comparing and contrasting
- communicating by email
- using adjective clauses—*who* or *that* as subject
- using adjective clauses—*who* or *that* as object
- using indefinite pronouns: *You, one, we,* and *some*
- using future passive

**Work-Out CD-ROM**

**Unit 10: Plug in and practice!**

# UNIT 1 SKILLS AND ABILITIES

**LESSON 2 Present Perfect vs. Simple Past** pages 6–7

| Present Perfect vs. Simple Past | |
|---|---|
| **Present Perfect** | **Simple Past** |
| We use the **present perfect** to talk about: | We use the **simple past** to talk about: |
| 1. an action that started in the past and is continuing now.<br><br>They **have lived** in Chicago since 2001. (They started living in Chicago in 2001, and they still live there now.) | 1. an action that ended in the past.<br><br>They **lived** in Chicago for two years. (They don't live there now.) |
| 2. an action that happened in a time period that isn't completed yet.<br><br>I **have taken** three English classes this year.<br>(It is still this year now.) | 2. an action that happened in a time period that is completed.<br><br>I **took** two English classes last year.<br>(Last year is completed.) |
| 3. an action that happened or did not happen at a non-specific time in the past.<br><br>Kato **has sent** me many confusing emails.<br>(We don't know the specific time that Kato sent the emails)<br><br>I **have never taken** an art class. | 3. an action that happened or didn't happen at a specific time in the past.<br><br>Kato **sent** me many confusing emails last week.<br>(We know when Kato sent the emails.)<br><br>I **didn't take** an art class last year. |
| *See page 228 for a list of the past participle forms of some irregular verbs. | |

**1** Complete the sentences. Use the simple past or the present perfect form of the verb in parentheses.

**1.** Laura _____has been_____ (be) an employee at Speedy Delivery for three years.

**2.** Last year, Laura _____ (learn) that she needed to improve her team skills.

**3.** In January, Laura _____ (decide) to take some continuing education classes.

**4.** She _____ (go) to the community college to register for a class.

**5.** She _____ (register) for Team Skills 101 at the end of January.

**6.** She _____ (take) five classes this year.

**7.** The classes _____ (really / help) her at work.

**8.** She _____ (learn) to be more cooperative and flexible.

**9.** She _____ (also / learn) to take responsibility at work.

**2** Read the facts about Sean and his goals for 2012. Then complete the paragraph with the verbs in parentheses. Use the simple past or the present perfect.

| January, 2012 | January to June, 2012 | January to Now, 2012 | Now: December, 2012 |
|---|---|---|---|
| New Year's Resolution: Be a better parent! Learn how to listen! | Take parenting class Read books | Practice every day! | Achieve goal! |

I'm a parent, but I ____have never been____ (be / never) a very good listener. Listening is an important part

*(1)*

of being a good parent, so at the beginning of the year, I _____ (decide) to do something

*(2)*

about my problem. In February, I _____ (take) a parenting class, and I _____

*(3)*                                                                                              *(4)*

(learn) how to really concentrate on what my kids are saying. I also _____ (read) some

*(5)*

books on good listening skills, and I _____ (learn) how to show speakers that I am listening.

*(6)*

Since the beginning of the year, my listening skills _____ (improve) a lot. I _____

*(7)*                                                                                   *(8)*

(practice) my new skills every day since January. Now I feel that I _____ (become) a better

*(9)*

parent and a better communicator.

**3** Write answers to the questions. Use the simple past and the present perfect.

**1.** What skills have you always been good at?

_____

**2.** What skills have you never been good at?

_____

**3.** What goals did you have at the beginning of the year?

_____

**4.** Have you achieved any of your goals yet? How have you achieved your goals?

_____

## Compound Sentences with *so, too, not either, neither,* and *but*

We use *so, too,* and *not either* to show **similarity** between two ideas or sentences.

|  |  | **Compound Sentence** |
|---|---|---|
| *so* | Dan **is** a good speaker. | Dan is a good speaker, and **so is** Kelly. |
| *too* | Kelly **is** also a good speaker. | Dan is a good speaker, and Kelly **is, too.** |
| *not either* | Dan **doesn't smile** much. | Dan doesn't smile much, and Kelly **doesn't either.** |
| *neither* | Kelly **doesn't smile** much. | Dan doesn't smile much, and **neither does** Kelly. |
| We use *but* to show **contrast** between two ideas or sentences. | | |
| *but* | Sara **makes** eye contact when she speaks. | Sara makes eye contact when she speaks, **but** Harry **doesn't.** |
| | Harry **doesn't make** eye contact when he speaks. | |

Note: When we combine sentences with *be,* we use a form of *be* in the second part of the sentence. When we combine sentences with other verbs, we use a form of *do* in the second part of the sentence.

**1** **Combine the pairs of sentences with the words in parentheses.**

**1.** Oscar always gets to work on time. Sue always gets to work on time. (so)

 *Oscar always gets to work on time, and so does Sue.*

**2.** Carlos isn't bilingual. Tara isn't bilingual. (neither)

_____

**3.** Wei doesn't have good computer skills. Jack doesn't have good computer skills. (not either)

_____

**4.** A smile communicates a positive attitude. Good posture communicates a positive attitude. (too)

_____

**5.** Kelly smiled during the interview. Asha didn't smile during the interview. (but)

_____

**6.** Rob looked defensive. Marta looked defensive. (too)

_____

**7.** Paolo is proficient in writing. Simon is proficient in writing. (so)

_____

**8.** Leila didn't do well at the interview. Steve didn't do well at the interview. (not either)

_____

### Either . . . or, Both . . . and, and Neither . . . nor

We use **either . . . or, both . . . and,** and **neither . . . nor** to join similar ideas.

| | | **Examples** |
|---|---|---|
| **either . . . or**<br>for two alternative ideas | You can pay your tuition in one payment.<br>You can pay your tuition in installments. | You can pay your tuition **either** in one payment **or** in installments. |
| **both . . . and**<br>for two affirmative ideas | Business letters should be concise.<br>Business emails should be concise. | **Both** business letters **and** business emails should be concise. |
| **neither . . . nor**<br>for two negative ideas | Business letters aren't private.<br>Business emails aren't private. | **Neither** business letters **nor** business emails are private. |
| | Jack doesn't like to drive.<br>I don't like to drive. | **Neither** Jack **nor** I like to drive. |

Note: With *either … or* and *neither… nor*, the verb agrees with the subject that is closer to it.
With *both … and*, we use a plural verb. *Both my sister and I* **are** *teachers*.

**1** Rewrite the sentences with *either . . . or, both . . . and,* or *neither . . . nor.*

**1.** You can call me or you can email me.

_____You can either call me or email me._____

**2.** You can request a copy of your transcript by writing a letter, or you can request a copy of your transcript by filling out a form.

_____

_____

**3.** We learned to write business reports, and we learned to do financial analyses.

_____

**4.** Business writing skills aren't hard to learn, and business speaking skills aren't hard to learn either.

_____

**5.** Listening is an important part of parenting, and teaching values is an important part of parenting.

_____

**6.** Mike doesn't have good writing skills yet, and Ling doesn't have good writing skills yet.

_____

**7.** We can go to the library to study, or we can study at my house.

_____

**8.** Sam isn't a good public speaker, and Julia isn't a good public speaker.

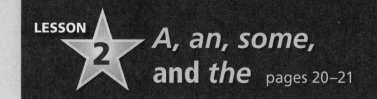

## A, an, some, and the

| | Notes | Examples |
|---|---|---|
| **a** **an** **some** | We use *a*, *an*, and *some* when we aren't thinking of a specific thing or person. | Tom has **a** good insurance policy. (We aren't thinking about a specific insurance policy.) |
| | We use *a* before count nouns that start with a consonant sound. | **a** car, **a** problem, **a** driver, **a** university |
| | We use *an* before count nouns that start with a vowel sound. | **an** alarm, **an** insurance policy, **an** accident, **an** hour |
| | We use *some* before noncount or plural nouns. | **some** problems, **some** trouble, **some** information |
| **the** | We use *the* when we are thinking of a specific thing or person. | Tom put **the** insurance policy in **the** glove compartment. (He has only one insurance policy.) |
| | We use *the* with singular and plural count and noncount nouns. | I remember **the** trouble Tom had with his insurance company. (We know what the trouble was.) |
| | We use *the* with plural family names and some names of places. | **the** Smiths, **the** Clintons, **the** United States, **the** Rocky Mountains, **the** Pacific Ocean |
| **No article** Ø | We don't use an article when we are talking about people or things in general. | **Drivers** who don't have insurance are asking for **trouble**. |
| | We don't use an article before people's names and most names of places. | **Mr. Smith** drove to **Los Angeles** last week. |

### ❶ Read the sentences. Circle *a* or *an*.

1. Tom bought **a** / **an** used Volkswagen from **a** / **an** online car dealer.

2. He heard about **a** / **an** insurance policy from **a** / **an** friend.

3. Tom made **a** / **an** phone call and got **a** / **an** company representative on the phone.

4. He asked for **a** / **an** policy with collision and bodily injury coverage.

5. The representative gave Tom **a** / **an** choice between paying once **a** / **an** year or paying monthly.

6. Tom decided to pay once **a** / **an** year, and he paid for his policy with **a** / **an** credit card.

7. As soon as he got off the phone, he took the Volkswagen for **a** / **an** ride to **a** / **an** new restaurant.

8. At **a** / **an** intersection, **a** / **an** driver made **a** / **an** illegal turn and hit Tom's new car.

**2** Complete the paragraph with *a, an, some,* or *the.*

Tom had _____ trouble today. He had _____*an*_____ accident on his way to _____
(1)                                          (2)                                              (3)

post office. He was driving his new Volkswagen when _____ car hit him at _____
                                                      (4)                          (5)

intersection of Smith and Main. Luckily, he has _____ insurance policy from _____
                                                  (6)                                 (7)

good insurance company. He called _____ company immediately and spoke to _____
                                     (8)                                            (9)

representative. _____ representative asked him _____ questions. She asked
                 (10)                                  (11)

Tom to describe _____ damage to his car. She also asked him for _____ name
                 (12)                                                    (13)

of _____ other driver and for _____ exact time that _____
    (14)                               (15)                        (16)

accident happened.

**3** Complete the accident report. Circle *a, an, the, some,* or Ø (no article).

## Department of Motor Vehicles Accident Report

### Section B - Description of What Happened

I was driving in [a / an / the /Ø] San Diego on March 19, 2012. I stopped for [a / an / the / Ø] red light at
                  (1)                                                            (2)

[a / an / the / some] intersection of Green and Oak. I was in [a / an / the / Ø] left-turn lane. There were
 (3)                                                           (4)

[a / an / the / some] cars in the opposite lane. When [a / an / the / Ø] light turned green, I started to make
 (5)                                                   (6)

[a / an / the / Ø] left turn. [A / An / The / Ø] car in [a / an / the / Ø] opposite lane was coming toward me,
 (7)                (8)                         (9)

even though I had [a / an / the / Ø] green light. [A / An / The / Ø] driver of [a / an / the / Ø] car hit
                   (10)                           (11)                         (12)

[a / an / the / Ø] passenger side of my car. We both pulled to [a / an / the / Ø] side of [a / an / the / Ø]
 (13)                                                           (14)                      (15)

road. The driver's name was [ a / an / the / Ø] Ron Taylor. He told me that he didn't have [a / an / the / Ø]
                             (16)                                                           (17)

insurance. I explained that [a / an / some / Ø] drivers in the United States have to have insurance. Then I
                            (18)

gave him [a / an / some / Ø] information about my insurance company.
          (19)

**4** Write a paragraph about an accident that you had or that you saw. Pay attention to your use of *a, an, the, some,* or no article.

# Indirect Questions pages 22–23

## Indirect Questions

**Indirect questions** are more polite than direct questions.

An indirect question can be:

- Part of a question: *Can you tell me what time it is?*
- Part of a statement: *I wonder what time it is.*

### Yes/No Questions

For indirect *yes/no* questions, use *if* or *whether* + subject + verb.

| Direct Questions | Indirect Questions |
|---|---|
| Is this the correct number? | Do you know **if** this is the correct number? |
| Does the bus stop here? | Could you tell me **whether** the bus stops here? |

### Wh- Questions

For indirect *wh-* questions, use question word + subject + verb.

| Direct Questions | Indirect Questions |
|---|---|
| Where is the bus stop? | Do you know **where** the bus stop is? |
| What time is it? | Can you tell me **what time** it is? |
| When does the bus leave? | I don't know **when** the bus leaves. |
| Why is he here? | I wonder **why** he is here. |

Note: We use statement word order in indirect questions.

**1** Rewrite each direct question as an indirect question. Use the words in parentheses.

**1.** (I wonder) Do they take credit cards? _____ I wonder if they take credit cards. _____

**2.** (I don't know) Do you want a round-trip ticket? _____

**3.** (Could you tell me) When does the next bus arrive? _____

**4.** (Ask them) Do they have change for a twenty? _____

**5.** (Can you tell me) What gate does the bus leave from? _____

**6.** (I wonder) When will the next bus come? _____

**7.** (Ask him) What's the arrival time? _____

**8.** (I don't know) Do we have enough money? _____

**2** Think of five things that you don't know about your classmates. Ask and answer indirect questions with a partner to find out.

**EXAMPLES:** *Do you know whether Luis has a car?*
*Do you know if Miriam speaks French?*
*Do you know where Luis lives?*

> ## May, Might, Could, Should, Ought to for Possibility and Probability
>
> We use **may, might,** or **could** + verb to talk about something that is **possible** in the present or future.
>
> EXAMPLES:
> | | |
> |---|---|
> | Mark **may be** struck in traffic. | = It's possible Mark is stuck in traffic. |
> | He **might not get** here on time. | = It's possible he won't get here on time. |
> | We **could miss** our flight. | = Maybe we will miss our flight. |
>
> We use **should** or **ought to** + verb to talk about something that will **probably** happen in the future.
>
> EXAMPLES:
> | | |
> |---|---|
> | Mark **should be** here in five minutes. | = It's probable he will be here in five minutes. |
> | He **ought to be** on time for the flight. | = It's probable he will be on time for the flight. |

**1** Write sentences with modals of possibility and probability. Use the cues in parentheses. More than one answer may be correct.

**1.** (possible: Otto will report the accident to his insurance company.)

     _Otto may report the accident to his insurance company._

**2.** (probable: The police will arrive in about 10 minutes.)

_____

**3.** (possible: Harry doesn't have a cell phone.)

_____

**4.** (probable: David knows what to do in a roadside emergency.)

_____

**5.** (possible): Janet won't be able to help us.

_____

**6.** (probable): The ambulance will be here very soon.

_____

**2** Write five sentences about what will possibly or probably happen to you this week. Use *may, might, could, should,* or *ought to.*

**Example:** *My brother may call me.*

**1.** _____

**2.** _____

**3.** _____

**4.** _____

**5.** _____

## *Must* for Logical Conclusion

We use *must* + verb to make a **logical conclusion** or to say that we are almost certain about something in the present.

EXAMPLES:

| | |
|---|---|
| Mark is 30 minutes late. | He **must be** stuck in traffic. |
| You keep biting your nails. | You **must feel** nervous. |
| They go to Florida every year. | They **must like** it there. |

**3** **Read the situations. Write a logical conclusion with *must*. Different answers are possible.**

**1.** Ana parked her car in a lot. When she came back, there was a big scratch on one side of the car.

_Ana must be upset._____

**2.** Katy's car won't move, and her gas needle is pointing to *Empty*.

_____

**3.** I see flares and a car with a raised hood on the roadside.

_____

**4.** Jack witnessed a car accident, but he drove away immediately and didn't help the drivers.

_____

**5.** Rick has never had an accident.

_____

**4** **Read the sentences. Underline the modal. Then check the correct box for each sentence.**

| | Possible | Probable | Almost Certain |
|---|:---:|:---:|:---:|
| **1.** We <u>might</u> be late for the party. | ⊗ | ○ | ○ |
| **2.** There could be an accident up ahead. | ○ | ○ | ○ |
| **3.** If there's an accident, we should see some flares or flashing lights. | ○ | ○ | ○ |
| **4.** There must be a problem up ahead because I see a lot of police cars. | ○ | ○ | ○ |
| **5.** Some people could be hurt. | ○ | ○ | ○ |
| **6.** I see five police cars! It must be a terrible accident! | ○ | ○ | ○ |

## Requests and Offers

We use **Would you** + verb to make polite **requests**.

EXAMPLES:
**Would you wait** here, please?
**Would you open** the door for me, please?

We use **Would you mind** + verb-**ing** to make polite **requests**.

EXAMPLES:
**Would you mind writing** your policy number down?
**Would you mind waiting** here?

We use **Could I** and **Why don't I** + verb to make polite **offers**.

EXAMPLES:
**Could I help** you with that suitcase?
**Why don't I get** you a cab?

**1** Change the orders to polite requests. Use *Would you* or *Would you mind*.

**1.** Turn off your cell phone. _____ *Would you turn off your cell phone, please?* _____

**2.** Stop here. _____

**3.** Call a taxi for me. _____

**4.** Slow down. _____

**5.** Tell me the directions. _____

**6.** Move your car. _____

**2** Make a polite offer for each situation. Use *Could I* or *Why don't I.*

**1.** Jan needs to go to the airport. You have a car.

  *Why don't I drive you to the airport?* _____

**2.** Ron just got a flat tire. He doesn't know how to change it.

  _____

**3.** Louisa is lost. She's looking for the highway entrance.

  _____

**4.** Mark wants to buy a train ticket from the machine, but he doesn't know how.

  _____

**5.** Your friend wants to get a driver's license, and he needs to study for the written test.

  _____

## Present Perfect Continuous

Use the **present perfect continuous** to talk about an action that started in the past and is continuing now.

| Statements | | | | Negative Statements | | | |
|---|---|---|---|---|---|---|---|
| I You | have | | | I You | haven't | | |
| He She | has | been waiting | for a long time. since10:00. | He She | hasn't | been waiting | very long. |
| We They | have | | | We They | haven't | | |

| Question with *How Long* | | | | Answers | | | |
|---|---|---|---|---|---|---|---|
| How long | have | you | been waiting? | **For** a long time. (*for* + length of time) | | | |
| | has | he | | **Since** 10:00 am. (*since* + point in time) | | | |

**1** **Complete the sentences. Use the present perfect continuous form of the verbs in parentheses. Use contractions or full forms.**

**1.** Raul _____has been having_____ (have) breathing problems since he was a child.

**2.** Ann _____ (feel / not) very well lately.

**3.** Asha _____ (work) as a pediatrician since 1997.

**4.** Jenny and Mark _____ (see) the same optometrist for the past five years.

**5.** The cardiologist _____ (treat) Ron for three years.

**6.** Lucia _____ (eat / not) very well since she got out of the hospital.

**7.** We _____ (go) to the physical therapist on Thursdays.

**8.** I _____ (exercise / not) enough lately.

**2** **Use the cues to write present perfect continuous questions with *How long* and short answers with *for* and *since*.**

**1.** Q: Janice / take vitamins _____How long has Janice been taking vitamins?_____

A: five years _____

**2.** Q: Mark / feel sick _____

A: three days _____

**3.** Q: The children / play outside _____

A: noon _____

**4.** Q: Sam / wait for the doctor _____

A: 9:00 A.M. _____

**5.** Q: you / work here _____

A: 1997 _____

**6.** Q: they / study _____

A: six hours _____

**7.** Q: we / drive _____

A: half a day _____

**8.** Q: Alice / go to nursing school _____

A: September _____

**❸ Complete the conversation. Use the present perfect continuous or the simple past forms of the verbs in parentheses. Use contractions or full forms.**

Mr. Green: Finally! I _____'ve been sitting_____ (sit) in that waiting room for a long time.
               ①

Dr. Patel: I'm so sorry! How long _____ you _____ (wait)?
                    ②

Mr. Green: I _____ (wait) for 45 minutes!
          ③

Dr. Patel: Again, I'm very sorry. So, how _____ you _____ (feel)?
              ④

Mr. Green: Not great. I _____ (have) heart pains again.
          ⑤

Dr. Patel: _____ you _____ (take) your medicine?
        ⑥

Mr. Green: Yes, I _____ (take) it, but I _____ (forget) to take it this morning.
          ⑦                  ⑧

Dr. Patel: _____ you _____ (exercise) a little every day?
        ⑨

Mr. Green: Not really. I _____ (take) a walk on Monday, but I _____
          ⑩                ⑪
(exercise / not) every day.

Dr. Patel: I see. _____ you _____ (eat) well?
          ⑫

Mr. Green: Well, I _____ (have) a salad for lunch yesterday, but I _____
          ⑬                ⑭
(eat) a hamburger and fries for dinner last night. I guess I _____ (take / not) good
                                    ⑮
care of myself.

## LESSON 3

# Gerunds vs. Infinitives as Objects of Verbs pages 36–37

## Gerunds vs. Infinitives as Objects of Verbs

We use a **gerund** (**verb-*ing***) after certain verbs.

EXAMPLES:

I **dislike canceling** appointments at the last minute.
Would you **consider coming** in on Monday?
We **recommend not showing up** late.

We use a gerund after these verbs:

| | | | | | | |
|---|---|---|---|---|---|---|
| admit | appreciate | avoid | consider | discuss | dislike | enjoy |
| finish | keep | miss | postpone | quit | recommend | suggest |

We use an **infinitive** (***to* + verb**) after certain verbs.

EXAMPLES:

I **need to change** my appointment.
She **promises to arrive** on time.
The doctor **decided not to come** in today.

We use an infinitive after these verbs:

| | | | | | | |
|---|---|---|---|---|---|---|
| agree | be able to | decide | expect | forget | hope | learn |
| need | plan | promise | refuse | try | want | would like |

Note: To make a negative gerund or infinitive, we put *not* before the gerund or infinitive.

**1** **Complete the sentences with the gerund form of a verb in the box. You can use some verbs more than once.**

| go | have | miss | see | take |
|---|---|---|---|---|

I had surgery on my back recently, and my doctor recommended _____*seeing*_____ a physical therapist.
**(1)**

She suggested _____ three times a week. I work full time, and I dislike _____ work
**(2)** **(3)**

for any reason. I discussed _____ time off for these appointments with my boss, but he said
**(4)**

I should avoid _____ work right now. We're in the middle of big project, and he said that he
**(5)**

would really miss _____ my help. I'll consider _____ to the therapist after the project
**(6)** **(7)**

is finished. I appreciate _____ a boss who thinks that I'm important, but in the meantime, my
**(8)**

back hurts!

**2** Complete the conversation. Use the infinitive form of the verb in parentheses.

Receptionist: What happened? We expected _____to see_____ (see) you yesterday.

Ms. Li: I'm so sorry! I forgot _____ (come). I would like _____ (schedule) another appointment.

Receptionist: Okay. I'll try _____ (find) something this week.

Ms. Li: Remember, I need _____ (have) a morning appointment.

Receptionist: Yes, I remember. Would you be able _____ (get) here by nine tomorrow?

Ms. Li: Yes, I'll be able _____ (do) that. And I promise _____ (be / not) late!

**3** Circle the gerund or the infinitive to complete the passage.

**Bay City Clinic**

**You doctor's name: Dr. Kline**

**Please describe the reason you need to see your doctor:**

I would like **seeing / to see** Dr. Kline because I need **getting / to get** my eyes checked. I have finished
① ②

**taking / to take** the medicine, and Dr. Kline recommended **coming / to come** in for another eye exam. I
③ ④

also want to discuss **getting / to get** new eyeglasses. I am able **coming / to come** on any Wednesday or
⑤ ⑥

Friday, and I would appreciate **having / to have** a morning appointment. I want **coming / to come** as soon as
⑦ ⑧

possible.

Thank you.

**4** Answer the questions. Then ask a partner the questions.

**1.** What is something you hope to do?

_____

**2.** What do you enjoy doing with your friends or family?

_____

**3.** What do you often avoid doing?

_____

**4.** What is something you would like to quit doing?

_____

## Used to

We use **used to** + **verb** to talk about something that was true in the past but is not true now.

Examples:

I **used to spend** hours on social networking sites. Now I only spend about an hour a day.

I didn't **use to*** **spend** much time on my homework. Now I spend a lot of time on it.

When did you **use to do** your homework?

A: Did you **use to spend** a lot of time on the computer?
B: Yes, I did.

*Notice the form *use to* with negative statements and questions.

Note: We use *be used to* + gerund to talk about something we are accustomed to. *I am used to spending hours at the* computer.

**1** **Complete the paragraph. Use *used to*, or *didn't use to*.**

My son, Marcos, is doing much better in school these days. He _____didn't use to_____ do so much

homework before, but now he does. He _____ watch a lot of TV, but now he spends more time
                                              (1)

on his homework. He _____ read very much, and he _____ go to the library, but
                      (2)                                          (3)                    (4)

now he seems to enjoy books. Before, he _____ spend hours surfing the net, but now he isn't
                                         (5)

allowed to. He _____ have a computer in his room, but we took it out. Marcos also
               (6)

_____ exercise, but now he plays soccer on a team. Before, we _____ monitor
(7)                                                                        (8)

how our children spent their time, but now we're better parents.

**2** **Write questions using the cues below, and write your answers. Then ask and answer the
questions with a partner.**

**When you were young . . .**

**1.** spend a lot of time with friends

Question: _____Did you use to spend a lot of time with friends?_____

Answer: _____Yes, I did._____

**2.** watch a lot of TV

Question: _____

Answer: _____

**3.** when / go to bed

Question: _____

Answer: _____

**4.** what / do for fun in the summertime

Question: _____

Answer: _____

| | Because, Since, and So | |
|---|---|---|
| | **Notes** | **Examples** |
| *because*<br>*since* | • *Because* and *since* introduce a clause.<br>• A clause with *because* or *since* introduces a cause or reason.<br>• When the clause with *because* or *since* comes first, we use a comma after it. | I went to visit Martha **because she was sick**.<br>   RESULT                       CAUSE<br>**Since she was sick**, I went to visit Martha.<br>   CAUSE                       RESULT |
| *so* | • *So* introduces a result clause.<br>• In sentences with *so*, we use a comma after the first clause.<br>• The clause with *so* can't come first. | Martha was sick, **so I went to visit her**.<br>   CAUSE                       RESULT |

**1** Combine each pair of sentences using *because*, *since*, or *so*. Use correct punctuation.

**1.** Ali hopes to become a pediatrician. He really enjoys working with children. (so)

        *Ali really enjoys working with children, so he hopes to become a pediatrician.*

**2.** Larry felt a sharp pain in his chest. He went to the emergency room. (so)

_____

**3.** He has health insurance. His hospital bill wasn't very high. (because)

_____

**4.** She is a licensed physical therapist. She got a good job at a health clinic. (since)

_____

**5.** Jim had a headache. He took some aspirin. (because)

_____

**6.** Marta finished her degree as a dietician. She is applying for a full-time job. (so).

_____

**7.** Laura was in the hospital for two weeks and couldn't come to class. I took our assignments to her. (since)

_____

**8.** Jin finally got a promotion at work. She is going to get a raise and will probably buy a house. (because)

_____

## Present Passive

A statement can be active or passive.

| **Active** | **Passive** |
|---|---|
| People <u>speak</u> <u>many languages</u> in the U.S. | <u>Many languages</u> <u>are spoken</u> in the U.S. |
|     VERB       OBJECT |     SUBJECT       VERB |

We use the passive when:

| | |
|---|---|
| • we don't know who does the action. | • A lot of equipment **is stolen** every year. |
| • it isn't important who does the action. | • Elections **are held** every November. |
| • it is obvious who does the action. | • A president **is elected** every four years. |

| **Passive Statements** | | | **Negative Passive Statements** | | |
|---|---|---|---|---|---|
| | *Be* | **Past Participle** | | *Be* | **Past Participle** |
| English<br>Many languages | is<br>are | **spoken** in the US. | The election<br>The elections | isn't<br>aren't | **held** in January. |

**1** Read the sentences. Write *A* (Active) or *P* (Passive).

**1.** __A__ Discrimination because of religion is illegal.

**2.** _____ In the United States, citizens are not required to vote.

**3.** _____ Citizens who are at least 18 years old have the right to vote in elections.

**4.** _____ In most states, students up to age 16 are required to attend school.

**5.** _____ The right to gather for a protest is called freedom of assembly.

**6.** _____ In the United Sates, free public education is provided for all children.

**7.** _____ An employer cannot pay a female employee less than a male employee.

**8.** _____ U.S. citizens can follow any religion they want.

**9.** _____ Parents are not allowed to leave their young children alone.

**10.** _____ Spanish is taught in many schools.

**2** Circle the correct form of the verb to complete the sentences.

1. In most states, children ages 5 to 16 (require / are required) to go to school.
2. When you (register / are registered) to vote, you fill out a form and mail it to a government office.
3. You cannot (discriminate / be discriminated) against because of age or race.
4. In most states, parents (allow / are allowed) to teach their children at home.
5. In the United States, we (have / are had) presidential elections every four years.
6. In some countries, elections (hold / are held) on a Sunday.
7. Some countries (require / are required) you to pay a fine if you don't vote.

**3** Complete the sentences. Use the passive form of the verb in parentheses.

1. The U.S. president _____is elected_____ (elect) every four years.
2. When you register to vote, your name _____ (add) to a list of voters.
3. Most elections _____ (hold) on the Tuesday after the first Monday in November.
4. In the United States, citizens _____ (allow) freedom of assembly.
5. U.S. citizens _____ (expect) to be tolerant of all religious beliefs.
6. In the United States, parents _____ (require) to educate their children.
7. U.S. citizens _____ (treat / not) differently because of their religion.
8. As soon as you _____ (register), you can vote in the next election.

**4** Work with a partner. Ask and answer the questions. Use complete sentences in your answers.

1. What are two things that you are required to do by law in your home country?

_____

_____

2. Are children required to attend school in your home country? Up to what age?

_____

3. What language is spoken in your home country?

_____

4. What are you required to do in this class?

_____

5. What are you not allowed to do in this class?

_____

## Past Passive

My parents **encouraged** me to participate in sports.     (Past active statement)
I **was encouraged** to participate in sports.     (Past passive statement)

| Subject | Was / were | Past Participle | |
|---|---|---|---|
| I<br>He | was<br>wasn't | told | to do homework every night. |
| We<br>You<br>They | were<br>weren't | required | to attend school on Saturdays. |

**1** **Change the present passive statements to the past passive.**

**1.** I am required to attend school on Saturdays.

_____ I was required to attend school on Saturdays. _____

**2.** Ana is expected to study math, science, music, and art.

_____

**3.** Parents are invited to the parent teacher conference.

_____

**4.** They are encouraged to study foreign languages in elementary school.

_____

**5.** Raul and I are sent to English classes every afternoon.

_____

**6.** Some children aren't encouraged to work hard in school.

_____

**2** **Compete the sentences. Use the simple past passive form of the verb in parentheses.**

When I was a child, I attended a coeducational school—boys and girls ____were required____ (require) to study
(1)

together. I _____ (require) to take math, science, languages, and music at my school.
(2)

The classes _____ (teach) by dedicated teachers. My parents participated in my education.
(3)

They _____ (require / not) to help out at the school or attend meetings, but
(4)

they _____ (encourage) to participate, and they enjoyed it. They_____
(5)                                                                                         (6)

(inform) about how I was doing in school, and I _____ (expect) to work hard. I think
(7)

they _____ (reward) for their involvement in my education because I _____
(8)                                                                                                      (9)

(consider) to be very good student.

**3** Read the timeline. Then complete the paragraph. Use the simple past passive form of the verbs in the box.

| 1990 | 1995 | 2005 | 2010 |
|------|------|------|------|
| birth | public school | private school | university |
| Spanish | Spanish | English, French | German |

| educate | require | send | speak |
|---------|---------|------|-------|

I was born in 1990. Spanish _____ was spoken _____ in our home when I was little. In 1995,
(1)

I _____ to a local public school, and Spanish _____ at that school.
(2) (3)

In 2005, I _____ to a private school. English _____ at the private school, and
(4) (5)

I _____ to take French, too. When I graduated from the private school, I _____
(6) (7)

to a German university, where, of course, only German _____. As a result,
(8)

I _____ in four languages.
(9)

**4** Work with a partner. Ask and answer the questions. Use complete sentences.

**1.** Where were you born?

_____

**2.** What language was spoken in your home when you were a child?

_____

**3.** What language was spoken in your first school?

_____

**4.** What kind of schools were you sent to when you were growing up?

_____

**5.** What were you required to study when you were in school?

_____

**6.** What were you not allowed to do when you were a child?

_____

**7.** What were you encouraged to do when you were a child?

_____

| Passive with Present Perfect | | | | | |
|---|---|---|---|---|---|
| **Statements** | | | **Negative Statements** | | |
| | *Has / have been* | Past Participle | | *Has / have been* | Past Participle |
| The decision | has already been | made. | The decision | hasn't been | made yet. |
| The decisions | have just been | | The decisions | haven't been | |
| ***Yes / No* Questions** | | | **Short Answers** | | |
| **Has** | everyone | **been informed** of the new rules? | Yes, they **have**. | | No, they **haven't**. |
| **Have** | the laws | **been passed**? | Yes, they **have**. | | No, they **haven't**. |

**1** Complete the sentences. Use the present perfect passive form of the verb in parentheses.

1. A new union leader _____ *has just been elected* _____ (elect/ just).

2. The important decisions _____ (make / not) yet.

3. The workers' rights _____ (protect) since the union was formed.

4. A union _____ (allow / never) at this company.

5. _____ the union rules _____ (approve) by all members?

6. _____ a union representative _____ (choose) yet?

**2** Complete the sentences. Use the present perfect passive form of the verb in parentheses.

**Come to a union information meeting on Thursday, June 4 at 7 P.M. to discuss the issues!**

- A union _____ *has not been formed* _____ (form / not) yet at Bay City Delivery.
  ①

- Some workers at Bay City Delivery feel that they _____ (discriminate)
  ②
  against.

- Not all workers _____ (treat) equally.
  ③

- Some employees _____ (pay / not ) for working extra hours.
  ④

- Benefits _____ (provide / not) for some workers.
  ⑤

- Problems _____ (solve / not) quickly.
  ⑥

## Passive with Modals

We can use modals (*can, could, should, may, might, must, ought to*) in passive sentences.

| Statements | | | | Negative Statements | | | |
|---|---|---|---|---|---|---|---|
| | | *be* | Past Participle | | | *be* | Past Participle |
| Employees' rights | should ought to must | be | protected. | Workers | should not must not | be | treated unfairly. |

**1** **Complete the sentences. Use the passive modal form of the words in parentheses.**

**1.** Safety equipment _____ must be provided _____ (must / provide) for all employees.

**2.** Immigrants _____ (must / not / take) advantage of.

**3.** Female workers _____ (must / pay) the same wages as male workers.

**4.** Pension plans _____ (must / provide) for all workers.

**5.** Workers _____ (must / not / discriminate) against because of their race, religion, or age.

**6.** Health benefits _____ (should / give) to all workers.

**7.** Transportation costs for getting to work _____ (should / pay) for by employers.

**8.** Children under the age of 18 _____ (should / not / allow) to work if they are still in school.

**2** **Work with a partner. Agree or disagree with the statements in Activity 1. Use passive modals and give reasons.**

**EXAMPLE:** *I don't think that transportation costs should be paid for by employers because it's too expensive for the company.*

_____

_____

_____

_____

_____

_____

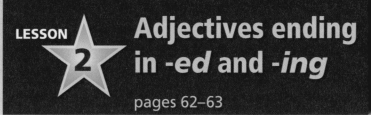

## Adjectives ending in -*ed* and -*ing*

| Notes | Examples |
|---|---|
| Adjectives that end in -*ed* describe a person that has a feeling. | John is **excited** about shopping. |
| Adjectives that end in -*ing* describe a person or a thing that causes a feeling. | Shopping is **exciting**. |

| Some Common -*ed* Adjectives | | Some Common -*ing* Adjectives | |
|---|---|---|---|
| amazed | excited | amazing | exciting |
| annoyed | exhausted | annoying | exhausting |
| bored | frightened | boring | frightening |
| confused | interested | confusing | interesting |
| depressed | satisfied | depressing | satisfying |
| disappointed | surprised | disappointing | surprising |

**1** Complete the sentences with the –*ed* or –*ing* form of the word in parentheses.

**1.** (frighten) The little girl is ___frightened___ because the movie she's watching is _____.

**2.** (bore) The student is _____ because the teacher's lecture is _____.

**3.** (confuse) The woman is _____ because the directions she's reading are _____.

**4.** (entertain) The boy is _____ because the book he's reading is
very _____.

**5.** (depress) Max is _____ because the bills that he's looking at are
very _____.

**6.** (exhaust) Oscar is _____ because shopping with his wife is _____!

**2** Circle the correct adjective.

**1.** I get **bored** / **boring** when I go shopping.

**2.** Sue is **annoyed** / **annoying** when a salesperson tries to pressure her.

**3.** Some people think shopping is very **entertained** / **entertaining**.

**4.** The store's refund policy is very **confused** / **confusing**.

**5.** I was **surprised** / **surprising** that there's a time limit for returning a purchase.

**6.** It's **disappointed** / **disappointing** to get only store credit if you want your money back.

**7.** Ron gets very **excited** / **exciting** whenever he sees a yard sale.

**8.** If you are not **satisfied** / **satisfying** with your purchase, you can return it for a refund.

**9.** The high prices at some stores are **frightened** / **frightening** !

**10.** Impulse shoppers often feel **depressed** / **depressing** after they buy things they don't need.

**3** Complete the conversation. Use the *-ed* or *-ing* form of the word in parentheses.

A: I'm _____depressed_____ (depress) because I couldn't find anything on sale today.
（1）

B: Me, too. It's really _____ (disappoint). This was supposed to be a big sale. I was really
（2）
_____ (excite) about it.
（3）

A: It's _____ (surprise) that we didn't find anything to buy!
（4）

B: Well, it was a _____ (bore) selection. Nothing _____ (interest) was on sale.
（5）                                              （6）

A: I'm pretty _____ (tire), too. How about you?
（7）

B: Me, too! Shopping is _____ (exhaust)!
（8）

A: How about those crowds! The other shoppers were very _____ (annoy)!
（9）

B: Some of the salespeople were _____ (annoy), too.
（10）

A: Well, it's over now. Now, let's find something really _____ (entertain) to do.
（11）

**4** Circle the correct adjective. Then complete the sentence.

**1.** When I go shopping, I am **surprised / surprising** by_____

_____

**2.** The most **amazed / amazing** purchase I ever made was_____

_____

**3.** One thing that is **bored / boring** about shopping is_____

_____

**4.** The most **exhausted / exhausting** kind of shopping is_____

_____

**5.** I am always **interested / interesting** in seeing new_____

_____

**LESSON 3**

# Tag Questions  pages 64–65

## Tag Questions with *Be*

We use tag questions to give an opinion that we think other people will agree with.

EXAMPLE: These cookies **are** fresh, **aren't** they?

We also use tag questions when we think the answer will be *yes*, but we want to check to be sure.

EXAMPLE: This **isn't** on sale, **is** it?

| Positive Statement | Negative Tag | Negative Statement | Positive Tag |
|---|---|---|---|
| She**'s** a smart shopper, | **isn't** she? | She **isn't** a smart shopper, | **is** she? |
| That**'s** a really good price, | **isn't** it? | That **isn't** a very good price, | **is** it? |
| These cookies **are** fresh, | **aren't** they? | These cookies **aren't** very fresh, | **are** they? |
| She **was** very helpful, | **wasn't** she? | She **wasn't** very helpful, | **was** she? |
| They **were** very helpful, | **weren't** they? | They **weren't** very helpful, | **were** they? |

Note: *That* changes to *it*, and *these* changes to *they* in the tag question.

**1** **Add tag questions to the statements.**

**1.** These bananas are ripe, _____*aren't they*_____?

**2.** The salesclerk was rude, _____?

**3.** The food wasn't very good, _____?

**4.** This isn't much fun, _____?

**5.** These shoes are beautiful, _____?

**6.** That wasn't a good sale, _____?

**7.** That's a good deal, _____?

**8.** They weren't very friendly, _____?

## Tag Questions with *Do*

| Positive Statement | Negative Tag | Negative Statement | Positive Tag |
|---|---|---|---|
| She **pays** her bills on time, | **doesn't** she? | She **doesn't pay** her bills on time, | **does** she? |
| You **have** your credit card, | **don't** you? | You **don't have** your credit card, | **do** you? |
| You **brought** your credit card, | **didn't** you? | They **don't have** their receipts, | **do** they? |
| They **have** their receipts, | **don't** they? | You **didn't bring** your credit card, | **did** you? |

**2** Match the statement and the tag question.

___e___ **1.** She wants to pay with a check,     a. do we?

_____ **2.** This comes with a warranty,     b. do they?

_____ **3.** They don't take checks,     c. doesn't it?

_____ **4.** We don't have much time,     d. don't you?

_____ **5.** You have your credit card,     e̶. doesn't she?

**3** Add a tag question to the statements.

**1.** They accept checks here, _____don't they_____?

**2.** You don't have your receipt, _____?

**3.** He doesn't have a credit card, _____?

**4.** He doesn't shop here, _____?

**5.** The store didn't close at 5:00, _____?

**6.** They bought a new TV, _____?

## Answering Tag Questions

| When someone asks: | The expected answer is: |
| --- | --- |
| This is a nice store, **isn't** it? | → Yes, it is. |
| These are really cheap, **aren't** they? | → Yes, they are. |
| This isn't very good, is it? | → No, it isn't. |
| These aren't very well made, are they? | → No, they aren't. |
| These grapes look delicious, **don't** they? | → Yes, they do. |

If you disagree with the person asking a tag question, it's polite to say "Actually" and give a reason why you disagree.

EXAMPLE:   A: This is really pretty, isn't it?
B: Actually, I don't really like the color that much. I prefer bright colors.

**4** Write your opinion about four things or conditions in your classroom. Use a statement with a tag question. Then ask and answer the questions with your partner.

Examples:   *A: It isn't very warm in here, is it?*          *A: Maya's shoes look uncomfortable, don't they?*
                   *B: No, it isn't.*                                              *B: Actually, I think they look fine.*

**1.** _____

**2.** _____

**3.** _____

**4.** _____

# LESSON 6
## Reported Speech pages 70–71

| Reported Speech with *Said* | | |
| --- | --- | --- |
| We use **reported** speech to tell what someone said. | | |
| **Rules** | **Quoted Speech** | **Reported Speech** |
| Simple present changes to simple past. | "The play set **is** nice," Jon said. "I **can't understand** the directions," Jane said. Bob said, "I **will help**." | Jon said (that)* the play set **was** nice. Jane said (that) she **couldn't understand** the directions. Bob said (that) he **would help**. |
| Present continuous changes to past continuous. | "I **am writing** a letter," she said. | She said (that) she **was writing** a letter. |
| *Am/is/are going to* changes to *was /were going to*. | "I**'m going to** get a new credit card," Don said. | Don said (that) he **was going to** get a new credit card. |
| **that* is optional | | |

**1** Change the quoted speech to reported speech. Be sure to change the verbs and pronouns.

1. "The music is great," Susan said.

   <u>Susan said (that) the music was great.</u>

2. "I'm going to buy a new MP3 player," Ricardo said.

   _____

3. "I am studying," Paolo said.

   _____

4. "I can't wait," Ms. Long said.

   _____

5. He said, "I need a new pair of shoes."

   _____

6. "I am having trouble with the homework," Victor said.

   _____

7. Cathy said, "I'm going to do my homework."

   _____

8. "We're going to take a vacation," Mr. Smith said.

   _____

## Reported Speech with *Asked* and *Told*

We use ***told*** + **object** to report what a person said to someone.

| Quoted Speech | Reported Speech |
|---|---|
| Sam said, "I'm going to call the manager." | Sam **told me** (that) he was going to call the manager. |
| | **us** |

We use ***asked*** or ***told*** + **object** + **infinitive** to report requests and commands.

| Quoted Speech | Reported Speech |
|---|---|
| "Can you help me?" Lily asked. | Lily **asked me to help** her. |
| "Open your books," the teacher said. | The teacher **told the students to open** their books. |

**2** **Change the quoted speech to reported speech. Use *asked* or *told*.**

**1.** Mary said to John, "I need some money."

<u>Mary told John that she needed some money.</u>

**2.** The teacher said to Barbara, "Can you please erase the board?"

_____

**3.** Bob said to his father, "I'm going to do my homework."

_____

**4.** The boss said to Mr. Thomas, "Can you finish the work?"

_____

**5.** John said to Nancy, "Wait for me at the coffee shop."

_____

**3** **Write sentences in reported speech. Use *told* if there is a listener. Change the pronouns and the verb forms.**

**1.** Asha: I'm unhappy with my purchase.

<u>Asha said she was unhappy with her purchase.</u>

**2.** Sam: I'll ask for a rain check.

_____

**3.** Ed told me: I'm going to return my purchase.

_____

**4.** Pete: The store can't give me a refund.

_____

**5.** Lucia told Pete: You need to do something to resolve the problem.

_____

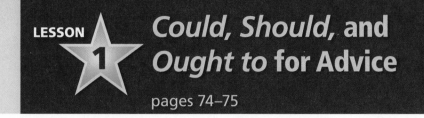

## *Could, Should,* and *Ought to* for Advice

We use **could, should,** and **ought to** to give advice. We use **should** to ask for advice.

| could | A: My car broke down. How am I going to get to work? |
| | B: You **could call** a taxi. |
| **should** | You **should listen** carefully in court. |
| | You **shouldn't daydream** during the testimonies. |
| | **Should** I **come** back tomorrow? |
| **ought to** | You **ought to stop** smoking. |

**1** Complete the email with *should, shouldn't,* or *ought.*

---

To: lruiz@email.com
From: RJones@email.com
Date: June 12, 2012
Re: Your Jury Duty Summons

Hi Lucia,

You asked me what you _____should_____ do about your jury summons. I received a jury summons last
①
year. You really _____ to follow the directions on the summons. You _____
②                                                                                    ③
ignore them. It usually says that you _____ call a phone number every night to see if
④
you _____ go to the courthouse the next day. It also says that you _____ fill
⑤                                                                                        ⑥
out the attached questionnaire and mail it back to the courthouse.

    When I got my summons, I called the number, and the message said that I _____ go to the
⑦
courthouse the next day. I had to go to work that day, so I called my boss. She said that I really _____
⑧
to go to jury duty because it was important. She also said that I _____ worry about missing
⑨
work. She told me I _____ take off as much time as I needed. I think if you have jury duty,
⑩
you _____ to ask your boss for time off from work, too.
⑪
Good luck!
Ron

---

**2** Unscramble the words to make questions.

1. leave / the jurors / immediately / Should / ?

   _____ Should the jurors leave immediately? _____

2. tomorrow / I / come back / the courthouse / to / Should / ?

   _____

3. we / When / call / should / the courthouse / ?

   _____

4. tell / she / should / What / her boss / ?

   _____

5. should / go / for / we / Where / jury duty / ?

   _____

6. What / should / go / time / he / to the courthouse / ?

   _____

**3** Read the situations. Write advice for each person. Use the modals in parentheses.

1. I got a summons for jury duty, but I have to go to work.

   (should) _____ .

2. The judge and the lawyers are interviewing me, but I don't understand their questions.

   (ought to) _____ .

3. I have to be at the courthouse at 9 A.M. every day this week, but I don't have a car.

   (should / shouldn't) _____ .

4. I bought a new cell phone last night, but this morning I found my old one.

   (should) _____ .

**4** Answer the questions. Then ask a partner the questions.

1. What should you wear to a courthouse?

   _____

2. Where should you go to pay a parking ticket?

   _____

## Should Have, Could Have, and *Must Have*

We use *should (not) have* + past participle to give an opinion on or to express regret about something in the past.

EXAMPLE
Matt **should have paid** the fine earlier. (Paying the fine early was advisable, but he didn't.)

We use *could (not) have* + past participle to say that something was possible or impossible in the past.

EXAMPLE:
He **could have gotten** a better lawyer. (It was possible to get a better lawyer, but he didn't.)

We use *must (not) have* + past participle to say that we are almost sure about something in the past.

EXAMPLE:
He **must not have crossed** at the crosswalk. (We are almost sure he did not cross at the crosswalk.)

**1** **Complete the sentences. Use *should have* or *shouldn't have* and the verb in parentheses.**

1. Sara's phone rang while she was in the courtroom. She _____should have turned_____ (turn) it off.

2. Ron got a ticket for speeding. He _____ (exceed) the speed limit.

3. Wei and Ping crossed the street in the middle of the block and almost got hit by a car.
   They _____ (cross) at the crosswalk.

4. Ann is in jail for a crime that she didn't commit. She _____ (get) a better lawyer.

5. Asha was talking on her cell phone, and she had a minor car accident. She _____ (use) her cell phone while she was driving.

**2** **Answer each question with a complete sentence. Use *could have* or *couldn't have*.**

1. Andrea left her computer in her car and someone stole it. What could she have done to avoid losing her computer?

   _____

2. Andy was walking down a dark street at night. Someone hit him on the head and took his wallet. What could he have done to avoid the assault?

   _____

3. Tranh tried to stop his car, but the streets were wet and he crashed into the car in front of him. What could Tranh have done (or not done) in this situation?

   _____

4. Ray was late for a meeting because he was speeding and a police officer stopped him. How could he have avoided this situation?

   _____

**3** **Read the situations and complete the sentences. Use *must have* or *must not have*.**

1. Jan committed a crime, but she only had to pay a fine. She _____*must have*_____ committed an infraction.

2. Ron was imprisoned for just under one year. He _____ committed a misdemeanor.

3. Sam's punishment was 50 hours of community service. He _____ committed a felony.

4. Robert was punished by ten years in prison. He _____ committed a felony.

5. A witness saw Luisa hit the victim on the head. Luisa _____ committed aggravated assault.

6. A police officer stopped Maria while she was driving, but he didn't give her a ticket. She _____ committed a traffic violation.

**4** **Read the news report. Then answer the questions**

> Last night, five teenagers were arrested in Green Park. The youths climbed over a wall and entered a "No Trespassing" area of the park. They spray-painted graffiti on the wall and left piles of soda cans and food wrappers everywhere.
>
> _____

1. Evan and his friends were arrested last night. What must they have done?

_____

_____

2. What should or shouldn't they have done?

_____

_____

# Be Supposed to  pages 80–81

## Be Supposed to

We use **be (not) supposed to** + verb to talk about expectations or what someone should do or shouldn't do. We use **be (not) supposed to** in the simple present or simple past only.

**Expectations:**
We **are supposed to call** the police if we see a suspicious person.
What time **was** the meeting **supposed to start?**

**What someone should/shouldn't do:**
What **are** Neighborhood Watch members **supposed to look out** for?
You're **not supposed to call** 911 in this situation.

**1** **Complete the conversations. Use the correct form of be (not) supposed to.**

1. A: How often ____*are*____ we ____*supposed to*____ have Neighborhood Watch meetings?

   B: We _____ meet once a month.

2. A: What _____ Neighborhood Watch members _____ do?

   B: They _____ look out for strange cars in the neighborhood.

3. A: What _____ I _____ do if I see a strange car in the neighborhood?

   B: You _____ call 911. We _____ talk to suspicious people ourselves; it's too dangerous.

4. A: _____ Neighborhood Watch members _____ arrest suspicious people?

   B: No, they _____; they _____ only _____ call the police.

5. A: What _____ we _____ do when we call 911?

   B: We _____ give our name and address.

6. A: What time _____ I _____ get there?

   B: You're very late. You _____ get here an hour ago.

**2** **Write three sentences about things you are supposed to do and three sentences about things you are not supposed to do in each situation. Use the words in parentheses.**

Example:   *You are supposed to be quiet in a courthouse.*

   **1.** (in a courthouse) _____

   **2.** (not / in a courthouse) _____

   **3.** (on a highway) _____

   **4.** (not / on a highway) _____

   **5.** (at school) _____

   **6.** (not / a school) _____

## *Had Better* and *Had Better Not*

We use ***had better (not)*** + **verb** for warnings. It means something bad will happen if you do or do not do something. We often contract ***had better*** to *'d better*.

EXAMPLES:

If you don't want to get a ticket, you**'d better stop** at the red light.
You**'d better not run** the red light, or you'll get a ticket.

**①** **Read the situations. Write what each person had better or had better not do.**

**1.** Jack is driving fast, and there's a red light at the intersection.

   *He'd better stop at the light . / He'd better not run the red light.*

**2.** Mary drove to the party and drank some alcohol.

   _____

**3.** There's a lot of crime in Binh's neighborhood.

   _____

**4.** Sam hit a car in the parking lot. There were witnesses.

   _____

**5.** Wei got a parking ticket, but he didn't pay it.

   _____

**6.** Sue has a full-time job, and she just got a jury duty summons.

   _____

**7.** When Ali woke up this morning, he felt sick. He's thinking of not going to work today.

   _____

**8.** Amanda saw a strange car driving though her neighborhood today.

   _____

**②** **Answer the questions about you.**

**1.** What is something that you'd better do this week? What will happen if you don't do it?

   _____

   _____

**2.** What is something that you'd better not do this week? What will happen if you do it?

   _____

   _____

**TARGET GRAMMAR: UNIT 6**   **177**

# UNIT 7 CAREER PATHS

## Past Perfect

We use the **past perfect** to talk about an action that happened **before** another action in the past.

EXAMPLES
I **had heard** the news by the time she **called**.

PAST PERFECT                    SIMPLE PAST

| Statements | | | | Negative Statements | | | |
|---|---|---|---|---|---|---|---|
| I<br>You<br>She<br>We<br>They | **had**<br>**hadn't** | **started** the<br>project | when the boss called. | I<br>You<br>She<br>We<br>They | **had not**<br>**hadn't** | **started** the<br>project | when the boss called. |

**1** Complete the sentences. Use the past perfect form of the verb in parentheses.

**1.** I _____ (not / see) Jane in ten years when she called me.

**2.** She _____ (send) her resume to several companies when she got her first interview.

**3.** Jan's supervisor _____ (warn) her several times by the time he fired her.

**4.** My friend was late to the interview because he _____ (forget) to set his alarm clock.

**5.** When Dimitri started college, he _____ (meet / not) his wife.

**6.** By the time Paul finished the project, everyone else _____ (go) home.

**7.** Was Joan reprimanded because she _____ (wear) jeans to work?

**8.** When did your boss notice that no one _____ (put) the tools away?

**2** Complete the sentences. Use the past perfect or the simple past forms of the verbs in parentheses.

**1.** I _____ (call) you four times yesterday, but you weren't home.

**2.** Susan _____ (finish) explaining the plan by the time Tom arrived at the meeting.

**3.** When I was young, I _____ (want) to go to law school.

**4.** We got stuck in traffic on our way to the airport. Our plane _____ (leave) by the time we arrived.

**5.** I _____ (start) working when the electricity went out.

**6.** John _____ (make) a phone call while he was walking to work.

## Past Perfect with *already, just,* and *yet*

We use the adverbs *already, just* and *yet* to say when an action happened.

| | |
|---|---|
| **already** = some time before now | We **had already eaten** when they arrived. |
| **just** = a short time before now | We **had just eaten** when they arrived. |
| **yet** = up to now; in negatives | When they arrived, we **hadn't eaten yet**. |

**3** Look at the timeline of Joe's morning. Then complete each sentence about Joe. Use the past perfect form of the verb in parentheses and *already, just,* or *yet*.

| 7:00 | 7:30 | 8:00 | 8:30 | 9:00 | 9:30 | 10:00 | 11:00 |
|---|---|---|---|---|---|---|---|
| Joe eats breakfast. | Joe's brother calls. | Joe leaves for work. | A package arrives at Joe's house. | Joe arrives at work. | Joe has a discussion with his boss. | The team meeting begins. | Joe calls his client. |

**1.** (arrive) By 8:45, Joe _____ hadn't arrived _____ at work _____ yet _____.

**2.** (eat) By 7:30, Joe _____ breakfast.

**3.** (leave) By 8:15, Joe _____ for work.

**4.** (arrive) Joe _____ at work by 9:10.

**5.** (have) At 9:15, Joe _____ a discussion with his boss _____.

**6.** (have) Joe _____ a discussion with his boss by 10:00.

**7.** (begin) At 10:00, the team meeting _____ .

**8.** (call) By 10:45, Joe _____ his client _____.

**4** Complete each sentence with information about you. Use a verb in the past perfect and *already, just,* or *yet.*

**1.** When I got to work, _____.

**2.** When I woke up this morning, _____.

**3.** By the time I got to class, _____.

**4.** When I got home last night, _____.

## Phrasal Verbs

**Phrasal verbs** are two- or three-word verbs that include a verb and a particle (*in, on, up, for, to, out at, back, through*, etc.). The particle changes the meaning of the verb.

EXAMPLES:
Could you please **drop off** Abby at school today?
Please **go over** this form tonight.

Here is a list of common phrasal verbs.

| | | |
|---|---|---|
| clean up | go away | play around |
| come back | go over | put away |
| come in | hand in | run into |
| drop in | hang up | show up |
| drop off | look into | start over |
| fill out | look up | think over |
| find out | pay off | work out |
| follow through | pick up | write up |

**1** **Complete each phrasal verb with the correct particle.**

**1.** I need to drop _____off_____ the kids at day care on my way to work.

**2.** Did you hand _____ your project?

**3.** Guess who I ran _____ the other day?

**4.** Did he show _____ for work today?

**5.** Don't hang _____ the phone!

**6.** I made a mistake on my report. I need to start _____ .

**7.** Please put _____ the projector when you're finished.

**8.** I really hope this idea works _____ .

**2** **Match each phrasal verb to its definition.**

| | | |
|---|---|---|
| __e__ **1.** go away | | **a.** complete (a form) |
| _____ **2.** follow through | | **b.** consider |
| _____ **3.** come back | | **c.** discover |
| _____ **4.** start over | | **d.** be worth the effort |
| _____ **5.** look into | | **e.** leave |
| _____ **6.** fill out | | **f.** begin again |
| _____ **7.** find out | | **g.** return |
| _____ **8.** pay off | | **h.** finish (a project or task) |
| _____ **9.** think over | | **i.** research |

## Separable and Inseparable Phrasal Verbs

**Inseparable phrasal verbs**
Some phrasal verbs cannot be separated.

EXAMPLES:
He **showed** up late.      He **looked into** the problem.

**Separable phrasal verbs**
Some phrasal verbs can be separated by an object. If the object is a pronoun, it must come between the verb and the particle.

EXAMPLES:
Clean up **the room**.      Clean **the room** up.      Clean **it** up.
　　　　　[object]　　　　　　　　　　[object]　　　　　　　　　[object]

| Separable Phrasal Verbs | | | | Inseparable Phrasal Verbs | | | |
|---|---|---|---|---|---|---|---|
| clean up | hang up | pick up | start over | come back | find out | go over | run into |
| drop off | look up | put away | think over | come in | follow through | look into | show up |
| fill out | pay off | put off | work out | drop in | go away | play around | |
| hand in | | send out | | | | | |

---

**3** Unscramble the sentences. Write two sentences where possible.

**1.** Paula / her resume / out / sent / last week.

　　　　*Paula sent her resume out last week. / Paula sent out her resume last week.*

**2.** find / you / out / did / the job / about

_____?

**3.** make sure / hand / your project / on time / in / you

_____.

**4.** them / off /am dropping / I / at / the station

_____.

**5.** problem / I'll / for you / look / that / into

_____.

---

**4** Underline the separable phrasal verbs. Draw two lines under the inseparable verbs. Circle the objects.

**1.** You shouldn't put off the trip any longer.

**2.** Please look into the problem now.

**3.** When I was in New York, I looked my old friends up.

**4.** Please fill the application out in ink.

**5.** We will go over your report tomorrow.

**6.** You should think over the offer before you accept it.

**7.** Will you fill out this form for me?

| **Past Perfect Continuous** | | |
|---|---|---|
| We use the **past perfect continuous** to talk about an action that was already in progress before another action in the past or before a specific time in the past. | | |
| **Statements** | | |
| I<br>You<br>He<br>She<br>They | **had been** | **talking** on the phone for an hour when the visitors arrived. |
| | | **working** there for 10 years by 2009. |

**1** Write sentences with the cues. Use the past perfect continuous in the first clause.

1. **action in progress:** we / live in Houston for ten years

   **specific time or event:** we / buy a house

   _____We had been living in Houston for ten years when we bought a house._____

2. **action in progress:** I / work on my report for an hour

   **specific time or event:** my boss / tell me to send it to him

   _____

   _____

3. **action in progress:** he / drive a truck for a long time

   **specific time or event:** he / lose his license

   _____

   _____

4. **action in progress:** he / work for the company for six years

   **specific time or event:** by 2009

   _____

   _____

5. **action in progress:** she / look for a job for months

   **specific time or event:** she / find a position at a bank

   _____

   _____

**2** Complete the sentences. Use the the past perfect continuous or the simple past form of the verb in parentheses.

I had an interesting day yesterday. I am a manager at a clothing store. I _____had been reviewing_____ (review)
(1)
the daily receipts last night when I _____ (notice) a problem. The amount of money in the drawer
(2)
didn't match the total on the receipts. According to the receipts, we had taken $522.83 in cash, but I counted
$722.83 in the drawer.

I couldn't understand what had happened. But then I remembered something. I _____ (work)
(3)
in the store all day when an unusual man _____ (come) in. He was out of breath, and
(4)
he looked at me a lot. I went into the stockroom to find a blouse for a customer. When I came back onto the
sales floor, the man was gone. I sold the blouse to my customer, and I saw two one hundred dollar bills under
the register. I put the bills into the register and forgot about them. A few minutes later, two police officers
came into the store. They told me that they _____ (chase) a thief when he
(5)
_____ (disappear) near my store.
(6)
When I remembered all of this, I called the police station. I asked them how much money the thief stole,
and they told me—$200! I realized that the thief _____ (wait) for me to leave the
(7)
sales floor when I _____ (see) him looking at me. He wanted to hide the money in
(8)
my store. That night, the police waited outside the store for the thief to come back for it. They
_____ (hide) outside the store for four hours when the thief finally
(9)
_____(arrive) . When he tried to break into the store, the police arrested him!
(10)

**3** Write five sentences using the past perfect continuous. Give information about yourself and your work. Use these verbs or use your own ideas.

Example:  *I had been working in customer service for a year when my boss offered me a promotion.*

| | | |
|---|---|---|
| ask | handle | take a break |
| assist | oversee | talk |
| call | prepare | think |
| discuss | process | train |
| drive | read | work |
| eat | study | write |

## Present Real Conditionals

Real conditional sentences tell what happens when or if something else happens. They show cause and result. We use **present real conditional** sentences to talk about facts and habits.

| If/When Clause<br>(*If* or *When* + simple present) | Result Clause<br>(simple present) |
|---|---|
| **When** he **needs** cash, | he **goes** to the ATM. |
| **If** you **pay** your bill in full, | you **don't pay** any interest. |

When the *if/when* clause comes second, we don't use a comma.
- He **goes** to the ATM **when** he **needs** cash.

**1** Read the article about credit card safety. Underline the *if* or *when* clauses and circle the result clauses.

You open your credit card bill and notice several charges for things you didn't buy. Someone else is using your name and your credit card number to buy things. You are a victim of credit card fraud.

Credit card fraud is a major problem. It costs cardholders and businesses hundreds of millions of dollars each year. If someone steals your credit card, they can use it to make purchases. Someone may also use your card if they find a receipt or statement with your credit card account number and expiration date.

Fortunately, there are some simple things you can do to protect yourself from credit card fraud. You should use secure websites. When you use secure websites, you are usually safe from fraud. You should also immediately report any mistakes on your bill. When you report a charge on your bill that you didn't make, your credit card company credits your account for the amount of the charge. Finally, immediately report a lost or stolen credit card. You avoid a lot of hassle if you report the loss or theft before someone uses your card. Also, if you report a theft right away, your credit card company has a better chance of catching a thief when he or she tries to use your card.

**2** Combine each pair of sentences to make a real conditional sentence. Use the word in parentheses and correct punctuation.

**1.** I have to pay a fee. I use my credit card. (when)

_____*I have to pay a fee when I use my credit card.*_____

**2.** We eat in restaurants. We always pay with cash. (when)

_____

**3.** You open a savings account at Statewide Bank. You get free checking. (if)

_____

**4.** I cut back my entertainment budget. My utility bills are high. (if)

_____

**5.** He works overtime.  He saves the extra money he makes. (when)

_____

**6.** I spend too much money on clothes. I don't have enough money for rent. (when)

_____

**7.** She works more hours. Her paycheck is bigger. (if)

_____

**8.** He has credit problems. He talks to a credit counselor. (when)

_____

**3** Complete each sentence with a result clause.

**1.** _____ if you don't pay your credit card bill on time.

**2.** When I get my paycheck, _____.

**3.** If you use a credit card for daily purchases,_____.

**4.** _____ when I shop for groceries.

**5.** When there's a big sale, _____.

**4** Complete each sentence with an *if* or *when* clause.

**1.** Employees get raises _____.

**2.** _____, the store gives you a discount.

**3.** I like to go shopping _____.

**4.** You lose a lot of time _____.

# Future Real Conditionals pages 106–107

| Future Real Conditionals | | | |
|---|---|---|---|
| We also use real conditional sentences to talk about something that will probably happen in the future as the result of an action. | | | |

| **If** Clause (**If** + simple present) | **Result Clause** (**am going to** or **will** + verb) | | |
|---|---|---|---|
| If housing prices **continue** to go down, | I | am going to <br> will | **buy** a house. |

When the *if* clause comes second, we don't use a comma.

| **Result Clause** | | | **If** Clause |
|---|---|---|---|
| She | is going to <br> will | **deposit** $100 each month | if she **opens** a savings account. |

**1** Unscramble each sentence. Notice the commas.

**1.** I'm / if I get paid / going to go / tomorrow, / out to dinner / .

<u>      If I get paid tomorrow, I'm going to go out to dinner.     </u>

**2.** with my taxes / I'll / if / I need help / call you / .

_____

**3.** to a different bank / I'm / doesn't stop charging me / going to go / if my bank / a maintenance fee / .

_____

**4.** a savings account, / every month / she'll put $200 in it / if she opens /.

_____

**5.** if his bank / he's / an account / at my bank / closes / going to open /.

_____

**6.** Jack will loan / if you / you some / need money, /.

_____

**7.** she'll / go to / go with you / the bank / if you / this afternoon, /.

_____

**8.** for grocery shopping, / if / go to the ATM / we / I'll / need money / .

_____

**2** Circle the errors in the sentences below. Rewrite each incorrect sentence. Some sentences don't have any errors.

1. If I get a bonus this month, I put it in my savings account.

    *If I get a bonus this month, I'll put it in my savings account.*

2. Jack will stop by this afternoon, if he needs to talk to you.

    _____

3. If we go to the movies twice this week, we go over our entertainment budget.

    _____

4. If we save enough money, we're going to take a family vacation this summer.

    _____

5. I get a second job if I need to make more money.

    _____

6. We're going to go over our budget, if we buy this TV.

    _____

7. If I decide to buy a car, I going to take out a loan.

    _____

8. If Mia will go to the bank today, she'll deposit her paycheck.

    _____

**3** Write real conditional sentences for a future possibility. Use the words in parentheses.

1. (make extra money this month)

    _____

2. (spend too much on food this month)

    _____

3. (save more than $500 by the end of this year)

    _____

4. (need more money next month)

    _____

5. (forget to pay your bills this month)

    _____

## Present Unreal Conditionals

We use **present unreal conditionals** to talk about an unreal situation with an imaginary result.

| *If* Clause (*If* + past simple) | Result Clause (*would* + verb) |
|---|---|
| If I **had** a lot of money,<br>If I **didn't have** a college degree, | I **would buy** a new house.<br>I **would go** back to school. |

In these sentences, the information in the *if* clause is NOT true.
**If I had** a lot of money = I **don't have** a lot of money.
**If I didn't have** a college degree = I **have** a college degree.

When the *if* clause comes second, we don't use a comma.
She**'d take** a trip if she **had** the time.

In unreal conditionals, if the verb is *be*, we use **were** for all subjects.

EXAMPLES
If I **were** 20 years younger, I **would try out** for professional soccer.
If Tony **were** here, we **would have** a great time.
I **would grow** my own vegetables if my yard **were** larger.

---

**1** Complete each present unreal conditional sentence. Use the correct form of the verb in parentheses.

**1.** If I (need) _____*needed*_____ a new checking account, I (open) _____*would open*_____ one at State Savings Bank.

**2.** We (use / not) _____ a credit card if we (have / not) _____ enough money to pay the bill.

**3.** Emily (buy) _____ a car if she (have) _____ enough money.

**4.** If I (be) _____ more creative, I (start) _____ my own business.

**5.** If they (buy) _____ a new house, they (choose / not) _____ one in the city.

**6.** Mark (be / not) _____ here if he (have / not) _____ the time.

**7.** If I (close) _____ my checking account, the bank (cancel) _____ my debit card.

**8.** If I (use / not) _____ coupons, my grocery bill (be) _____ much higher.

**2** Rewrite each sentence to make a present unreal conditional sentence.

**1.** I don't have a good credit rating, so I don't have a credit card.

_____If I had a good credit rating, I would have a credit card._____

**2.** We don't own a house, so we don't pay a mortgage.

_____

**3.** My rent is expensive, so I work two jobs.

_____

**4.** I don't have debt, so I don't have to talk to a credit counselor.

_____

**5.** I have a lot of debt, so I don't use credit cards.

_____

**6.** I have a good credit rating, so I get a low interest rate.

_____

**7.** I don't have money in my wallet, so I have to go to the ATM.

_____

**8.** I have $500, so I am able to open a savings account.

_____

**3** Write answers to the questions. Use the present unreal conditional. Then ask and answer the questions with a partner.

**1.** What would you do if you won the lottery?

_____

**2.** What would you do if you found $5,000 in a bag on the street?

_____

**3.** Where would you live if you were able to live anywhere in the world?

_____

**4.** If you won a vacation, where would you go?

_____

**5.** If you had the chance to change something in your community, what would you change?

_____

## Wish

| We use *wish* to talk about things that are not true now, but that we want to be true. | |
| --- | --- |
| **Notes** | **Examples** |
| We use the simple present form of **wish** and the simple past form of a verb. | I **wish** we **had** a better photocopier.<br>He **wishes** (that)* he **didn't have to** work today. |
| For the verb **be**, we use **were** for all subjects. | She **wishes** she **weren't** sick today.<br>**They** wish the kitchen **were** cooler. |
| We use **would** instead of **will**. | We **wish** Mark **would fix** the ventilation. |
| We use **could** instead of **can**. | I **wish** we **could** get new software. |

*\*that* is optional.

**1** Complete each sentence. Use the correct forms of *wish* and the verb in parentheses.

**1.** I _____ wish _____ I _____ had _____ (have) a better job.

**2.** I _____ I _____ (be) a sales manager.

**3.** I _____ I _____ (have to / not) work late tonight.

**4.** James _____ he _____ (can use) a computer.

**5.** Ellen _____ Mary _____ (will try) to be more punctual.

**6.** I _____ Susan _____ (be) here.

**7.** They _____ they _____ (be / not) in debt.

**8.** We _____ we _____ (can go) to the job fair.

**2** These sentences describe things that the speaker wants to change. Write sentences with *wish* to describe what the speaker wants.

**1.** I am not a supervisor. _____ I wish I were a supervisor. _____

**2.** I don't make a good salary. _____

**3.** I don't have a college degree. _____

**4.** I'm busy all the time. _____

**5.** I have to work two jobs. _____

## Be Going to and Will

| | Notes | Examples |
|---|---|---|
| **be going to** | We use **be going to** talk about future plans. | Jack is **going to talk** to Mr. Wong about his schedule this morning.<br><br>You **are going to work** for Susan tomorrow. |
| **will** | We use **will** to offer to help someone. | A: This box is very heavy!<br>B: **I'll carry** it for you. |
| | We use **will** to talk about future plans that are decided at the moment of speaking. | I feel really sick. I think I**'ll stay** home today. |

**❶ Read the sentences. For plans, write *P*. For offers to help, write *O*.**

___O___ **1.** I'll let you know if I hear about an opening for supervisor.

_____ **2.** Marco and Janice are going to help me with my project.

_____ **3.** I can't work late tonight. I'm going to go to a movie with a friend.

_____ **4.** I'll give you a ride to work.

_____ **5.** Carmen and I are going to meet Lisa at the office.

_____ **6.** I'll work for you on Saturday.

_____ **7.** We're going to be closed on Monday.

_____ **8.** I feel sick. I think I'll go see a doctor.

**❷ Complete the sentences with *will* or the correct form of *be going to*. Use contractions.**

**1.** A: Oh no! I forgot to call Matt about the meeting!

B: Oh, I _____'ll_____ call him. I have to make some calls, anyway.

**2.** A: Jackie _____ go into the office on Saturday. She has a lot of work to catch up on.

B: Does she need a ride? I _____ drive her there.

**3.** A: Did you hear about the new management position that's available? Luke and I _____ talk to Patty about it. How about you?

B: I _____ talk to her about it, too.

## Be Going to and Will—Yes/No Questions

We use *be going to* to ask about future plans.

| Are | you | | **ask** for a promotion? |
|-----|-----|----------|---------------------------|
| Is | he | **going to** | **switch** shifts with you on Tuesday? |
| Are | we | | **close** early on Sunday? |

We use *will* to ask someone for help.

| Questions | | | Answers |
|-----------|-----|---------------------------------|---------|
| **Will** | you | **switch** shifts with me on Saturday? | Sure. I'd be happy to. |
| **Will** | you | **help** me with this project? | Sorry. I don't have time now. |

**❸** Complete each sentence. Use *will* or the correct form of *be going to* and the verb in parentheses.

**1.** A: _____ Is _____ Alex _____ going to train _____ (train) the new employees on Monday?

B: Yes. He always trains the new employees.

**2.** _____ you _____ (ask) Jan to call me? I forgot to ask her.

B: Sure, no problem.

**3.** A: _____ you _____ (have) your interview next week?

B: Yes, and I'm very nervous about it.

**4.** A: _____ Alan _____ (be) in the office later today?

B: Yes, he should be here by noon.

**5.** A: _____ you _____ (explain) this employee evaluation to me? I don't understand some parts of it.

B: Sure. Which parts do you have trouble understanding?

**6.** A: _____ you _____ (talk) to Bill about being late? I would talk to him, but I have an appointment this morning.

B: Yes. I have an appointment to talk to him at 2:30 about some other issues.

**7.** A: _____ Lee _____ (work) for Janice tomorrow?

B: I think so. I heard Janice asking him about switching shifts with her.

**8.** A: _____ you _____ (stay) at work late tonight?

B: Yes. I already told my husband to expect me home late.

## Future Continuous

We use the **future continuous** to talk about actions that will be in progress at a specific time in the future.

| I | | working | at 9:00 tonight. | I | am | | | |
|---|---|---|---|---|---|---|---|---|
| You | | meeting | tomorrow. | He | is | going to be | working | at 9:00 tonight. |
| He She | **will be** **won't be** | | | She | | | | |
| We | | having lunch | when you arrive. | We | are | | | |
| They | | | | You They | | | | |

**1** Use the cues to complete sentences with the future continuous. Use *will* or *be going to*.

**1.** (check the safety gear / after lunch)

Sam _____ will be checking the safety gear after lunch. _____

**2.** (repair the ventilation system / Friday morning)

Workers _____

**3.** (switch shifts with Mia / for the rest of the month)

Tammy _____

**4.** (work the late shift / every night next month)

Jack _____

**5.** (talk to her supervisor about a promotion / this afternoon)

Anna _____

**6.** (discuss a raise / tomorrow morning)

Sara and I _____

**2** Complete the sentences about yourself.

**Example:** *Between 5:00 and 6:00 A.M. tomorrow,* _____ I will be sleeping. _____.

**1.** Between 5:00 and 6:00 A.M. tomorrow, I _____.

**2.** Between 7:30 and 8:00 A.M. tomorrow, I _____.

**3.** Between 12:30 and 1:30 P.M. tomorrow, I _____.

**4.** Between 7:00 and 8:00 P.M. tomorrow, I _____.

**5.** At 3:00 on Sunday afternoon, I _____.

# Expressing Result with *so . . . that* and *such . . . that* pages 122–123

| *so . . . that* and *such . . . that* |
| --- |
| We use *so* + **adjective or adverb** + *that* to show a result. |
| EXAMPLES: |
| Paula is **so creative that** <u>she comes up with new ideas every day</u>. <br>                                   RESULT |
| Paula thinks **so creatively** <u>that everyone looks to her for new ideas</u>. <br>                                   RESULT |
| We use *such* + **a/an** + *adjective* + *noun* + *that* to show a result. |
| EXAMPLES: |
| John is **such a productive employee** <u>that he does three times as much work as everyone else</u>. <br>                                   RESULT |

**❶ Complete each sentence with so or *such*.**

1. It was _____ such _____ a good job offer that he decided to move to Chicago.

2. The receptionist was _____ impolite when I called that I didn't apply for the job.

3. Doug's tie was _____ a bright color that it was distracting in the interview.

4. Marka is _____ satisfied with the company's family-friendly policies that she has stayed there for 14 years.

5. My job search became _____ confusing that I limited my search to one neighborhood.

6. Chris's vacation to Costa Rica was _____ tiring that he took a few more days off work.

7. We were all _____ surprised about Ed's retirement that we barely got any work done.

8. It was _____ a boring meeting that two people fell asleep.

**❷ Write sentences about people you know using *so* and *such*.**

1. _____

   _____

2. _____

   _____

3. _____

   _____

4. _____

   _____

## Adjective Clauses—*Who* or *That* as Subject

- An adjective clause gives more information about a noun in the main clause.
- An adjective clause starts with a relative pronoun. We use the relative pronoun *who* or *that* for people and *that* for things and people.
- *Who* and *that* are sometimes the subject of an adjective clause.

EXAMPLES:

The Oban Festival is an event **that** is celebrated in Japan.
                               ADJECTIVE CLAUSE

People honor their family members **who** have died.
                                  ADJECTIVE CLAUSE

An adjective clause can come after the subject of the main clause.

EXAMPLES:

Many people **who** live in Thailand celebrate Loy Krathong.
            ADJECTIVE CLAUSE

They float boats **that** are shaped like lotus flowers down rivers.
                 ADJECTIVE CLAUSE

**1** Match each main clause with an adjective clause.

___d___ **1.** Cinco de Mayo is a holiday _____.

_____ **2.** The people _____ are celebrating St. Patrick's day.

_____ **3.** The fifteenth day of the eighth lunar month is the day _____.

_____ **4.** A holiday _____ is Carnival.

_____ **5.** At a Carnival parade, you might see people _____.

_____ **6.** The woman _____ is my friend Anita.

_____ **7.** Loy Krathong is a festival _____.

_____ **8.** The Mid-Autumn festival is a holiday _____.

a. that is very popular in Brazil

b. who are wearing green

c. that is celebrated in Thailand

d̶. that celebrates Mexico's victory over the French

e. that the moon looks largest

f. who is wearing the blue costume

g. who are dressed up in colorful costumes

h. that takes place in the eighth lunar month

**2** Combine each pair of sentences to make a sentence with an adjective clause.

**1.** I host a lot of parties. The parties involve cooking and friends.

_____ *I host a lot of parties that involve cooking and friends.* _____

**2.** I like to cook food. The food is unusual.

_____

**3.** I use a lot of recipes. The recipes are from my grandmother's cookbook.

_____

**4.** My grandmother was a cook. The cook liked to experiment with different flavors.

_____

**5.** The people usually don't know each other. The people come to my parties.

_____

**6.** I know a lot of married couples. The couples met at one of my parties.

_____

**7.** One of the couples has three children. The couple met at my house.

_____

**8.** My sister is dating a man. The man came to one of my dinner parties.

_____

**3** Complete the adjective clauses with your own ideas.

Example: I have a friend who __lives in New York.__ _____

**1.** I have a friend who _____

**2.** I would like to own a car that _____

**3.** I live in a house / apartment that _____

**4.** I like the actor who _____

**5.** I lived in a city that _____

**6.** My favorite holiday is a holiday that _____

**7.** On my favorite holiday, we eat food that _____

**8.** Your own idea: _____

---

## Adjective Clauses—*Who* or *That* as Object

The relative pronouns **who** or **that** are sometimes the object of an adjective clause. We use **who** or **that** for people and **that** for things.

EXAMPLES:

You can talk about a book **that** <u>you've enjoyed recently</u>.

ADJECTIVE CLAUSE

It's not appropriate to bring someone **who** <u>your host is not expecting</u>.

ADJECTIVE CLAUSE

---

We can omit **that** and **who** when they are the object of the adjective clause.

EXAMPLES:

You can talk about a book ~~that~~ <u>you've enjoyed recently</u>.

It's not appropriate to bring someone ~~who~~ <u>your host is not expecting</u>.

---

An adjective clause can come after the subject of the main clause.

EXAMPLES:

The party <u>that you hosted</u> was fantastic.

The people <u>I met there</u> were interesting.

---

**1** Circle the pronoun at the beginning of each adjective clause. Write *S* for subject or *O* for object. Then rewrite the six sentences that have an object pronoun in the adjective clause. Omit the pronoun from your sentence.

_____O_____ **1.** On Friday night, I went to a dinner party (that) my friend Keri invited me to.

_____ **2.** I brought her some flowers that grew in my garden.

_____ **3.** I knew only two of the guests who were there.

_____ **4.** I'm usually nervous about talking to people that I don't know.

_____ **5.** However, everyone that I talked to at Keri's party was so friendly.

_____ **6.** The food that Keri served was delicious.

_____ **7.** I particularly enjoyed the chocolate cake that she baked herself.

_____ **8.** I think Keri's dinner was the best party that I've ever been to!

**1.** _____*On Friday night, I went to a dinner party my friend Keri invited me to.*_____

**2.** _____

**3.** _____

**4.** _____

**5.** _____

**6.** _____

**2** Combine each pair of sentences to make a sentence using an adjective clause with an object pronoun.

**1.** A friend invited me to a dinner party. I work with the friend.

_____A friend who I work with invited me to a dinner party._____

**2.** I brought her some flowers. She likes the flowers.

_____

**3.** I brought a friend to dinner with me. I've known the friend for a long time.

_____

**4.** A lot of people were at the party. I work with the people.

_____

**5.** There were also a lot of people at the party. I didn't know the people.

_____

**6.** I got to know a man. My friend works with the man.

_____

**7.** I really enjoyed the food. The host prepared.

_____

**8.** The dish was a fruit salad. I liked the dish the best.

_____

**3** Complete the adjective clauses with your own ideas.

**Example:** *I live in a city that I have always loved.*

**1.** I live in a city that I _____.
**2.** I saw a movie that you _____.
**3.** I have a friend who I _____.
**4.** I saw a movie that I _____.
**5.** I once visited a city that I _____.
**6.** I read a book that I _____.
**7.** I once had a job that I _____.
**8.** I live next door to a person who I _____.

**LESSON 4**

# Indefinite Pronouns: *You, One, We,* and *Some*  pages 136–137

| Indefinite Pronouns: *You, One, We,* and *Some* |
| --- |
| We use *you, one, we,* and *some* to talk about people in general. |
| EXAMPLES:<br>When **you** make assumptions about people, **you** may be guilty of stereotyping.<br>**One** should always try to avoid stereotyping others.<br>**We** stereotype because **we** like to organize people into categories.<br>Some people think stereotypes are harmless, but **some** think they are dangerous.<br><br>Note: *One* is very formal. We usually say *you*. |

**1** Complete each sentence. Use *you, one, we* or *some* and the correct form of the verb in parentheses.

1. _____We try_____ (try) to be careful, but it's easy to make unconscious assumptions about people.

2. _____ (like / not) it when other people make assumptions about us.

3. Most people are bothered by stereotyping, but _____ (be / not) bothered by it at all.

4. I think that _____ (should be) careful not to stereotype in any situation.

5. _____ (can know / not) if the person _____ (be) talking to will be offended.

6. When _____ (make) an effort to be conscious of what _____ (say) about people, _____ (be) more successful at avoiding stereotyping.

7. When _____ (stereotype), _____ (consider / not) the individual person.

8. Sometimes, _____ (assume) someone is not intelligent before _____ (get) to know them.

9. It's important to pay attention to the assumptions that _____ (make) about people.

**2** Read the sentences and look at the underlined pronouns. Write *I* next to the sentences with indefinite pronouns. Write *D* next to the sentences with definite pronouns.

_____ **1.** <u>We</u>'re going to a movie tomorrow night.

_____ **2.** <u>You</u> shouldn't assume Jack isn't intelligent.

_____ **3.** <u>You</u> should be nice to everyone, even people that you don't know.

_____ **4.** Some people enjoy talking to strangers, but <u>some</u> don't.

_____ **5.** <u>One</u> is enough for me. I can't eat two pieces of cake!

_____ **6.** When <u>we</u> are kind to other people, they are usually kind to us.

## Future Passive

We use the **future passive** when we don't know who will do the action or when we don't want to emphasize the person who will do the action.

| Active | | Passive |
|---|---|---|
| A school official will interview you tomorrow. | | You **will be interviewed** by a school official tomorrow. |
| Someone will ask the students to fill out a form. | | The students **will be asked** to fill out a form. |

**1** **Read each sentence. Write A for active or P for passive. Then rewrite the passive sentences to make active sentences.**

___A___ **1.** I'll start school in September.

_____

_____ **2.** Class schedules will be provided by your advisors.

_____

_____ **3.** The entrance exams will be graded by school administrators.

_____

_____ **4.** I'll help you study for your test tonight.

_____

_____ **5.** Students will be welcomed by the principal.

_____

**2** **Change each active sentence to make it passive. When the subject of the active sentence is *someone*, do not include *by* + noun.**

**1.** A school official will take the students to the auditorium.

   _Students will be taken to the auditorium by a school official._____

**2.** Applicants will submit college applications before May 15.

_____

**3.** Someone will require students to go to school for at least ten years.

_____

**4.** Exam results will determine a student's future education.

_____

**5.** Someone will grade the examinations before June 14.

_____

**6.** The Ministry of Education will make the admissions decisions.

_____

# ALL-STAR STUDENT BOOK 4 AUDIO SCRIPT

Note: This audio script offers support for many of the activities in the Student Book. When the words on the Student Book page are identical to those on the audio program, the script is not provided here.

## UNIT ONE

### Lesson 2, Activity 5: Listen and Identify (page 6)
*Listen to the conversations. For each conversation, check* **Good** *if the person is good at the skill or* **Not very good** *if the person is not good at it.*

1.
Ann: I need to talk to you about something, Mike.
Mike: Sure, what is it?
Ann: Well, I'm not happy about our conversation yesterday.
Mike: *What* about our conversation?
Ann: I said I'm not happy about it.
Mike: Oh, why?
Ann: Well, you weren't paying attention to what I was saying.
Mike: I'm sorry, what did you say, Ann?

2.
May: Excuse me, could you take a picture of us?
Doug: Sure.
May: Thanks. Okay, here, my camera's really simple to use. You just first um, have to, let's see, and then, right. You push the um, that thing. Then you have to wait before you push it.
Doug: Um, I'm sorry, what? I'm totally confused.

3.
Alan: We have three hours to set up for the party. If we all work together, we can get it done.
Sue: Well, the living room is a mess.
Bob: That's my fault. My friends and I were up late watching football. I'll clean up.
Alan: Sue, you're a really good cook, why don't you and I start making the food?
Sue: Sounds good.
Jan: I can go to the party store to get the supplies.

4.
José: I just got another email from Tom. I don't understand it at all.
Brian: What do you mean?
José: Well, first of all, it's so long. By the time I got to the end, I'd forgotten what the point was.
Brian: Yeah. He can be kind of wordy.
José: And confusing.

### Lesson 3, Activity 2: Listen for General Information (page 8)
*Listen to six telephone calls. Number them in order from first (1) to last (6).*

1.
A: You have reached the Smith residence. Please leave a message.
B: Hi, Pat. This is Leila calling. I just wanted to ask if you could give me a ride to the meeting tomorrow. My car isn't working again! Call when you can. 805-555-8724. Thanks. Bye.

2.
A: Hello?
B: Hi honey, it's me.
A: Hi, mom. What's up?
B: Is your dad there?
A: Not yet, why?
B: Well, I'm running a little late so I'm not going to be home for dinner.
A: Okay. I'm going over to Lisa's right now, but I'll leave dad a note.
B: Thanks, honey.
A: Sure, mom. Bye.
B: Bye.

3.
A: The Paper Shop.
B: Hi. Can I speak to Mr. Takase, please?
A: I'm sorry, but Mr. Takase just left the office. Can I take a message?
B: Well, this is John Lee with Safe Software. I'm returning Mr. Takase's call.
A: I see. Do you want him to call you back?
B: Well, I'm going to be in and out today. Do you know when he'll be back in the office?
A: He should be here between 2:00 and 5:00 today.
B: Okay, I'll try to call him back this afternoon, then.
A: Okay. I'll tell him you called.
B: Thank you.
A: You're welcome. Good-bye.
B: Good-bye.

4.
A: Hello.
B: Hi. Could I speak to Jan, please?
A: I'm sorry, but she's not at home right now.
B: Do you know when she'll be back?
A: No, I'm not sure.
B: Well, could you tell her that Maria called? I just wanted to apologize for missing the meeting today.
A: Okay. Do you want her to call you back?
B: No, that's not necessary. Tell her I'll see her next week.
A: Okay. Will do.
B: Thanks.
A: You're welcome. Bye.
B: Bye.

5.
A: Metro Supply. This is Joe speaking.
B: Could I speak with Tom Field, please?
A: I'm sorry, but he's in a meeting now. Can I take a message?
B: Sure. Could you tell him that Betty Grand called to invite him to a lunch meeting next Wednesday at noon?
A: Could you spell your last name, please?
B: Yes, that's G-r-a-n-d.

A: And you want to invite him to a lunch meeting next Tuesday at noon?

B: Um, that was *Wednesday* not Tuesday.

A: Yes, of course. *Next Wednesday* at noon. Does Mr. Field have your phone number?

B: Well, I think so. But let me give it to you anyway. It's 555-3345.

A: Ah, sorry. Could you repeat that?

B: Sure. 555-3345.

A: Thanks. I'll give him your message, Ms. Grand.

B: Thank you. Bye-bye.

A: Bye now.

6.

A: Southwest Roofing. This is Ginger speaking.

B: Hello. My name is Sam Sellers, and I'm calling about the sales job advertised in the newspaper.

A: Yes, you need to speak to Ms. Parker. Let me see if she's in her office. Can you hold for a second?

B: Sure.

A: I'm sorry, but she isn't in her office. Can I have her call you back?

B: Sure, when it's convenient for her.

A: Your name again, please?

B: Sam Sellers. S-e-l-l-e-r-s.

A: Thanks. And you're calling about the sales job?

B: Yes, that's right.

A: And your phone number?

B: It's 555-6688.

## Lesson 3, Activity 3: Listen for Specific Information (page 8)

*Read the telephone messages on page 9. Listen to the six telephone calls again. Add the missing information to the messages.*

## Lesson 4, Activity 4: Apply (page 11)

*Listen to the students discuss their goals and their plans for learning new skills. Complete the chart.*

1. Jan: Hi, I'm Jan Thompson. I'm a mom of three. I'm ready to go back to work. I'd like to be a real estate agent again. I have my license, but I haven't worked in more than three years. So I need to take some classes. I'd like to have more proficient Internet skills. It's important for realtors to have their own website these days. I'd also like to improve my oral communication skills. I've been talking mostly to children for a long time now! My plan is to take a basic computer skills course, a website design course and a public speaking course.

2. Maria: I'm Maria Lopez. I've worked at a day care for many years, but I want to be a teacher. My boss is flexible. He's letting me change my schedule so I can take classes in a certificate program at the community college. They offer a certificate in Child Development.
I also need to take some English classes. I can read really well in English, but I need to improve my writing skills.

3. Julio: I'm Julio Rodriguez. I just got out of the military. I'm ready to start my next career. I want to own my own business. My father always said that you have to take responsibility for your achieving your goals. So, I have a plan. First, I need to improve my communication skills, my math skills, and my writing skills. I know how important it is to be able to write clearly in any business. I'm going to take Writing II and Math III at the community college this fall. After that, I'm going to do a certificate program in business.

4. Frank: I'm Frank Romano. I work in a restaurant as a dishwasher. I want to be a cook. I love Italian food, and I love working in a kitchen. But I need to improve my cooking skills. So I'm going to take an Italian cooking course next fall. I also need to improve my listening skills. My boss always gets mad at me because I get distracted when he's talking to me, and it's hard for me to concentrate sometimes. I'm going to take business communications at the college. The teacher said that class covers listening skills.

## Lesson 7, Activity 1: Listening Review (page 16)

*Part 1: First, you will hear a question. Next listen carefully to what is said. You will hear the question again. Then choose the correct answer: A, B, or C. Use the Answer Sheet.*

1. Why is the man calling?

A: Serra Vista Community College? Can I help you?

B: Yes, I'm calling to find out if you offer classes in website design.

A: Yes, we do. We offer two website design classes this semester.

Why is the man calling?

A. He wants to get a job at the college.

B. He wants to take a class in website design.

C. He wants to use the computer lab at the college.

2. What time will the caller be home?

Hi sweetie, it's Mom. I'm running a little late. I had three meetings this afternoon, and now I have to get to the store before it closes at six. I should be home in an hour. It's five-thirty now.

What time will the caller be home?

A. six o'clock

B. six-thirty

C. three o'clock

3. What is Sharon worried about?
   A: Hey Sharon, are you ready for your presentation?
   B: Not really.
   A: Why not? What's wrong?
   B: Well, I'm just worried. I've never given a presentation before.
   A: Don't worry, you have good oral communication skills. Just relax.

   What is Sharon worried about?
   A. She has given a presentation before.
   B. She has never given a presentation before.
   C. She hasn't finished writing her presentation.

4. What does Josh need to do?
   A: I want to apply for a certificate course at the college, Mom.
   B: That's great idea, Josh. What are you going to study?
   A: Business.
   B: When do you start?
   A: Well, I have to get my records from high school first.

   What does Josh need to do?
   A. finish high school
   B. fill out an application form
   C. get his records from high school

5. What interpersonal skill is the speaker describing?
   It's very important that people understand you when you speak. When you tell someone important information, you should leave out unnecessary details. Be concise and speak slowly enough for people to understand you.

   What interpersonal skill is the speaker describing?
   A. oral communication skills
   B. team skills
   C. writing skills

## Lesson 7, Activity 1: Listening Review (page 16)
*Part 2: You will hear the first part of a conversation. To finish the conversation, listen and choose the correct answer: A, B, or C. Use the Answer Sheet.*

6.
   A: So, you're taking a Continuing Education class?
   B: Yes. It's a lot of fun.
   A: What course are you taking?
   B: I'm taking Pottery 1.
   A: Oh. What do you do in that class?

   A. We prepare food.
   B. We make vases and bowls.
   C. We fix machines.

7.
   A: Who wrote this report?
   B: Sara wrote it. Is there a problem?
   A: No. It's good. It's very clear.
   B: So, what do you think of her writing skills?

   A. I think she's very proficient.
   B. I think she's very distracted.
   C. I think she's very cooperative.

8.
   A: Hello. This is Raul Zayas. May I please speak to Ms. Green?
   B: Ms. Green isn't in right now. Would you like her to call you back?
   A: Yes, thank you.
   A: Does Ms. Green have your phone number?
   B: I think so, but let me give it to you anyway. It's 555-3345.
   A: Sorry. Could you repeat that?

   A. Certainly. Can you tell her to call me back?
   B. Certainly. It's R-A-U-L  Z-A-Y-A-S
   C. Certainly. It's 555-3345.

9.
   A: Were there any messages?
   B: Yes. Raul Zayas called.
   A: Oh. What did he say?
   B: He asked you to call him back.
   A: Did he leave his number?

   A. Yes. At 3:30.
   B. Yes. It's 555-3345.
   C. Yes. It's 454 Pine Street.

10.
   A: May I help you?
   B: Yes. I want to take one of your certificate programs.
   A: Which program are you interested in?
   B: I'm interested in the accounting program, but I'm not sure about the requirements.

   A. Well, you need to have a high school diploma or a GED.
   B. It takes one year to complete.
   C. GED stands for General Equivalency Degree.

## UNIT TWO

### Lesson 2, Activity 4: Listen (page 20)
*Listen to the conversations. Check (✓) True or False.*

1.
   A: Okay, I've got your insurance policy in front of me. How may I help you?
   B: Someone broke my car window. I'm calling to find out how much my deductible is.
   A: It's five hundred dollars.
   B: Thank you.

2.
   Thank you for calling Excellent Insurance Company. You can now submit claims online. First, go to member services and download the document called Member Claim Form. Fill it out online, then click "submit."

3.
- A: What happens if I get into an accident with someone and they get hurt?
- B: Well, you have bodily injury coverage of $3,000 for each person in the other car. Up to $6,000 per accident.

4.
- A: I'm sorry to say, Mr. Rideout, that even though you paid $30,000 for your car, it has depreciated. It's worth $10,000 now.

## Lesson 3, Activity 2: Listen. Put in Sequence
(page 22)

*Number the pictures about Tom and his accident in order from first (1) to last (5). Then listen to five conversations and check your numbers.*

1.

| | |
|---|---|
| Officer: | Can I see your license and registration, please? |
| Tom: | My registration? |
| Officer: | Yes. Your car registration. I need to see proof of insurance, too. |
| Tom: | Yes, of course. Just a minute. Oh, good, yes, here they are. |
| Officer: | Okay. Why don't you tell me what happened? |
| Tom: | Well, I, uh, I was driving along, but I wasn't speeding or anything. |
| Officer: | Of course. |
| Tom: | And then suddenly the car in front of me stopped. I mean, it all happened in an instant. I slammed on my brakes, but there was nothing I could do. |
| Officer: | I see. Good thing you were wearing your seat belt. |
| Tom: | Hmm. You're right. Oh, and officer? |
| Officer: | Yes. |
| Tom: | Could I get your name, please? |
| Officer: | Yes, of course. I'm Officer Bee Goode. |
| Tom: | Officer Bee Goode? |
| Officer: | Yes, that's right. |
| Tom: | Thank you for your help, Officer Goode. |

2.

Recording: You have reached Unified Insurance Company. If you have a question about a bill, press 8. If you need to make a claim, press 7.

[beep]

| | |
|---|---|
| Recording: | Please press the 15-digit number of your policy, then press the pound key. |
| Agent: | Hello. This is Yumiko Sazaki speaking. How can I help you? |
| Tom: | I'm calling to report an accident. |
| Agent: | Your name, please. |
| Tom: | Tom. Tom Rideout. |
| Agent: | Okay, Mr. Rideout. Could you please verify your policy number, address, and Social Security number? |
| Tom: | Yes, my policy number is 00044 44 244 4443 5. My address is 564 Philips Street in Miami, Florida; and my Social Security number is 123-45-6789. |

| | |
|---|---|
| Agent: | First of all, I'm sorry to hear about your accident. Please tell me who was driving the car. |
| Tom: | I was. |
| Agent: | Were there any injuries? |
| Tom: | No. Only damage to my car. |
| Agent: | And this was your 2009 Volkswagen Beetle? |
| Tom: | Yes. |
| Agent: | Okay. And what day did the accident happen? |
| Tom: | Today. This morning. |
| Agent: | And where did the accident take place? |
| Tom: | I was on Interstate 95 in Miami. |
| Agent: | And the weather conditions when the accident happened? |
| Tom: | The weather? Um, well, it was clear and sunny. |
| Agent: | And how did the accident happen? |
| Tom: | Well, I was driving along, and suddenly the driver in the car in front of me slammed on his brakes. |
| Agent: | I see. |
| Tom: | Yes, and then my car hit the back of his car. It was terrible! The police came, and I talked with Officer Bee Goode. |
| Agent: | Okay, Mr. Rideout. Can you give me a number where I can reach you? |
| Tom: | Yes. You can call my cell phone. The number is 555-3465. |
| Agent: | Thank you, Mr. Rideout. I'll be back in touch with you within the next 24 hours. |
| Tom: | Okay. Thanks. |
| Agent: | You're welcome. Bye-bye. |

3.

| | |
|---|---|
| Tom: | So do you think you can repair the engine by tomorrow? |
| Mechanic: | I don't think so. |
| Tom: | Why not? |
| Mechanic: | Well, I need to order some new parts, and I don't know when they'll arrive. |
| Tom: | What about the bumper and the hood? Can you fix them while you wait for the parts? |
| Mechanic: | I don't think so. We're going to have to order a new bumper and hood. That'll take about a week. |
| Tom: | Oh, but that's too long. |
| Mechanic: | You have to be somewhere? |
| Tom: | Yes, I have to get to Tampa. |
| Mechanic: | Well, there's a bus stop near by. I can get one of the guys to take you there if you want. It's just down the road. |
| Tom: | Would you? Thank you so much. |

4.

| | |
|---|---|
| Ticket Agent: | Next, please. |
| Tom: | I need to get to Tampa as quickly as possible. |
| Agent: | Let's see. Yes, the next bus to Tampa is at 4:10. |
| Tom: | 4:10? But it's only 2:00 now. |
| Agent: | Yes, well, I'm afraid you just missed the 1:45 bus to Tampa. |

| Tom: | This is terrible. So when does that bus get into Tampa? |
| Agent: | The 4:10? |
| Tom: | Yes. |
| Agent: | Hold on a minute. Okay, that bus gets into Tampa at 12:10. |
| Tom: | 12:10 in the morning? Oh, boy. Great. |
| Agent: | So do you want to buy a ticket? |
| Tom: | Well, I, well, yes, I guess so. |
| Agent: | One-way or round-trip? |
| Tom: | Round-trip. |

5.

| Bill: | Hello. |
| Tom: | Bill. It's Tom. |
| Bill: | Tom? Where are you? |
| Tom: | I'm in Miami. |
| Bill: | You're in Miami? What are you doing there? |
| Tom: | It's a long story. I'm at the bus station. |
| Bill: | Where's your car? |
| Tom: | I had an accident. |
| Bill: | Are you okay? |
| Tom: | Yes, I'm fine. |
| Bill: | Are you going to get here in time? |
| Tom: | Yeah, I think so. I was just wondering if I could ask two favors? |
| Bill: | Whatever you want. |
| Tom: | First, could you pick me up at the bus station at midnight tonight? |
| Bill: | Yeah. Sure. No problem. |
| Tom: | And can I borrow your car to get to the wedding tomorrow? |
| Bill: | Anything you want. |

## Lesson 3, Activity 3: Listen. Check (✓) *True* or *False*. (page 22)
*Read the statements. Then listen. Check (✓)* True *or* False.

## Lesson 7, Activity 1: Listening Review (page 30)
*Part 1: Listen to what is said. When you hear the question* Which is correct?, *listen and choose the correct answer: A, B, or C.*

1.
A: Can you explain the difference between collision and comprehensive coverage?
B: Sure, Ms. Santos. Collision covers crashes. Comprehensive covers crashes, break-ins, fires, or any other damage done to your car.

Which is correct?
A. The agent is explaining how the deductible works.
B. The agent is describing two different types of insurance coverage.
C. The agent is telling Ms. Santos how to fill out a claim form.

2.
A: Quality Car Insurance. How may I help you?
B: I'm calling because I was in a car accident last week with a driver who does not have car insurance.
A: Okay. Let me look up your policy and see if you're covered for that.

Which is correct?
A. The caller doesn't have collision insurance.
B. The caller needs assistance in a roadside emergency.
C. The caller had a collision with an uninsured motorist.

3.
A: Speedy Bus Transit, can I help you?
B: Yes, I need a round-trip ticket to Miami.
A: Okay, where are you traveling from?
B: Orlando.
A: Okay, let me see…

Which is correct?
A. The caller wants to take a bus to Miami.
B. The caller wants to take a bus to Orlando.
C. The caller wants to find out about train tickets.

4.
A: 9-1-1. Please state your location.
B: I'm near Exit 13 on Highway 181, and I just saw a car accident.
A: Is anyone hurt?
B: Yes, I think so.
A: Okay, are you in a safe place?
B: Yes.
A: You need to stay on the shoulder of the road away from traffic. Help is on the way.

Which is correct?
A. The caller should warn oncoming traffic.
B. The caller should stay on the side of the road.
C. The caller should try to help the hurt people.

5.
I like to travel by car because I can make my own schedule. I like to leave when I want to, stop when I want to, and keep going if I'm not tired. I don't want to be on anyone else's schedule.

Which is correct?
A. The speaker likes to drive so she can be independent.
B. The speaker likes to drive because it's cheap.
C. The speaker likes to drive because she likes to be alone.

## Lesson 7, Activity 1: Listening Review (page 30)
*Part 2: First you will hear a question. Next, listen carefully to what is said. Then choose the correct answer: A, B, or C. Use the Answer Sheet.*
6. Why is the driver going slowly?
A: Driver, why are we moving so slowly?
B: I'm going as fast as I can.

A: Well, I'm in a hurry.
B: I can't drive any faster. It's rush hour!

Why is the driver going slowly?
A. There's an accident.
B. There's a problem with the car.
C. There's a lot of traffic.

7. What kind of coverage does the driver have?
A: I was just in an accident. There's some damage to my car.
B: Did you get the other driver's insurance information?
A: He doesn't have insurance. Am I covered?
B: Yes, you're in luck. Your policy covers this sort of situation.

What kind of coverage does the driver have?
A. The driver has uninsured motorist coverage.
B. The driver has bodily injury coverage.
C. The driver has personal injury coverage.

8. Why does the driver only get 10,000 dollars to replace the car?
A: I just had a collision. I need to replace my car.
B: With your policy . . . let me see . . . O.K. you get enough money to cover the value of the car at the time of the accident.
A: And what is that?
B: Right now, the value is 10,000 dollars.
A: But I paid a lot more for that car!

Why does the driver only get 10,000 dollars to replace the car?
A. The driver doesn't have comprehensive coverage.
B. The driver doesn't have collision coverage.
C. The driver's car has depreciated.

9. For which bus does the customer buy a ticket?
B: Hi, I need to get to Miami as soon as possible.
A: Well, you just missed the 8:45 A.M. bus.
B: Oh, no! When does the next bus leave?
A: The next bus leaves at 11:55 A.M. There's another one that leaves this afternoon at 2 P.M.
B: When does the 2:00 bus get into Miami?
A: It arrives at 9 tonight.
B: No, that's too late. I'd like one round-trip ticket for the next bus, then.

For which bus does the customer buy a ticket?
A. the 8:45 bus
B. the 11:55 A.M. bus
C. the 2 P.M. bus

10. What happened to Erik?
B: Dad, It's Erik. I've run out of gas. What should I do?
A: Did you get off the road?
B: Yes. What else should I do?
A: Did you lift the hood?
B: Yes, I did.
A. Great. You're doing all the right things.

What happened to Erik?
A. He had an accident.
B. He had a roadside emergency.
C. He witnessed an accident.

## UNIT THREE

### Lesson 1, Activity 2: Put in Sequence (page 32)
*Listen. Write the number of the picture that matches the description you hear.*

1. The ambulance took him to the emergency room.
2. While he was in the hospital, the nurses took his vital signs frequently.
3. Oscar and Rita were at home playing cards.
4. Suddenly he felt a sharp pain in his chest.
5. In the emergency room, the doctors hooked him up to an IV.
6. The nurse wheeled Oscar out of the hospital.
7. Oscar collapsed on the floor. His wife ran to the phone and called 911.

### Lesson 3, Activity 2: Listen and Take Notes (page 36)
*Listen to conversations 1 through 4. Take notes in the chart.*

Conversation 1

| | |
|---|---|
| Appointment Desk: | Redfield Medical Clinic. How can I help you? |
| Patient: | I'm calling to make an appointment with Dr. Smith. |
| Desk: | Do you need to see her right away? |
| Patient: | No. I'm just making an appointment for my annual check-up. |
| Desk: | All right. Can you hold for a minute? |
| Patient: | Sure. |
| Desk: | Okay, let's see, Dr. Smith has an opening on Monday, November 15th at noon. |
| Patient: | Um, the 15th will work, but 1:00 would be better. Do you have an opening then? |
| Desk: | Yes, you're in luck. She does have an opening at 1:00. Your name, please? |
| Patient: | It's Jeff Bartell. |
| Desk: | How do you spell that? |
| Patient: | It's B-a-r-t-e-l-l. |
| Desk: | Okay. And your telephone number, Mr. Bartell? |
| Patient: | It's 555-4834. |
| Desk: | 555-4843. |
| Patient: | Excuse me, but I said 4834. |
| Desk: | Okay, 4834. Thank you. Well, Mr. Bartell, we'll see you on the 15th. |
| Patient: | Okay. See you then. Thank you very much. |
| Desk: | You're welcome. Bye-bye. |

Conversation 2

| | |
|---|---|
| Appointment Desk: | Redfield Medical Clinic. Can I help you? |

| Patient: | This is Shirley Bay calling. I have an appointment with Dr. Smith on the 15th that I need to cancel. |
|---|---|
| Desk: | Okay. Just a minute, please. Yes, I see. Your appointment is at 2:30. Would you like to reschedule that? |
| Patient: | No, not right now, thank you. I'll call back next week. |
| Desk: | Okay. I've canceled your appointment on the 15th. Anything else we can do for you? |
| Patient: | No, that's it for now. Thank you. |
| Desk: | Sure. Good-bye now. |

Conversation 3

| Appointment Desk: | Redfield Medical Clinic. How can I help you? |
|---|---|
| Patient: | I'm calling about a bill I just received from Dr. Baker. |
| Desk: | Can I have your name, please? |
| Patient: | It's June Waite. |
| Desk: | White? |
| Patient: | No, it's Waite. W-a-i-t-e. It rhymes with *gate*. |
| Desk: | Okay, Ms. Waite. Thank you. And your date of birth? |
| Patient: | 8-12-84. |
| Desk: | 8—12—74. |
| Patient: | That was 84, not 74. |
| Desk: | Sorry. I'm having a little trouble hearing you. And you said there was a problem with your bill? |
| Patient: | Yes, that's right. I just received a second bill for the checkup I had in July, but I already paid that bill. I paid it in August. |
| Desk: | Well, it's probably just a mix-up. Let me look into it, and I'll get back to you. |
| Patient: | Thanks. |

Conversation 4

| Appointment Desk: | McCoy Pediatrics, how may I help you? |
|---|---|
| Mrs. Wong: | This is May Wong. My son James is very sick. He's been coughing for a few days and now he has a fever. |
| Desk: | How old is your son? |
| Mrs.Wong: | He's six months old. |
| Desk: | How high is his fever? |
| Mrs. Wong: | It's 102. |
| Desk: | Okay. Can you bring him in an hour? |
| Mrs. Wong: | Yes. |

**Lesson 3, Activity 3: Listen for Specific Information (page 36)**
*Listen to the conversation. Look at the doctor's bill on page 37. Write the missing information.*

| Front Desk: | McCoy Pediatrics, how may I help you? |
|---|---|
| Mrs. Wong: | I'm calling about a bill that I received. My name is May Wong, and my son is James. |
| Front Desk: | What is the date on the bill? |
| Mrs. Wong: | The bill date is October 24th. The due date is November 24th. |
| Front Desk: | And the account number, Mrs. Wong? |
| Mrs. Wong: | 557892. |
| Front Desk: | And the date of service? You'll find this toward the bottom of the page. |
| Mrs. Wong: | Hang on. Oh, okay. It was August 6th. |
| Front Desk: | Okay, I have it here. The amount due is $160? |
| Mrs. Wong: | Yes, that's the right. But there's a problem. The total charge was $160 and my insurance paid $60. So the amount due should be $100, not $160. |
| Front Desk: | I'm sorry about that Mrs. Wong, you're right. We'll send you a corrected bill right away. |
| Mrs. Wong: | Thank you. |

**Lesson 7, Activity 1: Listening Review (page 44)**
*Part 1: First, you will hear a question. Next, listen carefully to what is said. You will hear the question again. Then choose the correct answer: A, B, or C. Use the Answer Sheet.*

1. Why is the woman calling?
   A: 9-1-1. Please state your emergency.
   B: My husband collapsed. I think he's having a heart attack.
   A: Okay, ma'am, I need you to remain calm. First, please give me your address.

   Why is the woman calling?
   A. to get help for her husband
   B. to ask about an emergency
   C. to get an address

2. What does the doctor specialize in?
   A: Dr. Callan's office, how may I help you?
   B: Uh, hi. I need to make an appointment with the doctor. I have a bad cough.
   A: Uh, I'm sorry, ma'am, Dr. Callan is a cardiologist. You need a primary care physician.

   What does the doctor specialize in?
   A. common illnesses
   B. diseases of the skin
   C. diseases of the heart

3. What did the billing department do wrong?
   A: McCoy Pediatrics, billing department. How can I help you?
   B: Hi, I'm calling about a bill I received today. My name is May Wong.
   A: Okay, Mrs. Wong, what seems to be the problem with your bill?

B: Well, you billed the wrong insurance company. I have Blue Star, not Redline insurance.

What did the billing department do wrong?
A. They billed the wrong patient.
B. They billed the wrong insurance company.
C. They billed the wrong amount.

4. Why is James eating more vegetables?
A: Hey, James. What's that?
B: It's my lunch.
A: It looks like a bag of vegetables.
B: It is. I'm trying to lose weight, so I'm eating more vegetables.

Why is James eating more vegetables?
A. He didn't bring a lunch.
B. He's trying to lose weight.
C. He lost too much weight.

5. What did Lisa do before she had children?
A: So, tell me, Lisa. Why are you interested in working in a hospital?
B: Well, before I had children, I used to work with sick elderly people, in their homes.
A: I see.
B: I really like to help people.

What did Lisa do before she had children?
A. She was sick, so she didn't work.
B. She worked in a hospital.
C. She worked with sick people.

***Part 2: You will hear the first part of a conversation. To finish the conversation, listen and choose the correct answer: A, B, or C. Use the Answer Sheet.***

6.
A: Did you hear about Sara? She just collapsed in the cafeteria.
B: Really? What happened?
A: Ted called 911.
B: Then what?

A. I hope he's feeling better.
B. An ambulance came and took her to the hospital.
C. He brought her to a dermatologist.

7.
A: Hi, Jim. How did your knee surgery go?
B: My doctors say it went well.
A: Will you be coming back to work soon?

A. Not yet. I have to work with a physical therapist first.
B. Yes, after I cancel the appointment.
C. No. They billed the wrong insurance company.

8.
A: Do you think this cereal looks good?
B: I don't know. How many calories per serving?

A: Oh, no… 400! And the first ingredient is sugar!

A. Since it's very healthy, let's try it.
B. You should read the food label.
C. Let's try to find something more healthy.

9.
A: I need to get more exercise.
B: Good idea. What kinds of exercise do you like to do?
A: That's the problem. I'm used to just sitting at home and surfing the Internet.

A. I used to be a smoker.
B. Oh, you've been spending too much time in front of your computer.
C. Should we call 9-1-1?

10.
A: Hey, Jen, how about joining an exercise class with me?
B: Um, maybe. When is it?
A: Tuesday evenings at 7.
B: Oh sorry, I can't. I work late on Thursdays.

A. No, that was Tuesday, not Thursday.
B. I've been taking exercise classes for three months.
C. You need to make an appointment.

## UNIT FOUR

### Lesson 2, Activity 3: Listen (page 48)
*Listen to four conversations. Then find the freedom or right that is discussed. Write the correct letter on the line.*

1.
A: Marin County Library, may I help you?
B: Yes, I'm calling to see if you have any voter registration forms.
A: We do. But you need to fill it out and send it in by Friday if you want to vote in the election.
B: Okay, thanks. I'll come by today and pick up a form.

2.
A: Do you have a minute, Ed?
B: Sure, Anna. What can I do for you?
A: Well, I'm not going to be able to attend the manager's luncheon you planned for us next Friday.
B: Why not?
A: Well, because of my beliefs, I can't be around alcohol or people drinking it.
B: That's fine, Anna. Please don't worry about it. We'll work something out.

3.
A: Doug, are you going to the protest this weekend?
B: I want to, but I don't know where we're meeting.
A: Grant Park, 8 A.M. Senator Michaels is going to give a speech. Then we're marching on the capitol building.
B: Sounds good. I'll be there.

4.
  A: Bamford Elementary, how can I help you?
  B: Hi, my name's Rosario Garcia. My cousin Elena is moving here next fall, and she has three children. They're 5, 8, and 10. I don't have any kids, and I've only lived in the states a few years, so I don't know how the school system works. Can my cousin's kids register for school here when they arrive?
  A: Of course, they can. Just have them call the school near their house when they're here.
  B: Okay, thanks.

## Lesson 3, Activity 2: Listen and Take Notes (page 50)
*Listen to four people's opinions. Summarize each opinion. Then check* Agree *if you agree or* Disagree *if you disagree.*

1.
*Woman*: The biggest problem with schools today is that parents don't take an active role in their kids' education. Maybe it's because they're too busy with work and other things, but the truth is, parents need to be more involved. I mean, they can volunteer and attend school meetings. And they can make sure their children do their school work. That's a parent's job.

2.
*Man*: I think students today spend too much time in extracurricular activities. When I was a child, we didn't have extracurricular activities. School was all about studying and learning. It wasn't about playing sports and having parties.

3.
*Woman*: I really don't think schools should be coeducational, especially for teenagers. When girls and boys are together in class, they don't think about studying. And when girls study with boys, they don't talk as much. Well, that's my opinion, anyway.

4.
*Man*: I just heard that students at the high school in my area can take dancing as an elective. I think that's great. School is about learning, not just history, math, and science, but about yourself, too. Music, dance, and other electives are a great way for kids to discover themselves.

## Lesson 3, Activity 3: Listen and Check Your Answer (page 50)
*Listen to five conversations. Check* They agree *if the people agree or* They disagree *if the people disagree.*

1.
  A: Do you think school should be required?
  B: Hmm. That's an interesting question. To be honest, I *don't* think it should be required.
  A: Yeah. Neither do I. I mean, when it's required, kids don't value it.

2.
  A: Do you think students should have more time for physical education?

  B: Yes, definitely. It's not good for children to sit in a chair all day. They need exercise. They need to move around.
  A: Really? I'm not sure I agree. I think school is for learning. Children can get exercise after school.
  B: Well, studies show that kids need a lot of exercise. It helps them learn better. Exercising is part of learning.

3.
  A: Do you think our high school should have a school newspaper?
  B: Yes. That's a great idea.
  A: Really? Why do you think so?
  B: Well, it gives students a real purpose for writing. I think they learn a lot from putting out a newspaper.
  A: Hmm, I don't know about that. I think writing should be taught in class, not by writing a newspaper.

4.
  A: What's your opinion of the extracurricular activities at the high school? Do you think we have enough?
  B: Yes, I guess so.
  A: Hmm. Me too.

5.
  A: What did you think of the PTA meeting last week?
  B: Oh, I didn't go. I think it's a waste of time.
  A: Why is that?
  B: Oh, I don't know. Nothing important ever happens.
  A: Well, next month we're going to discuss the new extracurricular activities. I think it should be interesting.
  B: Hmm.

## Lesson 7, Activity 1: Listening Review (page 58)
*Part 1: Listen to what is said. When you hear the question* Which is correct? *listen and choose the correct answer: A, B, or C. Use the Answer Sheet.*

1.
  A: This is KBBR national news radio, and I'm standing on the steps of city hall in Springtown, Oregon. There's a protest going on as you can hear in the background. The people of Springtown are marching on city hall because they are upset about a new parking law.

Which is correct?
  A. The reporter is speaking to the mayor of Springtown, Oregon.
  B. The people of Springtown are protesting at city hall.
  C. The reporter is upset because of parking in Springtown.

2.
  A: Mom, can I go over to Anton's?
  B: Have you done your homework?
  A: Not yet.
  B: Then you need to do your homework first.
  A: But it's too hard.
  B: I'll help you, then. Go get your books.

Which is correct?
  A. The mother is taking an active role in her son's education.
  B. The mother is expressing her right to free education.
  C. The son doesn't understand his right to a free education.

3.
  A: Hey, Carol, did you hear about the new school uniform rule?
  B: What?
  A: Starting next year, our kids have to wear uniforms to school.
  B: Oh, I think that's a great idea. Kids spend too much time worrying about their clothes.
  A: Really? I'm not sure I agree. I mean, kids love being unique. Uniforms are a bad idea.

Which is correct?
  A. The woman and the man disagree with each other.
  B. The woman and the man agree with each other.
  C. The woman and the man don't have opinions about school uniforms.

4.
  A: What are you doing after school today, Erin?
  B: I've got soccer practice.
  A: What about tomorrow?
  B: I have a baseball game. Then I have a guitar lesson.

Which is correct?
  A. Erin has a lot of extracurricular activities.
  B. Erin is taking a lot of electives.
  C. Erin has a lot of free time.

5.
  A: Hey, Doug, I saw you at the protest yesterday.
  B: Yep, I protested with the union outside of three big hotels.
  A: Why?
  B: Our vacation time was cut. They can't do that. We're union members.

Which is correct?
  A. Doug cut his vacation time.
  B. Doug took a vacation.
  C. Doug's employer cut his vacation time.

**Part 2: First you will hear a question. Next, listen carefully to what is said. You will hear the question again. Then choose the correct answer: A, B, or C. Use the Answer Sheet.**

6. What does the woman want to do?
  A: Hi. Can I help you with something?
  B: Yes. I want to vote in the election next month.
  A: Okay. You just need to fill out this form.
  B: Oh great, thanks. And should I bring it back here?
  A: No, you need to send it to the Board of Elections by next Tuesday.

What does the woman want to do?
  A. She wants to organize a peaceful protest.

  B. She wants to register to vote.
  C. She wants to register her child for school.

7. What is being compared?
  A: Hi, Dan. Have you registered for any classes this semester?
  B: Not yet. I have to take Business Communications and Beginning Programming. They're required. But I also want to take Art History or maybe Photography.
  A: Really? I hear the photography course is fun and the teacher is fantastic. Art History is really hard.

What is being compared?
  A. two electives
  B. two extracurricular activities
  C. two unions

8. What does Sara think about the union?
  A: What are you looking at, Sara?
  B: Some information about the union. I need to decide whether I want to join.
  A: Well, I'm going to join. I think unions protect workers' rights.
  B: Me too. Do you want to come with me to talk to the union representative?

What does Sara think about the union?
  A. The union is good for workers.
  B. The union treats employees unfairly.
  C. The union disagrees with the employers.

9. Why are the people protesting?
  A: Hey, what's going on over at V-Tech Electronics?
  B: Oh, there's a big protest today. The employees think they have the right to a better health care plan.
  A: What's wrong with the plan they have?
  B: I think the employers are only contributing half of the cost.

Why are the people protesting?
  A. They want more computers in the schools.
  B. They want their employer to pay for better health care.
  C. They think the employer is right.

10. What is the man's opinion?
  A: I heard that immigrants' rights group is saying that their employer discriminated against them.
  B: Oh yes, I heard about that. The company wouldn't give them benefits information in their native language.
  A: Right. I think the company took advantage of the employees.

What is the man's opinion?
  A. The employer has the right to free speech.
  B. The employees discriminated against the company.
  C. The employer was unfair.

## UNIT FIVE

### Lesson 2, Activity 3: Listen and Write (page 62)
*Listen to each conversation. Then complete each statement about what you heard. Use the highlighted words from page 63.*

1.
A: Hi there. Is there anything I can help you with?
B: No thanks. I'm just looking.
A: Okay. But let me show you this sweater. I think it would look great on you.
B: Oh. I don't really need a sweater. Thanks.
A: Really? This is a great deal. It's on sale, and look at this color. It's gorgeous. Would you like to try it on?

2.
A: Excuse me?
B: Yes.
A: If I buy this skirt for my sister and it doesn't fit her, can she bring it back?
B: She can, if she has the receipt. And she'll get store credit only.

3.
A: So, Ann, are you glad you came shopping with me?
B: No, I can't stand shopping. Can we get some lunch now?
A: In a minute. I think I'm going to get this cool set of pots and pans.
B: But you don't even cook!
A: But they're on sale. And they're a great color. I'm going to get them.

4.
A: Excuse me?
B: Yes, can I help you?
A: Well, I'm looking for rice.
B: Over there, in the large containers. You can just pour some into a bag and pay for it up front. We'll weigh it for you.
A: Okay, thanks.

### Lesson 3, Activity 2: Listen and Match (page 64)
*Listen to five conversations. Match each conversation to a picture on page 65. Write the number of the conversation in the circle.*

1.
Salesperson: Can I help you?
Customer:    Yes. I'd like to buy these.
Salesperson: And how would you like to pay?
Customer:    You take personal checks, don't you?
Salesperson: No, I'm sorry, we don't. We only accept cash or credit cards.
Customer:    Oh, no. Really?
Salesperson: Yes. That's the store policy.
Customer:    Oh, no. I don't have a credit card, and I don't have enough cash on me.
Salesperson: Well, there's an ATM right over there.
Customer:    Okay, good. I'll be right back.

2.
Salesperson: Can I help you?
Customer:    Yes, I'd like to return these.
Salesperson: Do you have your receipt?
Customer:    Yes. Um, here it is.
Salesperson: I'm sorry, but these items are nonreturnable.
Customer:    Excuse me?
Salesperson: You can't return these pants. They were a final sale.
Customer:    Are you sure?
Salesperson: I'm afraid so. It says right here on the receipt.

3.
Salesperson: Can I help you?
Customer:    Ah, no. No, thank you.
Salesperson: Have you seen our new suits? They just arrived, and they're on sale.
Customer:    No, thank you. I don't need a suit.
Salesperson: Are you sure? These won't last long. I've already sold three of them today.
Customer:    Ah, no, thank you. I'm just looking. I'll let you know if I need help.
Salesperson: Okay.

4.
A: Can you tell me where the olive oil is?
B: Olive oil. Hmm. I'm pretty sure that it's at the end of aisle 4, but I'm not absolutely certain. I'm new here.
A: Well, I'll look there. Thanks.
B: You're welcome.
A: I think this is aisle 4, but I'm not sure. I don't see a sign. Excuse me . . .

5.
Salesperson: Can I help you?
Customer:    Yes, I'd like some information about computers.
Salesperson: Okay. Do you need a desktop or a laptop?
Customer:    Well, it's possible that I'll need a laptop for travel, but I'm not sure.
Salesperson: Well, we have this lightweight, high-speed, wireless laptop. Here, hold this. It's light, isn't it?
Customer:    Yes. Does it come with a warranty?
Salesperson: I think so, but I'm not positive. I'll go check. Wait a minute, and I'll be right back.
Customer:    Okay. Thanks.

### Lesson 3, Activity 3: Listen for Specific Information (page 64)
*Listen to the conversations again. What does each customer want? Take notes in the chart.*

### Lesson 4, Activity 4: Apply (page 67)
*Listen. Check the correct boxes for each message. Write the number of bedrooms and the amount of rent in the last two boxes.*

1. Thank you for calling Express Rentals. We have one new rental. It's a 3-bedroom apartment on the Upper East Side

of Chicago. Pets are not allowed. The apartment is not furnished. Rent is $1,500 per month.

2. You have reached voice mailbox 55 at RoomMates and Rentals. This listing is for a large, 4-bedroom house with a big backyard. Pets are okay. The house is not furnished. Rent is $2,500 per month.

3. Thanks for calling. The apartment is still for rent. So here are the details. There is one bedroom and no furniture. The rent is $1,000 a month. Oh, and no pets.

4. You have reached the Orange County Real Estate message box for property OC154. The property is a gorgeous 4-bedroom, 5-bathroom, fully furnished home. The rent is $3,000 per month, and pets are welcome.

5. Hello. We have a condo for rent. It's a 2-bedroom on the north side. It's unfurnished, and pets aren't allowed. The rent is $1,400 a month. Please leave your name and number, and we'll get back to you.

6. You have reached the Grandview Apartments. We currently have a 1-bedroom apartment available on the top floor. It's furnished and pets are okay. The rent is $1,200 a month.

## Lesson 7, Activity 1: Listening Review (page 72)
*Part 1: You will hear the first part of the conversation. To finish the conversation, listen and choose the correct answer: A, B, or C. Use the Answer Sheet.*

1.
A: Do you like to shop?
B: Yes, I love going shopping.
A: Are you an impulse shopper?

A. No, I buy things even if I don't need them.
B. Yes, I think carefully about everything I buy.
C. No, I only buy things that I need.

2.
A: Would you like to buy that watch?
B: I think so. Does it come with a warranty?

A. Yes. If it breaks within a year, we'll fix it for you for free.
B. Yes, you can return it for store credit.
C. Yes, it's on sale for $85.

3.
A: Thanks for coming to the store with me, Tom.
B: No problem. You're looking for a sleeping bag, right?
A: Yes. Do you know where they are?

A. They're not over here, aren't they?
B. They're over here, aren't they?
C. They're over here, are they?

4.
A: What is your store's refund policy?
B: I think we have one, but I'm not positive.

A. Okay, so you're saying I can return this for a full refund?
B. Well, could you ask your manager?
C. Oh, you don't have one. That's too bad.

5.
A: Excuse me sir, can you help me?
B: Well, it's my first day, but I'll do my best.
A: Okay. Do you know where the footballs are?

A. Um. I'm pretty sure that they're over here, but I'm not absolutely certain.
B. Um. It's possible that they're over there, but I'm certain.
C. They aren't, are they?

*Part 2: Listen to what is said. When you hear the question,* **Which is correct?**, *listen and choose the correct answer: A, B, or C. Use the Answer Sheet.*

6.
A: Hey, look at what I just bought at May's! They're having a big sale.
B: Wow, that's a lot of sweaters.
A: Yeah, I bought two at the regular price, and I got the third one for 10 percent off!

Which is correct?
A. The man bought 2 sweaters.
B. The man bought 3 sweaters.
C. The many bought 10 sweaters.

7.
A: Hi. I'm calling about the two-bedroom apartment on State Street. I was wondering . . . is it furnished?
B: I'm afraid that one is no longer available. Would you be interested in a furnished 3-bedroom in the same building?

Which is correct?
A. The 2-bedroom is available.
B. The 3-bedroom is furnished.
C. The 3-bedroom is no longer available.

8.
A: Beech Realty. Thank you for calling. We have a 2-bedroom condo for rent that allows pets. It's unfurnished, and the rent is $1,450 a month.

Which is correct?
A. Beech Realty has an unfurnished, 2-bedroom apartment for rent.
B. Beech Realty has a furnished, 2-bedroom condo for rent.
C. Beech Realty has an unfurnished, 2-bedroom condo for rent.

9.
A: Do you want to go shopping with me?
B: No, I'm too tired.
A: Well, I know you don't like to shop anyway.
B: No. I think shopping is boring.

Which is correct?
    A. The woman is bored.
    B. The woman is tired.
    C. The woman thinks shopping is tiring.

10.
    A: I just called the store.
    B: What did they say?
    A: Well, the salesperson said that if the warranty is still good, the store will fix the laptop for free.

Which is correct?
    A. The woman will fix the laptop.
    B. The salesperson will fix the laptop.
    C. The store will fix the laptop.

## UNIT SIX

### Lesson 2, Activity 4:  Listen and Identify (page 76)
*Listen to the conversations. Check the type of crime you hear about.*

1.
    A: Okay, hold it right there.
    B: Darn!
    A: I said, "Stop!"
    B: I wasn't doing anything!
    A: Didn't you see the sign?
    B: What sign?
    A: The one that says "No Trespassing."
    B: There's no sign . . I didn't do anything wrong!
    A: You're trespassing on private property.
    B: But officer . . .
    A: It's clearly posted.
    B: Come on! I just didn't see the sign.
    A: You're under arrest. You have the right to remain silent . . .

2.
    A: Ms. Jones, will you describe to the jury what happened on the night of June 2nd?
    B: Um, yes. I was walking to my car. It was at the back of the parking lot. I heard a noise behind me. I ran to my car, and I started to open the door. Suddenly, the man grabbed me.
    A: Um, how did he grab you, Ms. Jones?
    B: By the collar of my coat.
    A: I see. Proceed.
    B: Then I felt something cold on my neck. It was a gun. I was scared.
    A: Then what happened?
    B: He pushed me to the ground. I dropped my car keys. He grabbed the keys, got into my car, and drove off.
    A: Thank you, Ms. Jones.

3.
    A: Rob, you're late. What happened?
    B: Mom, I got a ticket for jaywalking.

A: Jaywalking?!
    B: Yeah. I crossed State Boulevard in the middle of the block.
    A: Jeez! That's dangerous!
    B: I know . . .
    A: You shouldn't have jaywalked! You know that!
    B: I was in a hurry!
    A: Well, what's the fine?
    B: The fine? Um, the ticket says I have to pay $75.
    A: Well, you'll have to pay for that out of your own savings.
    B: I know . . .
    A: It'll be a good lesson for you.

### Lesson 2, Window on Pronunciation: Reduction of Past Modals (page 77)
*B Listen to the sentences. Write the missing words. Use the correct spelling.*

    1. I should have turned off my cell phone before I went into the courtroom.
    2. He shouldn't have crossed the street in the middle of the block.
    3. They could have paid the fine earlier.
    4. She should have slowed down at the intersection.
    5. You should have worn your seat belt.
    6. We couldn't have gotten a better lawyer.

### Lesson 3, Activity 2: Listen and Match (page 78)
*Listen. Write the number you press for the information.*
You have reached the County Clerk's automated information system.
For office hours, press 1.
For marriage license information, press 2.
For ceremony information, press 3.
For passport information, press 4.
For business license information press 5.

### Lesson 3, Activity 3: Listen for Specific Information (page 78)
*Listen to recorded messages about getting a marriage license and a driver's license. Check the things you have to do in the After listening column on page 79*
Part One: Marriage License

You have reached the County Clerk's automated information system.
For office hours, press 1.
For marriage license information, press 2.
For ceremony information, press 3.
For passport information, press 4.
For business license information press 5.

You have pressed 2.

To obtain a public marriage license, the couple must appear together at the county clerk's office with picture identification. You can use a passport, driver's license, naturalization form, resident alien card, or military ID showing your full legal name.

A blood test is not required. The fee for a public marriage license is $83.00. Your license only lasts for 90 days, so a marriage ceremony must take place within 90 days of receiving the license.

Part Two: Driver's License

You have pressed 1.

Thank you for calling the Department of Motor Vehicles. For information about obtaining a driver's license, press 1.

[sound of "1" key being pressed]

You have pressed 1.

To obtain a driver's license, you need to make an appointment at the DMV office. You will need to complete an application for a new license. The application must be signed in person at the DMV office. You will also need to provide proof of your birth date; your valid Social Security card; documents proving your true full name, such as an original certified copy of your birth certificate, an original passport, a military ID, or documents verifying proof of legal presence in the United States. The fee to obtain a new California driver's license is $24. You must take a vision test and a written test that consists of 25 multiple-choice questions. You may take the written test three times. Finally, you must supply proof of insurance and current registration for the vehicle used. Once all requirements are met and tests passed, you will be given a 60-day, temporary license until your new license is mailed to you. A fingerprint and photograph will be taken.

**Lesson 3, Activity 4: Listen and Take Notes** (page 78)
Read the questions in the *Note-Taking Chart* on page 79. Then listen again for the answers to the questions and take notes. After you listen, work with a classmate. Take turns asking and answering the questions.

**Lesson 4, Activity 3: Listen and Write** (page 81)
*Listen to the conversations. Write the problem.*
1.
  A: Did you see that car last night?
  B: No. What happened?
  A: Someone was driving a blue van up and down Grand Street.
  B: What were they doing?
  A: I don't know, but I didn't recognize the van. It didn't belong to the neighborhood.
  B: Did the people in the van force anyone to get in?
  A: No, but it was very suspicious.

2.
  A: Hey, what's that noise?
  B: It sounds like a cat.
  A: No, it's someone screaming.
  B: Yeah, you're right!
  A: It's someone shouting, "Help"!

  B: Is it coming from that car over there?
  A: No, it coming from the apartment house across the street.
  B: Let's call 9-1-1!

3.
  A: What's going on at the Lee's house?
  B: I don't know. No one is home there today.
  A: Well, I just saw someone there.
  B: Was he looking into the windows?
  A: No, actually, it looked like he was coming out the front door.
  B: That's odd. Was he carrying anything?
  A: As a matter of fact, yes. I think I'd better call the police.
  B: Good idea.

4.
  A: There's a guy sitting in a car next to the playground.
  B: Isn't that one of the parents?
  A: No. He's a stranger. I don't recognize the car, either.
  B: Who's he talking to?
  A: It looks like one of the Wilson's kids.
  B: I don't like that.
  A: Me, either.
  B: Let's get the cops over here right now.
  A: Good idea.

**Lesson 7, Activity 1: Listening Review** (page 86)
*Part 1: First you will hear a question. Next, listen carefully to what is said. You will hear the question again. Then choose the correct answer: A, B, or C. Use the Answer Sheet.*

1. What did the jury do?
  A: What was jury duty like?
  B: Well, first the lawyers interviewed us.
  A: Yes.
  B: Then they dismissed some people and told other people to stay.
  A: Uh-huh.
  B: Then we listened to the testimony of a lot of witnesses.

What did the jury do?
  A. dismissed the witnesses
  B. listened to testimony
  C. interviewed the defendant

2. What is the crime?
  A: Hold it!
  B: Yes, officer?
  A: You're not allowed to cross the street here. Cross at the corner.
  B: Okay. Sorry, officer.

What is the crime?
  A. trespassing
  B. jaywalking

C. littering

3. What is Ron's punishment?
A: What happened to Ron?
B: He committed a misdemeanor.
A: Does he have to go to prison?
B: No, but he has to do community service for six weeks.

What is Ron's punishment?
A. He has to go to prison.
B. He has to do community service.
C. He has to pay a fine.

4. What number do you press for business license information?
You have reached the County Clerk's automated information system.
For marriage license information, press 1.
For business license information, press 2.
For passport information, press 3.
What number do you press for business license information?
A. 1
B. 2
C. 3

5. When will the man get his new license?
A: When can I start driving?
B: Right away. You will receive a 60-day, temporary license until your new license is mailed to you.
A: Thanks.

When will the man get his new license?
A. in six days
B. in a month
C. in two months

*Part 2: You will hear the first part of the conversation. To finish the conversation, listen and choose the correct answer: A, B, or C. Use the Answer Sheet.*

6.
A: We listened to testimony for over a week.
B: Was the defendant guilty?

A. Yes, and now he will go to prison.
B. Yes, and the lawyers dismissed him.
C. Yes, and he received a summons in the mail.

7.
A: The police caught Amy littering at the beach last weekend.
B: Oh, no. What kind of offense is that?

A. It's a misdemeanor.
B. It's a felony.
C. It's an infraction.

8.
A: Hold it.
B: What is it, Officer?
A: You just jaywalked.
B: Gee, I'm sorry. What's the fine?

A. It's one month of community service.
B. It's $75.
C. It's imprisonment for one year.

9.
A: Do I need to show a Social Security card to get a marriage license?
B: No, it's not necessary.
A: So a Social Security card is not required?

A. That's right.
B. Thank you.
C. May I see your ID, please?

10.
A: Hey, what's that noise?
A: It's someone screaming.
B: Uh-oh. What should we do?

A. That's right.
B. We should have called 9-1-1.
C. Let's call 9-1-1.

## UNIT SEVEN

### Lesson 1, Activity 4: Listen and Match (page 88)
*Listen to the conversations and look at the picture. Match each conversation to the correct person.*

1.
Stu:   Hi, Mark. Anna told me that you wanted to speak to me.
Mark:  Yes, please come in. We need to discuss your work habits. I've seen you lying down during work hours.

2.
Mark:  I noticed that you violated a safety regulation today. You also used equipment improperly.
Tom:   Oh! What did I do?
Mark:  You were standing on top of a ladder to get a box. You're not supposed to stand on the top step of a ladder.

3.
Tim:   Hi, Mark. What do you want to talk to me about?
Mark:  Well, I saw that you were playing ball with Bob today. You shouldn't be playing games during work hours.
Tim:   I'm sorry, Mark. I won't do it again.

4.
Mark:  We need to discuss what you're wearing today.
Pete:  Why? Is something wrong?
Mark:  You're not supposed to wear shorts to work. You're supposed to wear your green uniform pants.

5.
Ken:   Hi, Mark. You wanted to talk to me?
Mark:  Yes, I did. You ignored your work duties today and were sitting down, reading the newspaper.
Ken:   Oh, I was on my break.

Mark: You need to take your breaks in the break room or outside of the store. Also, you had had a break just an hour before I saw you sitting down!

6.
Mark: You need to stop fighting with your co-workers.
Nina: But Phil started it. I asked him to help me with something, and he ignored me.
Mark: If someone makes you angry, come and talk to me. Don't start a fight in front of the customers.

## Lesson 2, Activity 3: Listen (page 90)
*Listen to the conversations. Which job is each person interviewing for? Check the correct position.*

1.
Interviewee: Can you tell me about some of the things I would be responsible for in this position?
Interviewer: Sure. First of all, you have to be able to provide good customer service. For example, you will deal with refunds and help customers.

2.
Interviewer: Tell me about your previous experience in retail.
Interviewee: I was a supervisor for three years at Lane's Department Store. In that position, I was responsible for the daily activities of the men's shoe department. I ordered all of the men's shoes for the store, and I reviewed the P & L reports.

3.
Interviewee: In my previous job, I was a team leader for a group of 30 sales associates. I also recruited and trained new sales associates for the store. I made sure that all of my sales associates were courteous and helpful to our customers.
Interviewer: It sounds like you've had a lot of experience in retail. How many years were you at your previous job?
Interviewee: I was a supervisor there for two and a half years.

4.
Interviewer: Why do you think you're the right person for this position?
Interviewee: Well, in my previous job, I was a supervisor in a department store. In that job, I was responsible for assisting customers, resolving customer complaints, taking care of shipments, and depositing money at the bank every night.

## Lesson 3, Activity 2: Listen for Specific Information (page 92)
*Listen to Roberta's interview and add the missing information to her job application on page 93.*

A: Can I help you?
B: Yes. I have an appointment to see Mr. Harrison.
A: And your name, please?

B: Roberta Madera.
A: Just a moment, Ms. Madera. I'll tell him you're here. He'll be with you in just a minute, Ms. Madera. Won't you have a seat?
B: Thanks.
C: Ms. Madera?
B: Yes.
C: Hello. I'm Mr. Harrison.
B: Hello, Mr. Harrison. It's nice to meet you.
C: Please come in.
B: Thank you.
C: Have a seat.
B: Thank you.
C: I have your application here, and I see here that you are applying for the assistant manager's position.
B: Yes, that's right. I was very excited to find a job opening at Sayer's.
C: And you'd be able to start on June 1st?
B: Yes, that's right.
C: I see that you went to Northeast Community College.
B: Yes, I've completed two years of work so far, and I hope to continue taking courses part time so I can get my degree.
C: Yes, I see that your major is business administration.
B: Yes. It's a good way to combine math and interpersonal skills.
C: That's true. But tell me, do you find it difficult to work full time and take courses at the same time?
B: It's challenging, but I just have to manage my time carefully.
C: Yes, I see. Let's see, now, why don't you tell me a little about your last job? It says that you worked at Floormart until last April. That's when the store moved out of state, isn't it?
B: Yes, that's right. They offered me a job if I was willing to move, but my family is here, so I decided against moving.
C: What was it like working at Floormart?
B: Well, as the assistant manager, I was able to do a lot of different things, from working with customers to financial planning. I like that. And I had an excellent boss. He was always willing to teach me new things and give me more responsibility.
C: Yes, I see. And, uh, what about your job at Reiko's?
B: Yes. That was my first full-time job. I was a clerk, then a supervisor. I think it was that job that made me realize that I liked being in charge. I mean, I liked being responsible for the store and making decisions. And I enjoyed working with and training the salespeople. I would have stayed there, but the job at Floormart came up, and I couldn't refuse it.
C: Yes, of course.

## Lesson 3, Activity 3: Listen and Evaluate (page 92)

*Read the questions. Then look at the pictures and listen to the interview again. Check (✓) your answers about Roberta. Now listen to Richard's interview. Answer questions 1–7 about him. Then compare the two interviews.*

A: Can I help you?

B: Yeah. I want to see Ms. Michaels.

A: Do you have an appointment?

B: Yeah.

A: And your name, please?

B: Richard.

A: Uh, and your last name?

B: Smith. Richard Smith.

A: Just a moment, Mr. Smith. I'll tell her you're here. She'll be with you in just a minute, Mr. Smith. Why don't you have a seat?

B: Okay.

C: Mr. Smith?

B: Yeah, that's me.

C: Why don't you come in? Have a seat.

B: Yeah, okay.

C: I have your application here, and I see that you worked for a travel agent for several years.

B: Yeah. It was so boring. And my boss was really mean. If I was even 10 minutes late in the morning, he'd yell at me. I was so glad when that place went out of business.

C: I see. Well, Mr. Smith. Thank you for coming in.

B: Is that all?

C: Yes.

## Lesson 7, Activity 1: Listening Review (page 100)

*Part 1: You will hear the first part of a conversation. To finish the conversation, listen and choose the correct answer: A, B, or C. Use the Answer Sheet.*

1.

A: Hi, Jane, how are you doing?

B: I'm great, thanks! I just got a new job at a department store.

A: Congratulations! Do you like your new job?

A. Yes, I did. I've been working there for three months.

B. Yes, I do. It's a really fun place to work.

C. Yes, I am. How do you like your new job?

2.

A: I see on your résumé that you worked at Mill City Hospital for two years.

B: Yes, that's right.

A: Can you tell me why you left that job?

A. Yes, I did. I left that job in 2009.

B. I had worked at the hospital for two years.

C. My husband's office moved us to a different city.

3.

A: Hi, Mr. Jenkins. Tracy told me that you want to talk to me.

B: Come in, Jack. Yes, there's a problem that I need to talk to you about. You violated a safety regulation today.

A: I'm sorry. What did I do?

A. You weren't wearing your safety goggles.

B. You were lying down during work hours.

C. You talked on the phone for two hours.

4.

A: Nina, can you come into my office for a minute?

B: Sure, Ted. Is something wrong?

A: Yes, Nina. We need to discuss your excessive absenteeism.

A. Oh, I'm sorry that I've missed so much work.

B. Jack and Sara were fighting again this afternoon.

C. I'll try to remember to take better care of the company equipment.

5.

A: Do you have any previous experience in retail?

B: Yes, I was a shift supervisor at Hale's for three years.

A: Oh, what kinds of things did you do there?

A. I handled customer refunds and processed the store's shipments.

B. I've been recruiting and training new sales associates for three years.

C. I had been working at Hale's for a year when I was promoted to shift supervisor.

*Part 2: Listen to what is said. When you hear the question, Which is correct?, listen and choose the correct answer: A, B, or C. Use the Answer Sheet.*

6.

A: Where have you been, Lisa?

B: I was on my lunch break.

A: You went to lunch at noon and it's already 1:45. You're supposed to take an hour for lunch.

Which is correct?

A. Lisa failed to observe the time limit for lunch.

B. Lisa didn't go to lunch when she was supposed to.

C. Lisa always goes to lunch at noon.

7.

A: Do you have any questions for me, Rose?

B: Yes, I do, Tim. Can you tell me about some of the benefits that your company offers?

A: Of course. Well, we offer full medical and dental insurance for all family members. And we also offer flextime and allow employees to telecommute once a week.

Which is correct?
   A. Rose is interviewing Tim.
   B. Tim is interviewing Rose.
   C. Rose is offering Tim a job.

8.
   A: What do you like best about your new job?
   B: Well, I like the people that I work with. They're really friendly.
   A: Do you get good benefits?
   B: Yes, I do. For example, I have a great 401k plan.

Which is correct?
   A. The company doesn't offer health benefits to new employees.
   B. The company offers excellent health benefits.
   C. The company offers an excellent retirement plan.

9.
   A: So, Bill, I see you've been a landscaper for over 10 years.
   B: Yes, that's correct.
   A: Can you tell me a little about your past job experience?
   B: Sure. In my last job, I was a supervisor. But in my previous job, I owned my own landscaping business.

Which is correct?
   A. Bill was a supervisor. Then he owned his own business.
   B. Bill owned his own business. Then he was a supervisor.
   C. Bill owned his own business and was a supervisor at the same time.

10.
   A: So, Matthew, can you tell me why you left your last job?
   B: Sure. I left because I didn't like it.
   A: I see.
   B: Also, it was really boring and my boss always got mad at me when I was late.

Which is correct?
   A. Matthew didn't have a positive attitude.
   B. Matthew was businesslike in his interview.
   C. Matthew didn't speak clearly.

## UNIT EIGHT

### Lesson 1, Activity 4: Listen (page 102)
*Check (✓)* **True** *or* **False.**

1. The Lee family spent their budgeted amount for entertainment.
2. The Lee family spent $40 more than they budgeted for utilities.
3. The Lees spent their budgeted amount for clothing.
4. They didn't have any debt this month.
5. They saved $50 on food this month.

6. The Lees spent $100 more than they budgeted for miscellaneous items.

### Lesson 3, Activity 2: Listen and Check (page 106)
*Read the questions about Seattle Banking checking accounts and home loans on page 107. Then listen to a conversation between a bank officer and a customer. Check (✓) four questions the customer asks.*

   A: Can I help you?
   B: Yes. I'd like to speak to someone about opening a new checking account.
   A: Can you have a seat? I'll see if Ms. Jeffries is available.
   B: Sure. Thank you.
   C: Hi. I'm Ms. Jeffries.
   B: Hi, Ms. Jeffries. I'm Sylvia Taylor.
   C: Nice to meet you, Ms. Taylor. Why don't you come over to my desk and have a seat?
   B: Thank you.
   C: How can I help you today?
   B: I just wanted to get some information about opening a checking account.
   C: Sure. Which kind of account are you interested in?
   B: Well, um, actually I'm not sure. I really don't know what your bank has to offer.
   C: Well, we have three types of checking accounts. There's the Circle Checking Account, the Green Checking Account, and the Basic Checking Account.
   B: I see. And, ah, how are they different?
   C: Well, the Circle Account is the only one that earns interest.
   B: That's nice.
   C: And the Circle Account is the only one that *doesn't* charge a fee when you use an ATM at other banks.
   B: I see.
   C: Yes. And the Circle Account is the only one that gives you free checks. You don't have to pay for *any* of your checks.
   B: That's great. So, um, how much money do you need to open a checking account?
   C: Well, for the Circle Account, you need $50, and for the other two you just need $25.
   B: That was $50 for the Circle Account and $25 for the Green Account and the Basic Account?
   C: That's right.
   B: And how much is the monthly maintenance fee?
   C: Well, for the Circle Account it's $15. But if you keep $5,000 in your account, you won't have to pay the monthly fee.
   B: Not much chance of that.
   C: Excuse me?
   B: Oh, nothing.
   C: And the Green Account is special because it's for online banking only, so there is no monthly maintenance fee. And the Basic Account has a $2.50 monthly fee.

B: Does this account provide free online banking?

C: Yes, it does. In fact, all three types of accounts provide free online banking. Each account also provides use of our own ATMs and a debit card at no additional charge.

B: I see. And I can pay my bills online free of charge?

C: Absolutely.

B: I'm also interested in buying a house. Can you give me some information about home loans?

C: Of course. We offer a 30-year fixed-rate loan at 5.5 percent.

B: So I would have 30 years to pay the loan?

C: That's correct. And you would pay 5.5 percent interest per year. So if you borrow $100,000, you will pay $5,500 in interest the first year.

B: What would my monthly mortgage payment be?

C: You would pay $567 a month. We also offer a 20-year fixed-rate loan at 5 percent interest per year.

B: How much interest would I pay each year?

C: With the 20-year mortgage, you would pay $5,000 in interest the first year and your mortgage payments would be $660 a month.

B: Well, I think that gives me the information I need. Thank you for your time.

C: Well, if there is anything else I can do for you, let me know. Here's my card.

B: Thanks.

C: Good-bye.

B: Good-bye.

## Lesson 3, Activity 3: Listen and Take Notes (page 106)
*Listen again. Add the missing information to the chart on page 107.*

## Lesson 4, Activity 2: Check True or False (page 108)
*Listen to the statements about Osvaldo's pay stub. Check (✓) True or False.*

1. Osvaldo's take-home pay this pay period is $1,103.78 [one thousand one hundred three dollars and seventy-eight cents].
2. The total amount deducted from his paycheck this pay period was $2,481.10 [two thousand four hundred eighty-one dollars and ten cents].
3. Osvaldo gets paid every two weeks.
4. From January 1 to March 15, Osvaldo earned $8,000 [eight thousand dollars].
5. Osvaldo has paid $208 [two hundred eight dollars] for federal income tax this year.
6. Osvaldo makes $80 [eighty dollars] an hour.
7. He has paid $41.60 [forty-one dollars and sixty cents] for Medicare this pay period.
8. Osvaldo's take-home pay so far this year is $5,518.90 [five thousand five hundred eighteen dollars and ninety cents].

## Lesson 7, Activity 1: Listening Review (page 114)
*Part 1: Listen to what is said. When you hear the question, Which is correct?, listen and choose the correct answer: A, B, or C. Use the Answer Sheet.*

1.
A: How much did we spend on food this month?
B: We spent $550.
A: What was our budget goal?
B: It was $500.

Which is correct?
A. They spent less than they had planned to spend.
B. They spent more than they had planned to spend.
C. They spent the amount that they had planned to spend.

2.
A: I paid my credit card late last month!
B: Did they charge a penalty fee?
A: Yes, they charged me $40. And my monthly payment is only $35!

Which is correct?
A. The credit card company charged a $40 penalty fee.
B. The credit card company charged a $35 penalty fee.
C. The credit card company didn't charge a penalty fee.

3.
A: What's wrong, Nancy?
B: I'm having credit card problems. I've maxed out all my credit cards.
A: Oh, no! You should call a consumer credit counseling service. And make sure you don't pay any of those bills late because they'll raise your interest rate.

Which is correct?
A. Nancy forgot to pay all of her credit card bills on time.
B. The credit card companies increased Nancy's interest rate.
C. Nancy has reached the credit limit on all her credit cards.

4.
A: Our Silver Account has a monthly maintenance fee of $5, but there is no fee with our Gold Account.
B: I see. And do both accounts provide free checks and free debit cards?
A: Both accounts provide free debit cards, but there is a check fee with the Silver Account.

Which is correct?
A. The Silver and Gold Accounts both charge a fee for checks.
B. The Silver and Gold Accounts both provide free checks.
C. The Gold Account provides free checks.

5.
A: How much is your paycheck, Mike?
B: Well, I worked 40 hours this week, so I made $1,000.
A: How much is your take-home pay?
B: It's $772.18.

A: That's great, because we have to pay our credit card bill by Thursday.

Which is correct?
  A. Mike's net pay for this pay period is $772.18.
  B. Mike's gross pay for this pay period is $772.18.
  C. Mike makes $40 an hour.

**Part 2: First you will hear a question. Next, listen carefully to what is said. You will hear the question again. Then choose the correct answer: A, B, or C. Use the Answer Sheet.**

6. What is the interest rate on the Silver Checking Account?
  A: You might be interested in our Silver Checking Account.
  B: Does it earn interest?
  A: Yes, it does. It earns 2 percent interest, and it comes with a free debit card and free online banking.
  B: That sounds perfect for me. And I only need $75 to open an account?

What is the interest rate on the Silver Checking Account?
  A. The Silver Account earns $75 interest a month.
  B. The Silver Account earns 2 percent interest.
  C. The Silver Account comes with a free debit card.

7. How much federal tax did Sara pay this pay period?
  A: Wow! Income tax is so high!
  B: I know! How much was deducted from your paycheck for California state taxes this pay period?
  A: $42.75.
  B: How about federal tax?
  A: $184.92! I'm only taking home $982.43!

How much federal tax did Sara pay this pay period?
  A. $42.75
  B. $184.92
  C. $982.43

8. What is wrong with Alex?
  A: What's the matter, Alex? You look upset.
  B: I am upset. We earn $3,000 a month, but our expenses are $3,200 a month! One of us needs to get a second job!
  A: Is there anything we can cut down on?
  B: Well, we spend about $400 a month on entertainment. I guess we could go out less often.

What is wrong with Alex?
  A. He has a budget deficit.
  B. He is tired because he has two jobs.
  C. He wants to spend more money on entertainment.

9. What fees are included with the Blue Account?
  A: What's the monthly maintenance fee for the Blue Account?
  B: It's $9 a month, and there is a fee for checks, but you won't be charged a fee if you use the ATM at other banks.

A: Is there a fee for debit cards?
B: No, the account comes with a free debit card.

What fees are included with the Blue Account?
  A. There is a fee for debit cards and checks.
  B. There is a maintenance fee and a fee for online banking.
  C. There is a maintenance fee and a fee for checks.

10. How much did the Lees spend on utilities this month?
  A: Our electric bill is really high this month! It's $230! We have to stop using the heater so much.
  B: I know. The phone bill is high, too. We made a lot of long distance calls.
  A: How much is it?
  B: It's $127. With our Internet cable bills, we're paying a total of $717 for utilities this month!

How much did the Lees spend on utilities this month?
  A. $437
  B. $717
  C. over a thousand dollars

## UNIT NINE

### Lesson 1, Activity 3: Listen and Write (page 116)
*Listen to the conversation. Then complete the Hazard Report Form.*
  A: Mr. Samson, can I talk to you for a minute?
  B: Sure, Alan, what's the problem?
  A: Well, one of the gas ovens isn't working properly. We have to light it by hand every time we want to use it.
  B: I see. Is it difficult to light?
  A: No, it only takes a couple of seconds to light it. But it's dangerous. I burned my finger lighting it yesterday.
  B: Oh, I see. Has anyone else been injured?
  A: I don't think so. But it smells like gas in the kitchen all the time. Mary said that the smell is making her feel sick.
  B: That's terrible. Also, if the gas is leaking out all over the kitchen, there could be a fire.
  A: Right, I hadn't thought of that.
  B: I'll need you to fill out a Workplace Hazard Report Form. Once you've filled it out, I'll take care of the problem right away.
  A: Great! Thanks, Mr. Samson.

### Lesson 2, Activity 4: Check True or False (page 118)
*Look at the schedule on page 119. Then listen. Check True or False.*
  1. Alan is working the evening shift on Wednesday.
  2. Jack switched shifts with Alan on Saturday.
  3. Mia is working for Jack on Friday.
  4. Mia has Saturday off.
  5. Jack switched shifts with Mia on Thursday.
  6. Pete switched shifts with Kim on Thursday.

## Lesson 3, Activity 2: Listen for General Information (page 120)

*Listen to the conversation. Look at pictures 1–3 on pages 120–121. Write the number of the picture that shows Sue.*

A: Thanks for meeting with me, Rick.

B: Of course, Sue. What did you want to discuss with me today?

A: Well, I've been working here at ShopMart for two years now, and I've really enjoyed it.

B: I'm happy to hear that. We've enjoyed having you here.

A: Thank you. I'm glad you feel that way. I've heard that a position has opened up in management, and I would like to be considered for it.

B: I see. Can you tell me why you feel you deserve a promotion?

A: Well, I have good interpersonal skills. I work well with all of the other salespeople.

B: That's true. You get along well with all of your co-workers.

A: Also, I've taken on a lot of extra responsibility in the last six months.

B: Can you tell me a little more about that?

A: Sure. I was hired as a salesperson, but I've been carrying out some managerial duties. For example, I've been ordering merchandise for the store and making the work schedules when Patty is too busy. I've also helped train three of the new salespeople.

B: Yes, and Patty has told me that you've done an excellent job training the new employees. I think you might have a good chance of getting the promotion, but the store manager is also responsible for accounting and hiring. You might have a better chance of getting the promotion if you take an accounting course or a management course at the community college.

A: Oh, that's a great idea. Thank you for the suggestion.

*Listen to the conversation. Look at pictures 4–6 on pages 120–121. Write the number of the picture that shows Dave.*

A: Can I talk to you for a minute, Rick?

B: Sure, Dave. What's on your mind?

A: Um, I'd like to discuss the possibility of getting a raise.

B: Oh, I see. Why do you feel you deserve a raise, Dave?

A: Well, I'm very organized. I also work well with customers. Several of them have sent me thank you notes.

B: That's all true, but you haven't been here very long.

A: I know. I've only been working here for six months, but I'm a very proficient salesperson. I've had the highest sales three months in a row.

B: You're right. You're an excellent salesperson, and the customers really enjoy working with you. Unfortunately, however, we have a policy here at ShopMart. You have to work here for at least a year before you can be considered for a raise.

A: Oh, I didn't know that. So I guess that means I have to wait at least six months before I can ask for a raise.

B: That's right. Also, you've been late for work a few times in the past.

A: I'm sorry about that. I have a class right before work.

B: I see. Well, maybe you can work with Patty to adjust your schedule, so it's easier for you to get to work on time.

A: Okay. Is there anything else I can do to improve my performance?

B: Well, I know that you're not comfortable working with computers. Patty might need your help with merchandise orders now and then, so it might be a good idea for you to take a basic computer skills class.

A: Okay, thanks. I'll do that.

## Lesson 3, Activity 3: Listen for Specific Information (page 120)

*Listen to the conversations again. Then complete the sentences.*

## Lesson 3, Window on Pronunciation: Stressing Important Words in Sentences (page 121)

The words you stress can change the meaning of your sentence.

B. Listen to the sentences. Underline the stressed words.

1. I'm <u>happy</u> to <u>hear</u> that.
2. <u>What's</u> on your <u>mind</u>?
3. I have <u>good</u> <u>interpersonal</u> skills.
4. I've been <u>carrying</u> <u>out</u> some <u>managerial</u> duties.
5. I've <u>trained</u> <u>three</u> of the new <u>employees</u>.
6. Is there anything <u>else</u> I can <u>do</u>?

## Lesson 7, Activity 1: Listening Review (page 128)

*Part 1: First you will hear a question. Next, listen carefully to what is said. You will hear the question again. Then choose the correct answer: A, B, or C. Use the Answer Sheet.*

1. What is the problem?
   A: Hi, John. Can I talk to you for a minute?
   B: Sure, what's on your mind?
   A: Well, every time I use the kitchen cleanser, I feel a little sick. I think we should start buying a different kind of cleanser.

What is the problem?
   A. The kitchen has inadequate ventilation.
   B. The kitchen cleanser doesn't clean very well.
   C. The kitchen cleanser is toxic.

2. What is the problem?
   A: What's going on, Terry?
   B: My computer is so slow!
   A: I know. My computer is really slow, too. I wish we had newer computers.
   B: I'm going to ask Mr. Lang to get us new computers next month.

What is the problem?
  A. The computers need to be updated.
  B. Terry doesn't know how to use her computer.
  C. Terry is trying to update her computer software.

3. What does Kelly want?
  A: Hi, Kelly. What did you want to talk to me about?
  B: Hi, Nick. I noticed that you have the late shift next Tuesday. Can you switch shifts with me? I have a doctor's appointment in the morning.
  A: Sure, I'll switch shifts with you. I like the early shift better anyway.

What does Kelly want?
  A. She wants to work the early shift on Tuesday.
  B. She wants to have Tuesday off.
  C. She wants to work the late shift.

4. Why does Dan feel he deserves a raise?
  A: What did you want to talk to me about, Dan?
  B: Um, I'd like to talk to you about the possibility of getting a raise.
  A: I see. Can you tell me why you feel you deserve a raise?
  B: Well, first of all, I always complete my projects on time. And second, I do what I have to do without being asked.

Why does Dan feel he deserves a raise?
  A. He's cooperative and punctual.
  B. H's dependable and shows initiative.
  C. He's polite and creative.

5. What is the problem?
  A: So, Mr. Miller, in general, you've received a good performance evaluation. You're very punctual, creative, and dependable.
  B: Thank you. I'm glad you feel that way. Is there anything I need to work on?
  A: Well, sometimes I've noticed that you're not very respectful to the customers. You need to be sure to treat everyone with respect.

What is the problem?
  A. Mr. Miller is not punctual or dependable.
  B. Mr. Miller did not receive a good performance evaluation.
  C. Mr. Miller is not polite to the customers.

*Part 2: You will hear the first part of a conversation. To finish the conversation, listen and choose the correct answer: A, B, or C. Use the Answer Sheet.*

6.
  A: Hey, Sandra. Can I talk to you for a minute?
  B: Sure, what's on your mind?
  A: I just found out that I have to go out of town on Friday. Can you work for me that day?

  A. I have that day off.
  B. I'm sorry. I need to have Saturday off.
  C. Sure, I'll work for you.

7.
  A: Mr. Ruiz, can I talk to you?
  B: Sure, Cathy. What can I help you with?
  A: The lights in the stockroom aren't bright enough, and it's difficult to see. I almost tripped over a box this morning because I didn't see it.

  A. Thanks for letting me know. This could be hazardous.
  B. Thanks for letting me know. It sounds like there's inadequate ventilation in the stockroom.
  C. I see. I'll make sure there are no toxic chemicals in the stockroom.

8.
  A: Have you met the new office manager yet?
  B: No, her name's Julie, right?
  A: Yeah, and she's great. It's only Wednesday, and she's already finished all of her projects for the week!

  A. Wow, she sounds really productive!
  B. That's great! She must be really creative!
  C. I'm impressed. We need a punctual office manager.

9.
  A: Let's go to a movie next Monday night.
  B: I can't. I work the late shift on Mondays.
  A: But next Monday is Memorial Day. Don't you have the day off?

  A. Oh, that's right. Lee is working for me that night.
  B. I'll ask Lee to switch shifts with me next Monday night.
  C. Oh, yeah! The office is closed for the holiday next Monday.

10.
  A: The office supplies keep disappearing! We spend so much money on new office supplies every month!
  B: I figured out a great way to save money on supplies at my office.
  A: Really? What did you do?
  B: I put a lock on the supply room door. Whenever someone wants more supplies, they have to ask me for them. Now people are more careful with their supplies.

  A. That's a really cooperative solution!
  B. That's a great solution! You're so creative!
  C. You're so productive! I'm going to do that at my office.

## UNIT TEN

### Lesson 2, Activity 3: Listen (page 132)
*Look at the information on page 133. Listen. Check* True *or False.*

1. Workers in Great Britain get 30 days of vacation after they've worked for a company for 10 years.
2. On average, workers in Japan get more vacation days than workers in the United States.
3. In China, women get 12 weeks of paid maternity leave.

4. In Japan, women receive 60 percent of their regular salary when they are on maternity leave.
5. The average worker in Mexico works 40 hours a week.
6. In the United States, fathers can take 12 weeks of unpaid paternity leave.

## Lesson 3, Activity 2: Listen for General Information (page 134)

*Read the article on page 135. Listen to the conversations. Then check whether Joe's behavior was appropriate or inappropriate. Don't complete the third column yet.*

1.
A: Can I ask your advice about something?
B: Sure, Joe, what's up?
A: One of my neighbors invited me to a dinner party at her house last night. I don't know her very well because I just moved into the building last month.
B: Okay, so what's the problem?
A: Well, I had never been to a dinner party in the United States before. I'm not sure that I behaved appropriately. Is it appropriate to bring a gift?
B: Sure, you could bring something small, like flowers or maybe a box of candy.
A: Oh. I brought a cake for dessert. Was that okay?
B: No, that wasn't really appropriate. You shouldn't bring food unless the host asks you to.
A: Oh, no.
B: Don't worry. I'm sure she wasn't offended.
A: I was really nervous that I wouldn't have anyone to talk to at the party. I was going to bring a friend with me, but I didn't.
B: Oh, you shouldn't bring anyone to a dinner party that the host isn't expecting.
A: Oh, good. I'm glad I didn't bring my friend along. Oh, can I ask you one more question?
B: Sure, what is it?
A: I sent her a thank-you card. Is that okay?
B: It's not necessary, but it's okay. I'm sure your neighbor was happy to receive a thank-you card.

2.
A: Sue, everything looks delicious!
C: I'm glad you think so!
A: I think I'll try this salad before everyone sits down to eat . . . Mmm, it's delicious!
C: Oh, thank you.
A: Okay, everyone, dinner is ready! Let's all sit down.
C: Joe, would you like some chicken?
A: Oh, no thank you. But I'd love some pasta.
C: Here you go.
A: Thanks!
C: So how do you like living in this neighborhood, Joe?
A: I think it's great! There are so many shops and restaurants nearby. And I really like to go to the park on Center Street.

C: I love that park, too. It's a great place to read.
A: How long have you lived in this building, Sue?
C: I've been here for about five years.
A: Oh, really? Do you pay the same rent as I do? Mine is $700 a month.
C: Uh, no, my rent is different. Uh, Alex, would you like some more salad?

## Lesson 3, Activity 3: Listen for Specific Information (page 134)

*Listen to the conversations again. Then complete the third column in the chart in Activity 2.*

## Lesson 3, Window on Pronunciation: Changing Stress with *That* (page 135)

B. Listen to the statements and questions. Circle *that* each time it is stressed.
1. (That's) the man that was on TV.
2. Remember the movie that I told you about? It's at (that) theater over there.
3. Did you meet the girl that Matt likes? (That's) her.
4. Not (that) book. I want the one that I gave you last week.
5. The neighbor that had an accident last week lives in (that) house.

## Lesson 4, Activity 4: Listen (page 137)

*Listen to the conversations. Complete the chart.*

1.
A: Hey, Tom, I'm having a problem with my computer. Can you help me?
B: Oh, sorry, I don't know anything about computers.
A: Really? I'm surprised. You seem like the computer type.
B: Why?
A: Well, you know, you wear glasses, and you like science fiction movies.

2.
A: Julie, can you give me a ride to the airport tomorrow?
B: Oh, sorry, I can't drive for a while.
A: Why, what happened?
B: I have too many traffic tickets. The police took away my driver's license last week.
A: Oh, no! That's horrible!
B: It's probably better for me. I'm not a very good driver.

3.
A: What are you doing this weekend, Anne?
B: I'm going to a baseball game with my husband.
A: Oh, I'm sorry.
B: What do you mean? I love going to baseball games.
A: Oh, I just assumed you wouldn't like baseball.
B: Why?
A: Well, my wife and my sisters don't like watching any sports.

**4.**

A: I can't believe Sarah is going out with that guy Mike.
B: Why not?
A: Sarah is so smart. She should go out with someone who is as intelligent as she is.
B: What makes you think Mike isn't intelligent?
A: I don't know. He's just so handsome. Didn't he used to be a model or an actor or something?
B: He was a model. He used the money to pay for graduate school.
A: Really?
B: Yeah, he has a Ph.D. in American history. He's a college professor.

## Lesson 7, Activity 1: Listening Review (page 142)

*Part 1: Listen to what is said. When you hear the question,* **Which is correct?**, *listen and choose the correct answer: A, B, or C. Use the Answer Sheet.*

**1.**

A: What are you doing this weekend, Tomiko?
B: My family and I are going to celebrate the Mid-Autumn Festival on Saturday night.
A: Oh, how do you celebrate?
B: We have dinner outside under the full moon.

Which is correct?
  A. Tomiko is going to a birthday party on Saturday night.
  B. Tomiko is going to celebrate the Mid-Autumn Festival tonight.
  C. The Mid-Autumn Festival is on Saturday night.

**2.**

A: How's your new job, Andy?
B: It's great! But now that my wife and I are both working, we're spending a lot of money on child care.
A: Oh, I know. Child care is so expensive!

Which is correct?
  A. Andy is part of a two-income household.
  B. Andy's wife is on maternity leave.
  C. Andy's wife is now back to work after maternity leave.

**3.**

A: How much paid vacation time do you get at your job, Paula?
B: I only get one week a year.
A: That's terrible! I thought two weeks of vacation was mandatory in the United States.
B: No, there's no mandatory vacation time in this country.

Which is correct?
  A. Paula gets two weeks of paid vacation a year.
  B. Businesses are required to offer two weeks of paid vacation per year.
  C. Paula gets one week of paid vacation a year.

**4.**

A: Hi, Marta.
B: Hi, Ken! I'm so glad you could make it to my dinner party!
A: Thanks. I hope you don't mind, but I brought my brother along.

Which is correct?
  A. Ken's brother was invited to the dinner party.
  B. Ken's brother was not invited to the dinner party.
  C. Marta was expecting Ken's brother to come to the dinner party.

**5.**

A: Hi, Brian. Are you going to Tammy's birthday party on Friday?
B: Yeah, I am. Is it okay if I give her money as a gift?
A: No, that wouldn't really be appropriate. She likes coffee. You could give her a bag of nice coffee instead.

Which is correct?
  A. Money is a good birthday gift for Tammy.
  B. Money is not a good birthday gift for Tammy.
  C. Brian doesn't want to go to Tammy's birthday party.

*Part 2: You will hear the first part of a conversation. To finish the conversation, listen and choose the correct answer: A, B, or C. Use the Answer Sheet.*

**6.**

A: Hey, Eric. Why are you all dressed in green today?
B: I'm celebrating St. Patrick's Day.
A: Oh, what's St. Patrick's Day?

  A. It's on March 17 every year.
  B. It's a holiday that is celebrated in England.
  C. It's a holiday that commemorates an Irish saint.

**7.**

A: Did you know that we only get four weeks of paid maternity leave at this company?
B: Really? When I lived in France, I got 16 weeks of paid maternity leave.
A: Wow, did your company have to give you that much paid maternity leave?

  A. Yeah, 16 weeks of maternity leave is mandatory in France.
  B. The amount of paid maternity leave varies from company to company.
  C. There are two wage-earners in my household.

**8.**

A: Can I ask you a question?
B: Sure, what's going on?
A: A woman that I work with invited me to her wedding. Is it appropriate to send a gift before the wedding?

A. No, it really wouldn't be appropriate to bring a guest with you.
B. Sure, that would be fine. I'm sure your friend would like to go to the wedding.
C. It's not necessary, but it would be okay. You can also bring a gift with you.

9.
A: Hey, Pat, can I get some advice?
B: Sure, Alan. What is it?
A: I've been invited to a dinner party tonight, but I have a doctor's appointment at 6:00 and the party starts at 7:00. Is it okay if I arrive at the dinner party late?
B: No, that wouldn't really be appropriate.

A. Oh, then I should reschedule my doctor's appointment.

B. Oh, then I should change my doctor's appointment to 7:00.
C. Good, then I'll keep my doctor's appointment.

10.
A: Are you going to celebrate Cinco de Mayo this year?
B: Yes, I'm going out to dinner with some friends to celebrate.
A: Cinco de Mayo is Mexican independence day, right?

A. Yes, that's a well-known legend.
B. No, that's a common misconception.
C. Actually, that's a customary activity.

# VOCABULARY LIST

Numbers in parentheses indicate unit numbers.

absenteeism (7)
account (3)
account (IRA) (8)
actual cash value (2)
actually (10)
addicted (3)
aggravated assault (6)
allow (5)
analgesic (3)
ancestors (10)
annual fee (8)
appropriate  (10)
assist (7)
assumptions (10)
attendance (9)
average (10)
balance (10)
bailiff (6)
battery (6)
belief (4)
boat trailer (2)
break the habit (3)
budget (8)
budget deficit (8)
businesslike (7)
buy in bulk (5)
calories (3)
can't help myself (3)
cardiologist (3)
carry a balance (8)
categories (10)
cautious (2)
celebrate (10)
certificate of deposit (CD) (8)
chiropractor (3)
claim (2)
cleanser (9)
clearly (1)
closed for a holiday (9)
coeducational (4)
collapse (3)
collision (2)
commemorates (10)
commit (6)
comprehend (1)
comprehensive (2)
concentrate (1)
concise (1)
concisely (1)
conclude (10)
consignment shops (5)
convince (5)
cooperative (1, 9)
costumes (10)
court reporter (6)
courteous (7)
coverage (2)

creative (9)
creativity (9)
credit counselor (8)
criminal (6)
customary (10)
debt (8)
deductible (2)
defendant (6)
defense attorney (6)
depreciate (2)
depressed (3)
dermatologist (3)
diagnose (3)
discipline (7)
discriminate against
    (someone) (4)
dismiss (6, 7)
disorderly (7)
distracted (1)
early shift (9)
election (4)
elective (4)
ensure (7)
entertainment (8)
excessive (7)
expect (1)
expense (8)
extracurricular activity (4)
fail (7)
felony (6)
fever (3)
find someone guilty (6)
first aid kit (3)
flares (2)
flat tire (2)
flexible (1)
freedom of assembly (4)
frequently (3)
furnish (5)
furnished (5)
garage sale (5)
gathering (4)
get together (4)
goggles (9)
guilty (6)
gynecologist (3)
handle (7)
have the day off (9)
hazard lights (2)
hazard triangle (2)
hazardous (9)
homemaker (10)
honor (10)
hood (2)
household (10)
ignorance (10)
ignore (7)

imprisonment (6)
impulse buyer (5)
inadequate (9)
inappropriate (10)
independence (9)
individual retirement (8)
inflation (8)
infraction (6)
initial (1)
initiative (9)
innocent (6)
installment plan (1)
insured (3)
interpersonal skills (9)
invest (8)
investment (8)
jaywalking (6)
judge (6)
jury (6)
lawyer (6)
leave out (1)
legend (10)
limousine (2)
lunar (10)
mandatory (10)
march (4)
march on (4)
maternity leave (10)
max out (8)
media (4)
merchandise (5)
miscellaneous (8)
mischief (10)
misconception (10)
misdemeanor (6)
motorist (2)
mounted police officer (4)
nutrient (3)
obstetrician (3)
offense (6)
optometrist (3)
overpass (2)
oversee (7)
paper jam (9)
parade (10)
paternity leave (10)
patrol (6)
pay a fine (6)
pay in full (8)
pediatrician (3)
penalty fee (8)
percent daily value (3)
performance (9)
physical therapist (3)
policy (2)
policyholder (2)
prefer (7)

premium (2)
prepare (7)
pressure (someone) into (5)
previous (7)
primary care physician (3)
prison (6)
probation (6)
productive (9)
proficient (1)
prosecutor (6)
protest (4)
psychiatrist (3)
psychologist (3)
punctual (9)
punishable (6)
purchases (5)
realize (3)
recruit (7)
refund policy (5)
register (4)
reimbursement (2)
reliability (9)
rely on (9)
report on (4)
reporter (4)
reprimand (7)
required (4)
responsibility (4)
retail (7)
right (4)
rush hour (2)
service (10)
serving size (3)
share (1)
shipment (7)
shoulder of the road (2)
side car (2)
side effect (3)
signal (2)
social networking sites (3)
specialize (3)
spine (3)
statistics (10)
stereotype (10)
stereotypical (10)
store credit (5)
summons (6)
surfing the Internet (3)
suspicious (6)
swallow (3)
switch shifts (9)
take advantage of
    (someone) (4)
take an active role in (4)
take responsibility for
    (something) (1)
testimony (6)

thrift stores (5)
time limit (5)
tolerant (4)
toxic (9)
traffic chopper (2)
transfusion (3)

treat (3)
unacceptable (7)
unconscious (10)
uninsured (2)
up to code (9)
update (9)

vary (8)
vehicle (2)
ventilation (9)
violate (7)
violation (6)
vital signs (3)

wage earner (10)
warranty (5)
wheel in a wheelchair (3)
witness (6)
work for (someone) (9)
yard sale (5)

# IRREGULAR VERBS

## Irregular Verbs

| Base Form | Simple Past | Past Participle | Base Form | Simple Past | Past Participle |
|---|---|---|---|---|---|
| be | was/were | been | keep | kept | kept |
| become | became | become | know | knew | known |
| begin | began | begun | leave | left | left |
| bleed | bled | bled | lend | lent | lent |
| break | broke | broken | lose | lost | lost |
| bring | brought | brought | make | made | made |
| buy | bought | bought | meet | met | met |
| choose | chose | chosen | pay | paid | paid |
| come | came | come | put | put | put |
| cost | cost | cost | read | read | read |
| cut | cut | cut | ring | rang | rung |
| do | did | done | run | ran | run |
| drink | drank | drunk | see | saw | seen |
| drive | drove | driven | sell | sold | sold |
| eat | ate | eaten | send | sent | sent |
| fall | fell | fallen | set | set | set |
| feel | felt | felt | shake | shook | shaken |
| fight | fought | fought | shut | shut | shut |
| find | found | found | sleep | slept | slept |
| forget | forgot | forgotten | speak | spoke | spoken |
| fry | fried | fried | speed | sped | sped |
| get | got | gotten | spend | spent | spent |
| give | gave | given | take | took | taken |
| go | went | gone | teach | taught | taught |
| grow | grew | grown | tell | told | told |
| have/has | had | had | think | thought | thought |
| hear | heard | heard | wear | wore | worn |
| hold | held | held | write | wrote | written |
| hurt | hurt | hurt | | | |

# CREDITS

## PHOTO CREDITS

**p. 2,** (1) Ron Chapple Stock/Alamy; (2) James Day/Taxi/Getty Images; (3) Kevin Dodge/Corbis; (4) moodboard/Corbis

**p. 3,** Antenna/Getty Images

**p. 7,** (1) ©BananaStock.Ltd; (2) Flying Colours Ltd/Digital Vision/Getty Images; (3) Punchstock/Image Source; (4) Jon Feingersh/Blend Images/Getty Images

**p. 8,** Ryan McVay/Getty Images

**p. 10,** Corbis - All Rights Reserved

**p. 13,** Allan Danahar/Digital Vision/Getty Images

**p. 24,** Martin Hospach/Getty Images

**p. 26,** Digital Vision/Alamy

**p. 28,** (left) L. Clarke/Corbis; (right) image 100/Alamy

**p. 35,** (1) Peter Widmann/Alamy; (2) Ryan McVay/Getty Images; (3) Brand X Pictures/PunchStock; (4) Guy Cali/Corbis; (5) Digital Vision/Getty Images; (6) Punchstock/Creatas; (7) Pixtal/age fotostock; (8) Geoff Manasse/Getty Images; (9) Getty Images

**p. 37,** ICHIRO/Digital Vision/Getty Images

**p. 38,** Werner Blessing/StockFood Creative/Getty Images

**p. 39,** Larsen & Talbert/FoodPix/Getty Images

**p. 41,** Digital Vision/Getty Images

**p. 49,** (1) AFP/Getty Images; (2) BananaStock/PunchStock; (3) The McGraw-Hill Companies, Inc./John Flournoy, photographer; (4) Rob Melnychuk/Digital Vision/Getty Images

**p. 50,** Tom Merton/Digital Vision/Getty Images

**p. 51,** (1) Photodisc/Punchstock; (2) Dennis MacDonald/Alamy; (3) Creatas; (4) Bob Rowan; Progressive Image/Corbis

**p. 55,** Getty Images/Photodisc

**p. 63,** (1) Corbis Super RF/Alamy; (2) Michael Newman/PhotoEdit; (3) David Sacks/Lifesize/Getty Images; (4) AFP/Getty Images; (5) Bill Aron/PhotoEdit; (6) Art Directors - Archive/Alamy

**p. 64,** (top) Digital Vision/Alamy; (bottom) Digital Vision/Getty Images

**p. 65,** (left) Paul Doyle/Alamy; (top right) Digital Vision/Getty Images; (bottom right) Danny Clifford/Alamy

**p. 70,** Bob Scott/Photonica/Getty Images

**p. 71,** NiKreationS

**p. 76,** (top) BrandX Pictures; (inset, top) Laurence Mouton/PhotoAlto Agency RF Collections/Getty Images; (inset, center) Don Farrall/Getty Images; (inset, bottom) RF/Corbis

**p. 78,** (top) Image Source/Getty Images; (center) Spencer Grant/PhotoEdit

**p. 80,** S. Meltzer/PhotoLink/Getty Images

**p. 85,** Stock Connection Distribution/Alamy

**p. 90,** (top) Anderson Ross/Getty Images; (bottom) Comstock/Getty Images

**p. 92,** (top) Stockbyte/Getty Images; (center) Left Lane Productions/Corbis

**p. 94,** LWA/Riser/Getty Images

**p. 97,** Courtesy of Chez Raginiak, 1Moment, LLC

**p. 104,** (1) Comstock Images; (4) Tony Freeman/PhotoEdit; (5) Jeff Greenberg/PhotoEdit; (6) Digital Vision/Getty Images; (7) Sheer Photo, Inc/Getty Images; (9) Getty Images

**p. 106,** (top) Eric Audras/Getty Images; (center) Stockbyte/Getty Images; (bottom) Image Source/Jupiter Images

**p. 107,** Stockbyte/Getty Images

**p. 111,** Brand X Pictures

**p. 122,** (top) John A. Rizzo/Getty Images; (bottom) Jose Luis Pelaez, Inc./Blend Images/Corbis

**p. 125,** Blend Images/Alamy

**p. 132,** Punchstock/Banana Stock

**p. 135,** Ryan McVay/Getty Images

**p. 136,** (top) Photodisc; (bottom) Eyewire/Photodisc/Getty Images

## TEXT CREDITS

**p. 55,** From the AFL-CIO Worker's Rights in America survey.

**p. 68,** "bulk" definition: From Rideout. *The Newbury House Dictionary of American English, Updated Edition with CD-ROM, 3E.* ©2000 Heinle/ELT, a part of Cengage Learning, Inc. Reproduced by permission.

**p.69,** "garage sale" "yard sale" "yard" definitions: From Rideout. *The Newbury House Dictionary of American English, Updated Edition with CD-ROM, 3E.* ©2000 Heinle/ELT, a part of Cengage Learning, Inc. Reproduced by permission.

**p, 136,** "stereotype" definitions: From Rideout. *The Newbury House Dictionary of American English, Updated Edition with CD-ROM, 3E.* ©2000 Heinle/ELT, a part of Cengage Learning, Inc. Reproduced by permission.

# SKILLS INDEX

## LEARNING LOGS

## LIFE SKILLS